WRITING DIASPORA

Arts and Politics of the Everyday

Patricia Mellencamp, Meaghan Morris, Andrew Ross,
series editors

WRITING DIASPORA

Tactics of Intervention in Contemporary
Cultural Studies

REY CHOW

INDIANA UNIVERSITY PRESS

Bloomington and Indianapolis

The paper used in this publication meets the minimum requirements of
American National Standard for Information Sciences—Permanence of
Paper for Printed Library Materials, ANSI Z39.48-1984.

♾™

Manufactured in the United States of America

Library of Congress Cataloging-in-Publication Data

Chow, Rey.
    Writing diaspora : tactics of intervention in contemporary
cultural studies / Rey Chow.
       p.   cm.—(Arts and politics of the everyday)
    Includes bibliographical references (p.   ) and index.
    ISBN 0-253-31366-X (alk. paper).—ISBN 0-253-20785-1 (pbk. :
alk. paper)
    1. China—Study and teaching—United States. 2. Culture—Study
and teaching—United States. I. Title. II. Series.
DS734.97.U6C47   1993
951'.0072—dc20   92-23064

1 2 3 4 5 97 96 95 94 93

For my family
Hong Kong—Minneapolis—Toronto—
Irvine

CONTENTS

ACKNOWLEDGMENTS

Except for the Introduction, all the chapters in this book were written during the period between late 1989 and mid-1991. My first note of thanks goes to Austin Meredith. He lives with me and, apart from providing the indulgences and conveniences we all selfishly seek from our companions, is always the first person to experience the tantrums and explosions that result from what I do to make a living—writing and speaking. The generosity and affection, as well as critical insights, of Sipra Jha, Tonglin Lu, and Mingbao Yue sustained me through many months of illness. Many conversations with Chris Cullens, Dorothea von Mücke, and Kwai-cheung Lo proved to be thought-provoking and useful.

I am indebted to my colleagues in the Department of Comparative Literature at the University of Minnesota—Nancy Armstrong, Peter Canning, Prabhakara Jha, Harvey Sarles, Jochen Schulte-Sasse, and Ronald Sousa—for giving me the most encouraging intellectual environment a junior faculty person can dream of in what are increasingly menacing bureaucratic times. I am indebted to the Center for Twentieth Century Studies at the University of Wisconsin—Milwaukee for its enthusiasm and support for my work: I thank in particular Kathleen Woodward, Carol Tennessen, and Patrice Petro; and Lynne Joyrich for introducing me to the center. (My visits there in 1990, 1991, and 1992 were made especially memorable by the hospitality of Herbert Blau, Jane Gallop, Dick Blau, Andrew Martin, Panivong Norindr, and Marina Pérez de Mendiola.) I am grateful to Giulia Colaizzi and Jenaro Talens for inviting me to conferences in Valencia, Spain, in 1990 and 1991. My sincere thanks also to Michael Clark and two anonymous readers, who provided comments and suggestions that significantly facilitated the final revisions.

The idea of this book was Leonard Tennenhouse's. (He is, of course, not responsible for what I did with it.) To him and Nancy Armstrong, I owe innumerable instances of professional, intellectual, and personal help, which they always give generously with large doses of that lifesaving ingredient, humor.

Most of the book was completed when I was a holder of the McKnight-Land Grant Professorship at the University of Minnesota. For the McKnight Foundation's magnanimous financial assistance, I shall always remain thankful.

My gratitude, finally, to Meaghan Morris, Andrew Ross, and especially Patricia Mellencamp for making the publication of this book possible.

Chapters that were previously or are simultaneously published are reprinted here with permission. They have all been modified or revised, and edited for this book. Chapter 2 can be found in *Displacements: Cultural Identities in Question*, ed. Angelika Bammer (Bloomington and Indianapolis: Indiana University Press, forthcoming). Chapter 3 was first published in Spanish under the title "Autómatas postmodernos" in *Feminismo y teoría del discurso*, ed. Giulia Colaizzi (Madrid: Ediciones Cátedra, Colección Teorema, 1990), 67–85, and then in English in *Feminists Theorize the Political*, ed. Judith Butler and Joan Scott (New York: Routledge, 1992), 101–17. Chapter 4 was published in *Dialectical Anthropology* 16: 3 (1991), 191–207, ed. Donald Nonini and Judith Farquhar. Chapter 5 can be found in *Gender and Sexuality in Twentieth-Century Chinese Literature and Society*, ed. Tonglin Lu (Albany: SUNY Press, forthcoming). Chapter 6 was published in *differences* 2: 3 (Fall 1990): 29–51. A shorter version of chapter 7 was published in *Discourse* 13: 1 (Fall/Winter 1990–91): 129–48. The Spanish version of chapter 8 can be found in *Velocidad y comunicación*, ed. Jenaro Talens (Madrid: Ediciones Cátedra, forthcoming).

WRITING DIASPORA

I

INTRODUCTION
LEADING QUESTIONS

Orientalism and East Asia: The Persistence of a Scholarly Tradition

The sinologist Stephen Owen wrote a controversially negative essay about "world poetry" not too long ago in the pages of *The New Republic*.[1] While ostensibly reviewing the English translation of the collection *The August Sleepwalker* by the mainland Chinese poet Bei Dao, Owen attacks "third world" poets for pandering to the tastes of Western audiences seeking "a cozy ethnicity" (Owen, p. 29). Much of what is written by non-Western poets is, he complains, no longer distinguished by a true national identity but is instead "supremely translatable" (Owen, p. 32):

> most of these poems translate themselves. These could just as easily be translations from a Slovak or an Estonian or a Philippine poet. . . . We must wonder if such collections of poetry in translation become publishable only because the publisher and the readership have been assured that the poetry was lost in translation. But what if the poetry wasn't lost in translation? What if this is it?
> This *is* it. (Owen, p. 31; emphasis in the original)

As a sinologist, Owen's biggest concern is that contemporary Chinese writers are sacrificing their national cultural heritage for a "translation" that commodifies experiences of victimization. He warns:

> And there is always a particular danger of using one's victimization for self-interest: in this case, to sell oneself abroad by what an inter-

national audience, hungry for political virtue, which is always in
short supply, finds touching. (Owen, p. 29)

Like other "new poetries" such as new Hindi poetry and new
Japanese poetry (Owen, p. 29), the "disease of modern Chinese
poetry" (Owen, p. 30) is that it is too Westernized. For Owen, the
most important question is therefore: "is this Chinese literature, or
literature that began in the Chinese language?" (Owen, p. 31).[2]
In her criticism of Owen's essay, Michelle Yeh points out the
obvious contradictions that underlie what appears to be an objective
and scholarly discussion:

> On the one hand, he is disappointed at the lack of history and culture
> that would distinguish China from other countries. On the other
> hand, the historical context essential to the writing and reading of
> contemporary Chinese poetry is not taken seriously and is used only
> as an occasion for chastising the poet who writes "for self-interest".
> . . . The cynicism is oddly out of step with the high regard in which
> Professor Owen holds poetry, for it not only ignores personal and
> literary history but also underestimates the power of poetry as a vital
> means of spiritual survival, of affirming individual dignity and faith
> when virtually all else fails.[3]

For readers who know something about China, Owen's attitude
is not a particularly novel one. It is typical of the disdain found in
many relatively recent American scholarly reactions toward the lib-
eralized China of the 1980s. Harry Harding has written informa-
tively about this kind of "debilitating contempt" that succeeded the
euphoric China fever of the 1960s and 1970s.[4] But more is at stake
here. What kind of cultural politics is in play when a professor from
Harvard University accuses the men and women from the "third
world" of selling out to the West? While he criticizes poets like Bei
Dao for succumbing to the commodifying tendencies of transnational culture out of "self-interest," what is absent from Owen's
musings is an account of the institutional investments that shape his
own enunciation. This *absence* constitutes a definite form of power
by not drawing attention to itself and thus not subjecting itself to
the harsh judgment of "self-interest" that is so useful in criticizing

others. The elaboration and fortification of this kind of absence amounts to the perpetuation of a deeply ingrained Orientalism in the field of East Asian studies, of which Owen's practice is but one example. Because this is an Orientalism at which many East Asia scholars, *both* native and non-native, connive, it is of some urgency to mobilize criticism of it.

Colin MacKerras writes about Edward Said's *Orientalism*: "Although designed specifically as a critique of the Western study of West Asian civilizations, its main points are equally applicable to the study of China."[5] Precisely because of this, the arguments against Said's work in the East Asian field are often similar to their counterparts in South Asian and West Asian studies. Critics like Said, it is often said, belittle and ignore the work that is being done by specialists of these non-Western cultures and that has produced knowledge about peoples whose traditions would otherwise perish. I have indicated elsewhere that we need to acknowledge the significance of this type of work as sharing an *episteme* with primatology.[6] It is, however, not enough simply to align a field like East Asian studies with primatology and compare the salvational motives of their respective practitioners. What needs to be foregrounded is the nature and extent of the self-interestedness involved in the disapproval of the critique of Orientalism as a transcultural phenomenon.

Although Owen in his piece is not directly criticizing Said's work, his arguments clarify many of the current feelings in his field. Basic to Owen's disdain toward the new "world poetry" is a sense of loss and, consequently, an anxiety over his own intellectual position. This anxiety can be understood in part through Sigmund Freud's analysis of melancholia.[7] For Freud, we remember, the melancholic is a person who cannot get over the loss of a precious, loved object and who ultimately introjects this loss into his ego. What Freud emphasizes throughout his discussion as the unique feature of the melancholic, who differs from other kinds of mourners, is that he exhibits the symptoms of a delusional belittling of himself. Because the nature of the loss remains unconscious to the patient, the loss is directed inward, so that he becomes convinced of his own worthlessness as if he has been unjustly abandoned.

In his essay, Freud is concerned with the relationship between the self and the lost loved object. Freud's construction involves two parties, subject and object, and does not go on to show how the melancholic acts in regard to other subjects. Postcoloniality here offers a use of Freud that necessitates a rethinking of his theory about the melancholic disorder. In the case of the sinologist's relationship with his beloved object, "China," melancholia is complicated by the presence of a third party—the living members of the Chinese culture, who provide the sinologist with a means of *externalizing* his loss and directing his blame. What Freud sees as "self"-directed denigration now finds a concrete realization in the denigration of others.

For Owen, the inferior poetic skills of Bei Dao are, ostensibly, what he considers to be signs of the "third world" poet's inability to rise to the grandeur of his own cultural past. But this moralistic indictment of the other's infidelity masks a more fundamental anxiety. This is the anxiety that the Chinese past which he has undertaken to penetrate is evaporating and that the sinologist himself is the abandoned subject. What this means, significantly, is that a situation has been constructed in which the historical relation between the "first world" and the "third world" is reversed: writers of the "third world" like Bei Dao now appear not as the oppressed but as oppressors, who aggress against the "first world" sinologist by robbing him of his love. Concluding his essay sourly with the statement, "Welcome to the late twentieth century," Owen's real complaint is that *he* is the victim of a monstrous world order in front of which a sulking impotence like his is the only claim to truth.

Characteristic of this Orientalist melancholia are all the feelings proper to nineteenth-century Anglo-German Romanticism: the assumption that literature should be about depth and interiority, that expression of emotional truth should be modest, if not altogether wordless, and that being cultured means being hostile toward any form of reification and exhibitionism. Notably, Owen is not insensitive to oppression and suffering (he repeatedly points to the injustice caused by Western imperialism and Western cultural hegemony), but such sensitivity demands that oppression and suffering should not be announced loudly or even mentioned too often by those who are undergoing it, for that would amount to poor taste and insincerity. Reading him, one has the sense that in order to be good, poetry must be untranslatable because any translation would be suspect of *betraying* the truth. By implication, human language itself is a prime traitor to preverbal phenomena/sentiments.[8]

Confined to a discursive space that is theoretically at odds with the comparative tenets of contemporary cultural studies, the sinologist holds on to the language of the nation-state as his weapon of combat. This is one of the major reasons why "history," in the sense of a detailed, factographic documentation of the local, the particular, and the past (understood as what has already happened and been recorded), enjoys such a prioritized disciplinary status in East Asian cultural politics. The hostility toward the critique of Orientalism currently heard in some East Asian scholarly circles is a direct consequence of this language of the nation-state. But if the critique of Orientalism is rejected, as is often the argument, for its "universalizing" overtones, then the idea of China, Japan, or "East Asia" as distinct historical entities is itself the other side of Orientalism. In a discussion about how universalism and particularism reinforce and supplement each other, Naoki Sakai writes:

> Contrary to what has been advertised by both sides, universalism and particularism reinforce and supplement each other; they are never in real conflict; they need each other and have to seek to form a symmetrical, mutually supporting relationship by every means in order to avoid a dialogic encounter which would necessarily jeopardize their reputedly secure and harmonized monologic worlds. Universalism and particularism endorse each other's defect in order to conceal their own; they are intimately tied to each other in their accomplice [*sic*]. In this respect, *a particularism such as nationalism can never be a serious critique of universalism, for it is an accomplice thereof.*[9]

Of Japan, for instance, Sakai writes specifically:

> Japan did not stand *outside* the West. Even in its particularism, Japan was already implicated in the ubiquitous West, so that neither historically nor geopolitically could Japan be seen as the *outside* of the West. This means that, in order to criticize the West in relation to Japan, one has necessarily to begin with a critique of Japan. Likewise, the critique of Japan necessarily entails the radical critique of the West.[10]

What these passages indicate is that Orientalism and a particularism like nationalism or nativism are the obverse and reverse of the same coin, and that criticism of one cannot be made without criticism of the other. The tendency in area studies, nonetheless, is to play them off against each other with nationalism/nativism gaining the upper hand. This has led to what Gayatri Spivak calls a "new culturalist alibi,"[11] by which some seek to avoid the pitfalls of the earlier Orientalism simply by particularizing their inquiries as meticulously as possible by way of class, gender, race, nation, and geographical locale. We see this in a title construction such as "*Funu, Guojia, Jiating* [Chinese women, Chinese state, Chinese family]."[12] The use of "Chinese" as a specifier signals a new kind of care and a new kind of attentiveness to the discursive imperatives—"Always contextualize! Never essentialize!"—of cultural pluralism. But *funu, guojia, jiating* are simply words in the Chinese language that mean women, state, family. Had the title been "la femme, l'état, la famille," would it be conceivable to append a phrase like "French woman, French state, French family"? In the name of investigating "cultural difference," ethnic markers such as "Chinese" easily become a method of differentiation that precisely blocks criticism from its critical task by reinscribing potentially radical notions such as "the other" in the security of fastidiously documented archival detail. A scholarly nativism that functions squarely within the Orientalist dynamic and that continues to imprison "other cultures" within entirely conventional disciplinary boundaries thus remains intact.

At a conference on gender issues in twentieth-century China, my commentator, an American female anthropologist who has done pioneering work on rural Chinese women, told the audience that what I said about the relation between China studies and Western cultural imperialism made her feel politically uncomfortable. Instead, she suggested, we should focus on the "internal colonization" of Chinese women by Chinese patriarchy. This person was thus still illustrating, in 1991, the point G. Balandier made in 1951, namely that "Out of a more or less conscious fear of having to take into consideration . . . the society of the colonial power to which they themselves belong," Western anthropologists persistently neglect the "colonial situation" that lies at the origin of their "field of research" in most parts of the world.[13]

These examples of pressures to focus on the "internal" and the specifically "Chinese" problems are examples of how what many profess to be "cross-cultural" study can remain trapped within a type of discourse that is geographically deterministic *and hence* culturally essentialist. "China," "Japan," and "East Asia" become signs of "difference" that reaffirm a sense of identity as originary self-identicalness. The problems posed by women and imperialism in the East Asian field are thus often subordinated, philosophically, to a local native tradition (in which any discussion of women alone would be guilty of coloniality) and, institutionally, to "area studies," where imperialism as a transnational phenomenon is dismissed as irrelevant. What this means is that, while plenty of work is done on East Asian women, much of it is not feminist but nationalist or culturalist; while plenty of work is done on the modern history of East Asia, much of it is not about East Asia's shared history with other orientalized cultures but about East Asia as a "distinct" territory with a distinct history. What is forgotten is that these notions of East Asia are fully in keeping with U.S. foreign policy in the post-Second World War period, during which the older European Orientalism was supplanted by the emergence of the U.S. as the newest imperialist power with major military bases in countries such as Japan, Korea, Taiwan, the Philippines, and Vietnam.

What is also missed is that when we speak against Orientalism and nativism, we understand them as *languages* which can be used by natives and non-natives alike. A critique of the Orientalism in East Asian pedagogy neither implies that only "natives" of East Asian cultures are entitled to speaking about those cultures truthfully nor that "natives" themselves are automatically innocent of Orientalism as a mode of discourse.

The most crucial issue, meanwhile, remains Orientalism's general and continuing *ideological* role. Critics of Said in the East Asian field sometimes justify their criticism by saying that Said's theory does not apply to East Asia because many East Asian countries were not, territorially, colonial possessions. This kind of positivistic thinking, derived from a literal understanding of the significance of geographical captivity, is not only an instance of the ongoing anthropological tendency to deemphasize the "colonial situation" as I mention above; it also leaves intact the most important aspect of Orientalism—its legacy as everyday culture and value. The ques-

tion ought, I think, to be posed in exactly the opposite way: *not*
how East Asia cannot be understood within the paradigm of Orientalism because it was not everywhere militarily occupied, but how,
in spite of and perhaps because of the fact that it remained in many
cases "territorially independent," it offers even better illustrations
of how imperialism works—i.e., how imperialism as ideological
domination succeeds best without physical coercion, without actually capturing the body and the land.

Here, the history of China vis-à-vis the West can be instructive
in a number of ways.[14] Unlike India or countries in Africa and
America, most parts of China were, in the course of European imperialism, never territorially under the sovereignty of any foreign
power, although China was invaded and had to grant many concessions throughout the nineteenth century to England, France, Germany, Russia, Japan, and the U.S. Major political movements in
China, be they for the restoration of older forms of government
(1898) or for the overthrow of the dynastic system (1911), be they
led by the religious (1850–1864), the well educated (1919), the anti-
foreign (1900, 1937–1945), or Communists (1949), were always conducted in terms of China's relations with foreign powers, usually
the West. However, my suggestion is that the ability to preserve
more or less territorial integrity (while other ancient civilizations,
such as the Inca, the Aztec, India, Vietnam and Indochina, Algeria,
and others, were territorially captured) as well as linguistic integrity (Chinese remains the official language) means that as a "third
world" country, the Chinese relation to the imperialist West, until
the Communists officially propagandized "anti-imperialism," is seldom purely "oppositional" ideologically; on the contrary, the point
has always been for China to become as strong as the West, to
become the West's "equal." And even though the Chinese Communists once served as the anti-imperialist inspiration for other "third
world" cultures and progressive Western intellectuals, that dream
of a successful and consistent opposition to the West on ideological
grounds has been dealt the death blow by more recent events such
as the Tiananmen Massacre of 1989, in which the Chinese government itself acted as viciously as if it were one of its capitalist enemies.[15] As the champion of the unprivileged classes and nations of
the world, Communist China has shown itself to be a failure, a

failure which is now hanging on by empty official rhetoric while its people choose to live in ways that have obviously departed from the Communist ideal.

The point of summarizing modern Chinese history in such a schematic fashion is to underscore how the notion of "coloniality" (together with the culture criticisms that follow from it), when construed strictly in terms of the *foreignness* of race, land, and language, can *blind* us to political exploitation as easily as it can alert us to it. In the history of modern Western imperialism, the Chinese were never completely dominated by a foreign colonial power, but the apparent absence of the "enemy" as such does not make the Chinese case any *less* "third world" in terms of the exploitation suffered by the people, whose most important colonizer remains their own government. China, perhaps because it is an exception to the rule of imperialist domination by race, land, and language involving a foreign power, in fact highlights the effects of the imperialistic *transformation of value and value-production* more sharply than in other "third world" cultures. Unlike, say, India, where the British left behind insurmountable poverty, a cumbersome bureaucracy, and a language with which to function as a "nation," but where therefore the sentiment of opposition can remain legitimately alive because there is historically a clearly identifiable *foreign* colonizer, the Chinese continue to have "their own" system, "their own" language, and "their own" problems. The obsession of Chinese intellectuals remains "China" rather than the opposition to the West. The cultural production that results is therefore narcissistic, rather than simply oppositional, in structure. Whatever oppositional sentiment there exists is an oppositional sentiment directed toward itself—"China," the "Chinese heritage," the "Chinese tradition," the "Chinese government," and variants of these.

To give to Chinese and East Asian studies the critical energy they need is therefore to articulate the problems of *narcissistic value-production within*—rather than in negligence of—the larger context of the legacy of *cultural imperialism*. Neither of these alone suffices for a genuine intervention. The work that has yet to be done in the field of East Asia is not a matter of sidestepping the critique of Orientalism in order to talk about what are "authentically" East Asian historical issues. Instead, putting the myth of "authenticity" within the history of a mutually reinforcing universalism and particularism, we must demand: Why were questions of Orientalism not asked earlier, and why are they being avoided even now?

Sanctifying the "Subaltern": The Productivity of White Guilt

The Orientalist has a special sibling whom I will, in order to highlight her significance as a kind of representational agency, call the Maoist. Arif Dirlik, who has written extensively on the history of political movements in twentieth-century China, sums up the interpretation of Mao Zedong commonly found in Western Marxist analyses in terms of a "Third Worldist fantasy"—"a fantasy of Mao as a Chinese reincarnation of Marx who fulfilled the Marxist promise that had been betrayed in the West."[16] The Maoist was the phoenix which arose from the ashes of the great disillusionment with Western culture in the 1960s and which found hope in the Chinese Communist Revolution.[17] In the 1970s, when it became possible for Westerners to visit China as guided and pampered guests of the Beijing establishment, Maoists came back with reports of Chinese society's absolute, positive difference from Western society and of the Cultural Revolution as "the most important and innovative example of Mao's concern with the pursuit of egalitarian, populist, and communitarian ideals in the course of economic modernization" (Harding, p. 939). At that time, even poverty in China was regarded as "spiritually ennobling, since it meant that [the] Chinese were not possessed by the wasteful and acquisitive consumerism of the United States" (Harding, p. 941).

Although the excessive admiration of the 1970s has since been replaced by an oftentimes equally excessive denigration of China, the Maoist is very much alive among us, and her significance goes far beyond the China and East Asian fields. Typically, the Maoist is a cultural critic who lives in a capitalist society but who is fed up with capitalism—a cultural critic, in other words, who wants a social order opposed to the one that is supporting her own undertaking. The Maoist is thus a supreme example of the way desire works: What she wants is always located in the other, resulting in an identification with and valorization of that which she is not/does not have. Since what is valorized is often the other's deprivation—"having" poverty or "having" nothing—the Maoist's strategy becomes in the main a *rhetorical* renunciation of the material power that enables her rhetoric.

In terms of intellectual lineage, one of the Maoist's most important ancestors is Charlotte Brontë's Jane Eyre. Like Jane, the Maoist's means to moral power is a specific representational position—the position of powerlessness. In their reading of *Jane Eyre*, Nancy Armstrong and Leonard Tennenhouse argue that the novel exemplifies the paradigm of violence that expresses its *dominance through a representation of the self as powerless*:

> Until the very end of the novel, Jane is always excluded from every available form of social power. Her survival seems to depend on renouncing what power might come to her as teacher, mistress, cousin, heiress, or missionary's wife. She repeatedly flees from such forms of inclusion in the field of power, as if her status as an exemplary subject, like her authority as narrator, depends entirely on her claim to a kind of truth which can only be made from a position of powerlessness. By creating such an unlovely heroine and subjecting her to one form of harassment after another, Brontë demonstrates the power of words alone.[18]

This reading of Jane Eyre highlights her not simply as the female underdog who is often identified by feminist and Marxist critics, but as the intellectual who acquires power through a moral rectitude that was to become the flip side of Western imperialism's ruthlessness. Lying at the core of Anglo-American liberalism, this moral rectitude would accompany many territorial and economic conquests overseas with a firm sense of social mission. When Jane Eyre went to the colonies in the nineteenth century, she turned into the Christian missionary. It is this understanding—that Brontë's depiction of a socially marginalized English woman is, in terms of ideological production, fully complicit with England's empire-building ambition rather than opposed to it—that prompted Gayatri Spivak to read *Jane Eyre* as a text in the service of imperialism. Referring to Brontë's treatment of the "madwoman" Bertha Mason, the white Jamaican Creole character, Spivak charges *Jane Eyre* for, precisely, its humanism, in which the "native subject" is not created as an animal but as "the object of what might be termed the terrorism of the categorical imperative." This kind of creation is imperialism's use/travesty of the Kantian metaphysical demand to "*make* the heathen into a human so that he can be treated as an end in himself."[19]

In the twentieth century, as Europe's former colonies became independent, Jane Eyre became the Maoist. Michel de Certeau describes the affinity between her two major reincarnations, one religious and the other political, this way:

> The place that was formerly occupied by the Church or Churches vis-à-vis the established powers remains recognizable, over the past two centuries, in the functioning of the opposition known as leftist. . . .
>
> [T]here is vis-à-vis the established order, a relationship between the Churches that defended an *other world* and the parties of the left which, since the nineteenth century, have promoted a *different future*. In both cases, similar functional characteristics can be discerned. . . .[20]

The Maoist retains many of Jane's awesome features, chief of which are a protestant passion to turn powerlessness into "truth" and an idealist intolerance of those who may think differently from her. Whereas the great Orientalist blames the living "third world" natives for the loss of the ancient non-Western civilization, his loved object, the Maoist applauds the same natives for personifying and fulfilling her ideals. For the Maoist in the 1970s, the mainland Chinese were, in spite of their "backwardness," a puritanical alternative to the West in human form—a dream come true.

In the 1980s and 1990s, however, the Maoist is disillusioned to watch the China they sanctified crumble before their eyes. This is the period in which we hear disapproving criticisms of contemporary Chinese people for liking Western pop music and consumer culture, or for being overly interested in sex. In a way that makes her indistinguishable from what at first seems a political enemy, the Orientalist, the Maoist now mourns the loss of her loved object— Socialist China—by pointing angrily at living "third world" natives. For many who have built their careers on the vision of Socialist China, the grief is tremendous.

In the "cultural studies" of the American academy in the 1990s, the Maoist is reproducing with prowess. We see this in the way terms such as "oppression," "victimization," and "subalternity" are now being used. Contrary to Orientalist disdain for contemporary native cultures of the non-West, the Maoist turns precisely the "disdained" other into the object of his/her study and, in some cases, identification. In a mixture of admiration and moralism, the Maoist sometimes turns all people from non-Western cultures into a generalized "subaltern" that is then used to flog an equally generalized "West."[21]

Because the representation of "the other" as such ignores (1) the class and intellectual hierarchies within these other cultures, which are usually as elaborate as those in the West, and (2) the discursive power relations structuring the Maoist's mode of inquiry and valorization, it produces a way of talking in which notions of lack, subalternity, victimization, and so forth are drawn upon indiscriminately, often with the intention of spotlighting the speaker's own sense of alterity and political righteousness. A comfortably wealthy white American intellectual I know claimed that he was a "third world intellectual," citing as one of his credentials his marriage to a Western European woman of part-Jewish heritage; a professor of English complained about being "victimized" by the structured time at an Ivy League institution, meaning that she needed to be on time for classes; a graduate student of upper-class background from one of the world's poorest countries told his American friends that he was of poor peasant stock in order to authenticate his identity as a radical "third world" representative; male and female academics across the U.S. frequently say they were "raped" when they report experiences of professional frustration and conflict. Whether sincere or delusional, such cases of self-dramatization all take the route of self-subalternization, which has increasingly become the assured means to authority and power. What these intellectuals are doing is robbing the terms of oppression of their critical and oppositional import, and thus depriving the oppressed of even the vocabulary of protest and rightful demand. The oppressed, whose voices we seldom hear, are robbed twice—the first time of their economic chances, the second time of their language, which is now no longer distinguishable from those of us who have had our consciousnesses "raised."

In their analysis of the relation between violence and representation, Armstrong and Tennenhouse write: "[The] idea of violence as representation is not an easy one for most academics to accept. It implies that whenever we speak for someone else we are inscribing her with our own (implicitly masculine) idea of order."[22] At present, this process of "inscribing" often means not only that we "represent" certain historic others because they are/were "oppressed"; it often means that *there is interest in representation only when what is represented can in some way be seen as lacking.* Even though the Maoist is usually contemptuous of Freudian psychoanalysis because it is "bourgeois," her investment in oppression and victimization fully partakes of the Freudian and Lacanian notions of "lack." By attributing "lack," the Maoist justifies the "speaking for someone else" that Armstrong and Tennenhouse call "violence as representation."

As in the case of Orientalism, which does not necessarily belong only to those who are white, the Maoist does not have to be racially "white" either. The phrase "white guilt" refers to a type of discourse which continues to position power and lack against each other, while the narrator of that discourse, like Jane Eyre, speaks with power but identifies with powerlessness. This is how even those who come from privilege more often than not speak from/of/as its "lack." What the Maoist demonstrates is a circuit of productivity that draws its capital from others' deprivation while refusing to acknowledge its own presence as endowed. With the material origins of her own discourse always concealed, the Maoist thus speaks as if her charges were a form of immaculate conception.

The difficulty facing us, it seems to me, is no longer simply the "first world" Orientalist who mourns the rusting away of his treasures, but also students from privileged backgrounds Western *and* non-Western, who conform behaviorally in every respect with the elitism of their social origins (e.g., through powerful matrimonial alliances, through pursuit of fame, or through a contemptuous arrogance toward fellow students) but who nonetheless *proclaim* dedication to "vindicating the subalterns." My point is not that they should be blamed for the accident of their birth, nor that they cannot marry rich, pursue fame, or even be arrogant. Rather, it is that they choose to see in others' powerlessness an idealized image of themselves and refuse to hear in the dissonance between the content and manner of their speech their own complicity with violence. Even though these descendents of the Maoist may be quick to point out the exploitativeness of Benjamin Disraeli's "The East is a career,"[23] they remain blind to their own exploitativeness as they make "the East" *their* career. How do we intervene in the productivity of this overdetermined circuit?

Tactics of Intervention

Between Orientalism and nativism, between the melancholic cultural connoisseur and the militant Maoist—this is the scene of postcoloniality as many diasporic intellectuals find it in the West. "Diasporas are emblems of transnationalism because they embody the question of borders," writes Khachig Tölölyan.[24] The "question of borders" should not be a teleological one. It is not so much about the transient eventually giving way to the permanent as it is about an existential condition of which "permanence" itself is an ongoing fabrication. Accordingly, if, as William Safran writes, "diasporic consciousness is an intellectualization of [the] existential condition"[25] of dispersal from the homeland, then "diasporic consciousness" is perhaps not so much a historical accident as it is an intellectual reality—the reality of being intellectual.

Central to the question of borders is the question of propriety and property. Conceivably, one possible practice of borders is to anticipate and prepare for new proprietorship by destroying, replacing, and expanding existing ones. For this notion of borders—as margins waiting to be incorporated as new properties—to work, the accompanying spatial notion of a field is essential. The notion of a "field" is analogous to the notion of "hegemony," in the sense that its formation involves the rise to dominance of a group that is able to diffuse its culture to all levels of society. In Gramsci's sense, revolution is a struggle for hegemony between opposing classes.

While the struggle for hegemony remains necessary for many reasons—especially in cases where underprivileged groups seek equality of privilege—I remain skeptical of the validity of hegemony over time, *especially if it is a hegemony formed through intellectual power.* The question for me is not how intellectuals can obtain hegemony (a question that positions them in an oppositional light against dominant power and neglects their share of that power through literacy, through the culture of words), but how they can resist, as Michel Foucault said, "the forms of power that transform [them] into its object and instrument in the sphere of 'knowledge,' 'truth,' 'consciousness,' and 'discourse.' "[26] Putting it another way, how do intellectuals struggle against a hegemony which already includes them and which can no longer be divided into the state and civil society in Gramsci's terms, nor be clearly demarcated into national and transnational spaces?

Because "borders" have so clearly meandered into so many intellectual issues that the more stable and conventional relation between borders and the "field" no longer holds, intervention cannot simply be thought of in terms of the creation of new "fields."[27] Instead, it is necessary to think *primarily* in terms of borders—of borders, that is, as *para-sites* that never take over a field in its entirety but erode it slowly and *tactically*.

The work of Michel de Certeau is helpful for a formulation of this para-sitical intervention. De Certeau distinguishes between "strategy" and another practice—"tactic"—in the following terms. A strategy has the ability to "transform the uncertainties of history into readable spaces" (de Certeau, p. 36). The type of knowledge derived from strategy is "one sustained and determined by the power to provide oneself with one's own place" (de Certeau, p. 36). Strategy therefore belongs to "an economy of the proper place" (de Certeau, p. 55) and to those who are committed to the building, growth, and fortification of a "field." A text, for instance, would become in this economy "a cultural weapon, a private hunting preserve," or "a means of social stratification" in the order of the Great Wall of China (de Certeau, p. 171). A tactic, by contrast, is "a calculated action determined by the absence of a proper locus" (de Certeau, p. 37). Betting on time instead of space, a tactic "concerns an operational logic whose models may go as far back as the age-old ruses of fishes and insects that disguise or transform themselves in order to survive, and which has in any case been concealed by the form of rationality currently dominant in Western culture" (de Certeau, p. xi).

Why are "tactics" useful at this moment? As discussions about "multiculturalism," "interdisciplinarity," "the third world intellectual," and other companion issues develop in the American academy and society today, and as rhetorical claims to political change and difference are being put forth, many deep-rooted, politically reactionary forces return to haunt us. Essentialist notions of culture and history; conservative notions of territorial and linguistic propriety, and the "otherness" ensuing from them; unattested claims of oppression and victimization that are used merely to guilt-trip and to control; sexist and racist reaffirmations of sexual and racial diversities that are made merely in the name of righteousness—all these forces create new "solidarities" whose ideological premises remain unquestioned. These new solidarities are often informed by a *strategic* attitude which repeats what they seek to overthrow. The weight of old ideologies being reinforced over and over again is immense.

We need to remember as intellectuals that the battles we fight are battles of words. Those who argue the oppositional standpoint are not *doing* anything different from their enemies and are most certainly not directly changing the downtrodden lives of those who seek their survival in metropolitan and nonmetropolitan spaces alike. What academic intellectuals must confront is thus *not* their "victimization" by society at large (or their victimization-in-solidarity-with-the-oppressed), but the power, wealth, and privilege that ironically accumulate from their "oppositional" viewpoint, and the widening gap between the professed contents of their words and the upward mobility they gain from such words. (When Foucault said intellectuals need to struggle against becoming the object and instrument of power, he spoke precisely to this kind of situation.) The predicament we face in the West, where intellectual freedom shares a history with economic enterprise, is that "if a professor wishes to denounce aspects of big business, . . . he will be wise to locate in a school whose trustees are big businessmen."[28] Why should we believe in those who continue to speak a language of alterity-as-lack while their salaries and honoraria keep rising? How do we resist the turning-into-propriety of oppositional discourses, when the intention of such discourses has been that of displacing and disowning the proper? How do we prevent what begin as tactics—that which is "without any base where it could stockpile its winnings" (de Certeau, p. 37)—from turning into a solidly fenced-off field, in the military no less than in the academic sense?

The Chinese Lesson

The ways in which modern Chinese history is inscribed in our current theoretical and political discourses, often without our knowing about them, are quite remarkable. I can think of at least three major instances. First, post-structuralism's dismantling of the sign, which grew out of a criticism of phonetic logocentrism from within the Western tradition and which was to activate interest in "text" and "discourse" across humanistic studies, began in an era when Western intellectuals, in particular those in France (Jacques Derrida, Julia Kristeva, Philippe Sollers, Roland Barthes, Louis Althusser, to name a few) "turned East" to China for philosophical and political alternatives. Chinese "writing" has been a source of fascination for European philosophers and philologists since the eighteenth century because its ideographic script seems (at least to those who do not actually use it as a language) a testimony of a different kind of language—a language without the mediation of sound and hence without history.[29] Second, the feminist revolutions of the 1960s and 1970s drew on the Chinese Communists' practice of encouraging peasants, especially peasant women, to "speak bitterness" (*suku*) against an oppressive patriarchal system. The various methods of "consciousness-raising" that we still practice today, inside and outside the classroom, owe their origins to the Chinese "revolution" as described in William Hinton's *Fanshen*.[30] Third, the interest invested by current culture criticism in the socially dispossessed rejoins many issues central to the founding ideology of the Chinese Communist party, which itself drew on Soviet and other Western philosophies.[31] As I indicate in the chapter "Against the Lures of Diaspora," the one figure that is represented and discussed repeatedly in modern Chinese writings since the turn of the twentieth century has been none other than the "subaltern."

To prioritize modern Chinese history this way—to say that "modern China" is, whether we know it or not, the foundation of contemporary cultural studies—is not to glorify "Chinese wisdom." Rather, my aim is to show how the "fate" of an ancient civilization turned modern epitomizes and anticipates many problems we are *now* facing in the West, which in many ways is condemned to a kind of belated consciousness of what its forces set in motion in its others, which usually experience the traumas much earlier. In this regard, the impasses long felt by modern Chinese intellectuals vis-à-vis "their" history, which not only comprises a language used by over a quarter of the world's population but also a long tradition of writing, printing, publishing, examinations, revolutions, and state bureaucracy, can serve as a model for the West's future in the negative sense, that is, a future whose disasters have already been written.

To give one example, the sanctification of victimization in the American academy and its concomitant rebuke of "theory" as intellectualist and elitist parallel, in an uncanny fashion, the treatment of intellectuals during the Cultural Revolution, when labels of "feudalist," "reactionary," "Confucianist," and the like led to murder and execution in the name of salvaging the oppressed classes. This alleged separation of intellectuals from life continues today, not so much in China, where intellectuals are poorly paid, as in places where part of the power enjoyed by intellectuals comes precisely from "bashing" themselves from an anti-intellectual position of "solidarity with the masses." Terry Eagleton's recent diatribe against "American" intellectuals—even though his own publications are bestsellers in the American intellectual market—is a good example of this kind of Cultural Revolution thinking inside capitalist society. Eagleton's attitude is consistent with the typical European intellectual disdain toward "America" and with British intellectual disdain toward "French thought." This is how he uses the Tiananmen incident to target *his own* enemies:

> Viewed from eight thousand miles off, [the new historicist] enthusiasm for Foucault has a good deal to do with a peculiarly American left defeatism, guilt-stricken relativism and ignorance of socialism— a syndrome which is understandable in Berkeley but, as I write, unintelligible in Beijing. The unconscious ethnocentrism of much of the U.S. appropriation of such theory is very striking, at least to *an outsider*. What seems on the surface like a glamorous theory of the Renaissance keeps turning out to be about the dilemmas of ageing 1960s radicals in the epoch of Danforth Quayle. I write this article while the Chinese students and workers are still massing outside the Great Hall of the People; and I find it rather hard to understand why the neo-Stalinist bureaucrats have not, so far anyway, moved among the people distributing copies of Derrida, Foucault and Ernesto Laclau. For the Chinese students and workers to learn that their

actions are aimed at a "social totality" which is, theoretically speaking, non-existent would surely disperse them more rapidly than
water cannons or bullets.[32]

The claim to being an "outsider" is a striking one, bringing to
mind not only Jane Eyre's self-marginalization but also nineteenth-
century Britain's "splendid isolation." Needless to say, it remains
the case that the "people" of the "third world" are invoked only in
the form of an indistinguishable mass, while "first world" intellectuals continue to have names.

Growing up in the 1960s and 1970s in Hong Kong, that "classic
immigrant city" and "junction between diaspora and homeland,"[33]
I experienced Chinese communism differently from many of my
colleagues in the American academy and as a result am incapable
of drawing from it the sense of revolutionary conviction that still
infuses the speeches of Marxist intellectuals in the West. If Gramsci
writing in prison "might have been Mao announcing the Cultural
Revolution," then the problem of Mao, for many Chinese, was precisely that he "did what Gramsci thought."[34] My most vivid childhood memories of the Cultural Revolution were the daily reports
in 1966 and 1967 of corpses from China floating down into the Pearl
River Delta and down into the Hong Kong harbor, of local political
unrest that led to disruption of school and business, and of the
brutal murder of Lam Bun, an employee of Hong Kong's Commercial Radio (a pro-British institution, as were many of Hong Kong's
big financial enterprises of that time) whose work during that period involved reading a daily editorial denouncing leftist activities.
On his way to work with his brother one day in 1967, Lam Bun was
stopped by gangsters, who barred them from getting out of his car
and burned them alive. There are also memories of people risking
their lives swimming across the border into Hong Kong and of people visiting China with "the little red book" but also with supplies
of food and clothing. This was a period of phenomenal starvation
in China. Some people from Hong Kong were going in the hope
that, if not searched by border authorities, they could leave behind
the food and clothing for needy relatives. (One woman, I recall,
wore seven pairs of pants on one of her trips.)

What I retain from these memories is not a history of personal
or collective victimization but the sense of immediacy of a particular

diasporic reality—of Hong Kong caught, as it always has been since the end of the Second World War, between two dominant cultures, British colonial and Chinese Communist, neither of which takes the welfare of Hong Kong people into account even though both would turn to Hong Kong for financial and other forms of assistance when they needed it. This marginalized position, which is not one chosen by those from Hong Kong but one constructed by history, brings with it a certain privilege of observation and an unwillingness to idealize oppression. To find myself among colleagues from the U.S., Europe, India, and Africa who speak of Chinese communism in idealized terms remains a culture shock. My point, however, is not that of denouncing communism as an error of human history.[35] With the collapse of communism in the Soviet Union and the waning of communism in China, it is easy to bash Marxists and Communists as "wrongdoers" of the past two centuries. This would be like saying that Christians and the church misrepresent the true teachings of the Bible. To the contrary, I think an understanding of what "went wrong" would be possible only if we are willing to undertake what Foucault advocates as a historical analysis of "fascism," a term which, as Foucault said, has been used as a floating signifier with which we blame the other for what goes wrong.[36] The first step in this analysis is not, for instance, to show how the Soviet Union has woken up to its error of the past seventy-four years but to acknowledge that what happened in the Soviet Union and China are necessary events of a positive present of which we, living in the other half of the globe in "capitalistic freedom," are still a functioning part. To pose the "Gulag question," Foucault said, means:

> [r]efusing to question the Gulag on the basis of the texts of Marx or Lenin or to ask oneself how, through what error, deviation, misunderstanding or distortion of speculation or practice, their theory could have been betrayed to such a degree. On the contrary, it means questioning all these theoretical texts, however old, from the standpoint of the reality of the Gulag. Rather than of searching in those texts for a condemnation in advance of the Gulag, it is a matter of asking what in those texts could have made the Gulag possible, what might even now continue to justify it, and what makes it [*sic*] intolerable truth still accepted today. The Gulag question must be posed not in terms of error (reduction of the problem to one of theory), but in terms of reality.[37]

The hardest lesson from Chinese communism, as with Soviet communism, is that it has *not* been an accident but a process in the history of modern global enlightenment. This is a process that strategizes on the experiences of the "subalterns" while never truly resolving the fundamental division between intellectual and manual labor, nor hence the issues of hierarchy, inequity, and discrimination based on *literate* power. What the Chinese Cultural Revolution accomplished in a simplistic attempt to resolve that fundamental division was a *literal* destruction of intellectuals (as bearers of the division). While actual lives were thus sacrificed *en masse*, literate power as social form and as class division lives on. If indeed the "subalterns" were revolutionized, then why, we must ask, are we still hearing so much about problems in China that obviously indicate the opposite, such as the sexual oppression of women, the persistent illiteracy of the peasants, the abuse of bureaucratic power by those in charge of the welfare of the people—all in all what amounts to continued class injustice in a supposedly classless society?

Writing Diaspora

Each of the preceding sections contains questions that are part of that "intellectualization" of a "diasporic consciousness." The history of Hong Kong predisposes one to a kind of "border" or "parasite" practice—an identification with "Chinese culture" but a distantiation from the Chinese Communist regime; a resistance against colonialism but an unwillingness to see the community's prosperity disrupted. The advantage of a continuous and complete institutional education, even when that education was British colonial and American, means that unlike many people who have no means of leaving Hong Kong before the Chinese Communist takeover in 1997, I have not been "subordinated." Even though my "personal" history is written with many forms of otherness, such otherness, when combined with the background of my education, is not that of the victim but of a specific kind of social power, which enables me to speak and write by wielding the tools of my enemies.

When its term of colonization by the British comes to an end in 1997, Hong Kong will, in a way that makes it unique in the history of Western imperialism, be handed over to a new colonial power called "its mother country." (It will share this peculiar condition with neighboring Macau, currently a Portuguese colony.) Squeezed between West and East, Hong Kong currently has a democracy that is as fragile as its citizens' ethnic ties to China are tenacious. As Martin Lee, the most outspoken leader for democracy in Hong Kong, describes it: "Imagine a paper door. Of course you can walk through it. It is only useful if you respect the people behind it, and open it and enter only after you've been invited. Democracy in Hong Kong is that paper door, hoping that China will respect us and will not therefore barge in."[38] While China already shows its will to exercise authoritarian rule—the leading example being that of imposing the building of a nuclear power reactor in Daya Bay, in close proximity to utterly unevacuable Hong Kong—Hong Kong citizens themselves remain fascinatingly contradictory in their "diasporic consciousness."

Two recent examples. First, during May 1989, more than half a million of Hong Kong's citizens took to the streets to give support to the student demonstrations in Beijing. We now know that many of the Chinese democracy leaders who escaped from China in subsequent months did so under the auspices of the "Yellow Bird Operation," a secret network of Hong Kong intellectuals who collaborated with the underground triad societies in Asia for the cause of their "compatriots." (The effect of the Beijing government's military violence was that civilians and criminals formed a united front.)[39] Second, in the summer of 1991, when an unprecedented flood disaster struck the majority of Chinese provinces, it was once again the citizens of Hong Kong who, by the end of that summer, had collectively donated more than HK $0.7 billion (approximately U.S. $90 million) to the China flood relief.[40]

My deliberate attempt to chronicle the major role played by Hong Kong in these happenings in China is not, however, an attempt to promote "Chinese" solidarity, which is what fueled and continues to fuel the recent events. And here I write as a kind of diasporic person in diaspora, a Hong Kong person in North America. Many in Hong Kong, like other Chinese communities overseas, are inspired by a sense of their "Chineseness"—many claimed, in June 1989, to have awakened to their "Chinese" identity, and the fund-raising activities in 1991 were conducted under slogans such

as "Blood is Thicker than Water." In the absence of a national religion, a strong single political regime, an identity based on national
unity, and often the possibility of ever living in China, the claims
to ethnic oneness—sinicization—suffice as a return home and are
as practically effective as they are illusory and manipulative. Like
all myths of origin, sinicization is usually "exploited for a variety of
political and social purposes by the diaspora, the homeland, and
the host society."[41] David Yen-ho Wu defines it this way:

> For centuries the meaning of being Chinese seemed simple and
> definite: a sense of belonging to a great civilization and performing
> properly according to the intellectual elites' norm of conduct. This
> is what Wang Gungwu referred to as the Chinese "historical iden-
> tity." The Chinese as a group traditionally believed that when a larger
> Chinese population arrived in the frontier land, Sinicization was the
> only possible course. It was inconceivable that any Chinese could
> be acculturated by the inferior non-Chinese "barbarians"; however,
> such acculturation has been a common course of development for
> Chinese in the frontier land and overseas, although people still insist
> that an unadulterated Chinese culture is maintained by the Chinese
> migrants.[42]

I call the current political sentiments in Hong Kong "contradictory" because the forces of sinicization are unbelievably strong precisely at a time when Hong Kong's historical difference from China
should stand as the most uncompromisable opposition to the mainland. While that difference is always invoked (even by the Chinese
authorities themselves, who promise a "one country, two systems"
rule after 1997), one has the feeling that the actual social antagonisms separating China and Hong Kong—such as a firmly instituted
and well-used legal system, emerging direct elections, the relative
freedom of speech, and so forth, all of which are present in Hong
Kong but absent in China—are often overwritten with the myth of
consanguinity, *a myth that demands absolute submission because
it is empty.* The submission to consanguinity means the surrender
of agency—what is built on work and livelihood rather than blood
and race—in the governance of a community. The people in Hong
Kong can sacrifice everything they have to the cause of loving
"China" and still, at the necessary moment, be accused of not being

patriotic—of not being "Chinese"—enough. (The same kind of logic was behind the guilt-tripping purges of the Cultural Revolution: Sacrifice everything, including your life, to the party, but it remains the party's decision whether or not you are loyal.) Going far beyond the responsibility any individual bears for belonging to a community, "Chineseness," as I show in some of the pages that follow, lies at the root of a violence which works by the most deeply ingrained feelings of "bonding" and which—even at the cost of social alienation—diasporic intellectuals must collectively resist.

Part of the goal of "writing diaspora" is, thus, to *unlearn* that submission to one's ethnicity such as "Chineseness" as the ultimate signified even as one continues to support movements for democracy and human rights in China, Hong Kong, and elsewhere. Such support must be given regardless of one's ethnic "roots." The essays in this book are not essays "for" China or Chinese or East Asian "specificity." While China and Asia are the focus of many of them, the related discussions are, I believe, germane to other disciplines where similar kinds of problems exist and need to be articulated. Nor should the book be read as a volume of "collected essays" demonstrating some unified body of ideas. My goal is to set up a discourse that cuts across some of our new "solidarities" by juxtaposing a range of cultural contradictions that make us rethink the currently dominant conceptualizations of the solidarities themselves. If there is something from my childhood and adolescent years that remains a chief concern in my writing, it is the tactics of dealing with and dealing in dominant cultures that are so characteristic of living in Hong Kong. These are the tactics of those who do not have claims to territorial propriety or cultural centrality. Perhaps more than anyone else, those who live in Hong Kong realize the opportunistic role they need to play in order, not to "preserve," but to negotiate their "cultural identity"; for them opportunity is molded in danger and danger is a form of opportunity. Their diaspora is a living emblem of the cryptic Chinese term *weiji*, which is made up of the characters for "danger" and "opportunity," and which means "crisis."

Vera Schwarcz recently wrote that "contemporary Chinese intellectuals have become fractured vessels—broken-hearted witnesses to their own and their countrymen's suffering." But, she goes on to say, "Fidelity to historical memory . . . requires intellectuals to acknowledge their own complicity in China's long-standing autocracy. This is an important and also a rather bleak responsibility."[43] One of the chapters in this book, "Pedagogy, Trust, Chinese Intellectuals in the 1990s," was written with the sense of this "bleak responsibility." This essay was presented in my absence at a major conference in late 1990. My discussant was someone who is a graduate from Harvard and a faculty member of a university in the U.S. In the original essay I had made a mistake in my translation from the Chinese. On the basis of this mistake, my discussant trashed the entire essay, commenting to the audience that, after all, "she's from Hong Kong."[44] The question behind this statement of the *fact* of my geographical origin, I suppose, was: How can this Westernized Chinese woman from colonial Hong Kong, this cultural bastard, speak for China and Chinese intellectuals? Had it been my ambition to represent China or be authentically Chinese, I would have been shattered in shame. What remains useful from this episode in diaspora is its lesson about a persistent and pernicious form of centrism.[45] Like many of his contemporaries in mainland China, this person who attacked me lived through the hardships of the Cultural Revolution, which disrupted and hampered the institutional education process of the Chinese youths of that time. He should have been quicker than most to recognize the cultural violence in the words which spoke him. That someone like him should survive the experience of such a vast oppression so politically, ethnically, and linguistically centrist and so adamantly devoted to the perpetuation of such centrism is a foremost example of the *strategized* realities challenging contemporary Chinese and all other intellectuals today.

II

WHERE HAVE ALL THE NATIVES GONE?

The Inauthentic Native

A couple of years ago, I was serving on a faculty search committee at the University of Minnesota. The search was for a specialist in Chinese language and literature. A candidate from the People's Republic of China gave a talk that discussed why we still enjoy reading the eighteenth-century classic *The Dream of the Red Chamber*. The talk was a theoretical demonstration of how no particular interpretation of this book could exhaust the possibilities of reading. During the search committee's discussion of the various candidates afterward, one faculty member, an American Marxist, voiced his disparaging view of this particular candidate in the following way: "The talk was not about why we still enjoy reading *The Dream of the Red Chamber*. It was about why she enjoys reading it. She does because she likes capitalism!"

This colleague of mine stunned me with a kind of discrimination that has yet to be given its proper name. The closest designation we currently have for his attitude is racism, that is, a reduction of someone from a particular group to the stereotypes, negative *or* positive, we have of that group. But what is at stake here is not really "race" as much as it is the assumption that a "native" of Communist China ought to be faithful to her nation's official political ideology. Instead of "racial" characteristics, Communist beliefs became the stereotype with which my colleague was reading this candidate. The fact that she did not speak from such beliefs but instead from an understanding of the text's irreducible plurality (an understanding he equated with "capitalism") greatly disturbed him; his lament was that this candidate had betrayed our expectation of what Communist "ethnic specimens" ought to be.

My colleague's disturbance takes us to the familiarly ironic scenarios of anthropology, in which Western anthropologists are uneasy at seeing "natives" who have gone "civilized" or who, like the anthropologists themselves, have taken up the active task of shaping their own culture. Margaret Mead, for instance, found the interest of certain Arapesh Indians (in Highland New Guinea) in cultural influences other than their own "annoying" since, as James Clifford puts it, *"Their* culture collecting complicated hers."[1] Similarly, Claude Lévi-Strauss, doing his "fieldwork" in New York on American ethnology, was affected by the sight, in the New York Public Library reading room where he was doing research for his *Elementary Structures of Kinship*, of a feathered Indian with a Parker pen. As Clifford comments:

> For Lévi-Strauss the Indian is primarily associated with the past, the "extinct" societies recorded in the precious Bureau of American Ethnology *Annual Reports*. The anthropologist feels himself "going back in time". . . . In modern New York an Indian can appear only as a survival or a kind of incongruous parody.[2]

My colleague shares the predicament of Mead and Lévi-Strauss insofar as the stereotypical "native" is receding from view. What confronts the Western scholar is the discomforting fact that the natives are no longer staying in their frames. In the case of the faculty search at Minnesota, what I heard was not the usual desire to *archaize* the modern Chinese person[3] but rather a valorizing, on the part of the Western critic, of the official political and cultural difference of the PRC as the designator of the candidate's supposed "authenticity." If a native from the PRC espouses capitalism, then she has already been corrupted. An ethnic specimen that was not pure was not of use to him.

The Native as Image

In the politics of identifying "authentic" natives, several strands of the word "identification" are at stake: How do we identify the native? How do we identify with her? How do we construct the native's "identity"? What processes of identification are involved? We cannot approach this politics without being critical of a particular relation to *images* that is in question.

In his volume of essays exploring film culture, Fredric Jameson writes that "The visual is *essentially* pornographic. . . . Pornographic films are . . . only the potentiation of films in general, which ask us to stare at the world as though it were a naked body."[4] This straightforward definition of the visual image sums up many of the problems we encounter in cultural criticism today, whether or not the topic in question is film. The activity of watching is linked by projection to physical nakedness. Watching is theoretically defined as the primary agency of violence, an act that pierces the other, who inhabits the place of the passive victim on display. The image, then, is an aggressive sight that reveals itself in the other; it is the site of the aggressed. Moreover, the image is what has been devastated, left bare, and left behind by aggression—hence Jameson's view that it is naked and pornographic.

For many, the image is also the site of possible change. In many critical discourses, the image is implicitly the place where battles are fought and strategies of resistance negotiated. Such discourses try to inhabit this image-site by providing alternative sights, alternative ways of watching *that would change the image*. Thus one of the most important enterprises nowadays is that of investigating the "subjectivity" of the other-as-oppressed-victim. "Subjectivity" becomes a way to change the defiled image, the stripped image, the image-reduced-to-nakedness, by showing the truth behind/beneath/around it. The problem with the reinvention of subjectivity as such is that it tries to combat the politics of the image, a politics that is conducted on surfaces, by a politics of depths, hidden truths, and inner voices. The most important aspect of the image—its power precisely as image and nothing else—is thus bypassed and left untouched.[5] It is in this problematic of *the image as the bad thing to be replaced* that I lodge the following arguments about the "native."

The question in which I am primarily interested is: Is there a way of "finding" the native without simply ignoring the image, or substituting a "correct" image of the ethnic specimen for an "incorrect" one, or giving the native a "true" voice "behind" her "false" image? How could we deal with the native in an age when there is no possibility of avoiding the reduction/abstraction of the native as image? How can we write about the native by not ignoring the defiled, degraded image that is an inerasable part of her status—i.e., by not resorting to the idealist belief that everything would be all right if the inner truth of the native is restored because the inner truth would lead to the "correct" image? I want to highlight the native—nowadays often a synonym for the oppressed, the marginalized, the wronged—because I think that the space occupied by the native in postcolonial discourses is also the space of error, illusion, deception, and filth. How would we write this space in such a way as to refuse the facile turn of sanctifying the defiled image with pieties and thus enriching ourselves precisely with what can be called the surplus value of the oppressed, a surplus value that results from *exchanging* the defiled image for something more noble?

The Native as Silent Object

The production of the native is in part the production of our postcolonial modernity. Before elaborating on the relation between "native" and "modernity," however, I want to examine how current theoretical discussions of the native problematize the space of the native in the form of a symptom of the white man. Following Lacan, I use "symptom" not in the derogatory sense of a dispensable shadow but in the sense of something that gives the subject its ontological consistency and its fundamental structure. Slavoj Žižek explains the non-pejorative sense of "symptom" this way:

> If, however, we conceive the symptom as Lacan did in his last writings and seminars, namely as a particular signifying formation which confers on the subject its very ontological consistency, enabling it to structure its basic, constitutive relationship towards enjoyment (*jouissance*), then the entire relationship [between subject and symptom] is reversed, for if the symptom is dissolved, the subject itself disintegrates. In this sense, "Woman is a symptom of man" means that man himself exists only through woman qua his symptom: his very ontological consistency depends on, is "externalized" in, his symptom.[6]

As the white man's symptom, as that which is externalized in relation to the white-man-as-subject, the space occupied by the native is essentially object-ive, the space of the object.

Because of the symptomatic way non-white peoples are constructed in postcoloniality, and because "symptom" is conventionally regarded in a secondary, derivative sense, many critics of colonialism attempt to write about these peoples in such a way as to wrest them away from their status as symptom or object. The result is a certain inevitable subjectivizing, and here the anti-imperialist project runs a parallel course with the type of feminist project that seeks to restore the truth to women's distorted and violated identities by theorizing female subjectivity. We see this in Frantz Fanon's formulation of the native. Like Freud's construction of woman (which, though criticized, is repeated by many feminists), Fanon's construction of the native is Oedipal. Freud's question was "What does woman want?" Fanon, elaborating on the necessity of violence in the native's formation, asks "What does the black man want?"[7] The native (the black man) is thus imagined to be an angry son who wants to displace the white man, the father. While Freud would go on to represent woman as lack, Fanon's argument is that the native is someone from whom something has been stolen. The native, then, is also lack.

This Oedipal structure of thinking—a structure of thinking that theorizes subjectivity as compensation for a presumed lack—characterizes discourses on the non-West in a pervasive manner, including, occasionally, the discourse of those who are otherwise critical of its patriarchal overtones. In her reading of Julia Kristeva's *About Chinese Women*, for instance, Gayatri Spivak criticizes Kristeva's ethnocentric sense of "alienation" at the sight of some Chinese women in Huxian Square. Kristeva's passage goes as follows:

> An enormous crowd is sitting in the sun: they wait for us wordlessly, perfectly still. Calm eyes, not even curious, but slightly amused or anxious: in any case, piercing, and certain of belonging to a community with which we will never have anything to do.[8]

Citing this passage, which is followed a few pages later by the question, "Who is speaking, then, before the stare of the peasants at Huxian?",[9] Spivak charges Kristeva with being primarily interested in her own identity rather than in these other women's. While I agree with this observation, I find Spivak's formulation of these other women's identity in terms of "envy" troubling: "Who is speaking here? An effort to answer that question might have revealed more about the mute women of Huxian Square, *looking with qualified envy* at the 'incursion of the West.' "[10] Doesn't the word "envy" here remind us of that condition ascribed to women by Freud, against which feminists revolt—namely, "penis envy"? "Envy" is the other side of the "violence" of which Fanon speaks as the fundamental part of the native's formation. But both affects—the one of wanting to *have* what the other has; the other, of destroying the other so that one can *be* in his place—are affects produced by a patriarchal ideology that assumes that the other at the low side of the hierarchy of self/other is "lacking" (in the pejorative, undesirable sense). Such an ideology, while acknowledging that a lack cannot be filled, also concentrates on how it might be filled (by the same thing), even if imperfectly. The fate of the native is then like that of Freud's woman: Even though she will never have a penis, she will for the rest of her life be trapped within the longing for it and its substitutes.

What we see in the accounts by Kristeva and Spivak is a battle for demonstrating the *unspeaking* truth of the native. While Spivak shows how the articulation of the Western critic is itself already a sign of her privileged identity, for Kristeva it is the limits of Western articulation and articulation itself that have to be recognized in the presence of the silent Chinese women. Throughout Kristeva's encounter with these women, therefore, we find descriptions of the others' looking—their "calm eyes," their "indefinable stare,"[11] and so on—that try to capture their undisturbed presence. If these others have been turned into objects, it is because these objects' gaze makes the Western "subject" feel alienated from her own familiar (familial) humanity:

> They don't distinguish among us man or woman, blonde or brunette, this or that feature of face or body. As though they were discovering some weird and peculiar animals, harmless but insane.[12]
>
> I don't feel like a foreigner, the way I do in Baghdad or New York. I feel like an ape, a martian, an *other*.[13]

Between a critical desire to subjectivize them with envy and a "humble" gesture to revere them as silent objects, is there any alternative for these "natives"?

Kristeva's way of "giving in" to the strangeness of the other is a philosophical and semiotic gesture that characterizes many European intellectuals, whose discourse becomes self-accusatory and, *pace* Rousseau, confessional when confronted by the other.[14] When that other is Asia and the "Far East," it always seems as if the European intellectual must speak in absolute terms, making this other an utterly incomprehensible, terrifying, and fascinating spectacle. For example, after visiting Japan, Alexandre Kojève, who had asserted that history had come to an end (he was convinced of this in the United States, where he thought he found the "classless society" predicted by Marx as the goal of human history), wrote a long footnote to the effect that his experience with the Japanese had radically changed his opinion about history. For Kojève in 1959, as for Roland Barthes about a decade later, the formalized rituals of Japanese society suggested that the Japanese had arrived at the end of history three centuries earlier. As Barthes would say, semiologically, that Japanese culture is made up of empty signs, Kojève writes:

> all Japanese without exception are currently in a position to live according to totally *formalized* values—that is, values completely empty of all "human" content in the "historical" sense. Thus, in the extreme, every Japanese is in principle capable of committing, from pure snobbery, a perfectly "gratuitous" *suicide*. . . . [15]

Michel Serres, on the other hand, also finds "the end of history" when he goes east, but it is in agricultural China that he finds the absolute totality of the other. Confronted with the Chinese who have to make use of every bit of land for cultivation, Serres comments with statements like the following in an essay called "China Loam":

> Farming has covered over everything like a tidal wave.
>   It is the totality.

> This positiveness is so complete, so compact, that it can only be expressed negatively. There is no margin, no gap, no passes, no omission, no waste, no vestiges. The fringe, the fuzzy area, the

refuse, the wasteland, the open-space have all disappeared: no surplus, no vacuum, no history, no time.[16]

Here the utmost limit of what we call history had already been
reached a thousand years ago.[17]

To the extent that it is our own limit that we encounter when we
encounter another, all these intellectuals can do is no more than
render the other as the negative of what they are and what they
do. As Serres puts it, the spectacle of China's total rationality is so
"positive, so rational, so well-adapted that one can only speak of it
in negative terms."[18] As such, the "native" is turned into an absolute
entity in the form of an image (the "empty" Japanese ritual or
"China loam"), whose silence becomes the occasion for *our*
speech.[19] The gaze of the Western scholar is "pornographic" and
the native becomes a mere "naked body" in the sense described by
Jameson. Whether positive or negative, the construction of the native remains at the level of image-identification, a process in which
"our" own identity is measured in terms of the degrees to which
we resemble her and to which she resembles us. Is there a way of
conceiving of the native beyond imagistic resemblance?

This question is what prompts Spivak's bold and provocative
statement, "The subaltern cannot speak."[20] Because it seems to cast
the native permanently in the form of a silent object, Spivak's statement foreseeably gives rise to pious defenses of the native as a
voiced subject and leads many to jump on the bandwagon of de-
claring solidarity with "subalterns" of different kinds. Speaking sin-
cerely of the multiple voices of the native woman thus, Benita Parry
criticizes Spivak for assigning an absolute power to the imperialist
discourse:

> Since the native woman is constructed within multiple social rela-
> tionships and positioned as the product of different class, caste and
> cultural specificities, it should be possible to locate traces and testi-
> mony of women's voice on those sites where women inscribed them-
> selves as healers, ascetics, singers of sacred songs, artisans and
> artists, and by this to modify Spivak's model of the silent subaltern.[21]

In contrast to Spivak, Parry supports Homi Bhabha's argument that
since a discursive system is inevitably split in enunciation, the colo-

nist's text itself already contains a native voice—ambivalently. The colonial text's "hybridity," to use Bhabha's word, means that the subaltern has spoken.[22] But what kind of an argument is it to say that the subaltern's "voice" can be found in the *ambivalence* of the imperialist's speech? It is an argument which ultimately makes it unnecessary to come to terms with the subaltern since she has already "spoken," as it were, in the system's gaps. All we would need to do would be to continue to study—to deconstruct—the rich and ambivalent language of the imperialist! What Bhabha's word "hybridity" revives, in the masquerade of deconstruction, anti-imperialism, and "difficult" theory, is an old functionalist notion of what a dominant culture permits in the interest of maintaining its own equilibrium. Such functionalism informs the investigatory methods of classical anthropology and sociology as much as it does the colonial policies of the British Empire. The kind of subject-constitution it allows, a subject-constitution firmly inscribed in Anglo-American liberal humanism, is the other side of the process of image-identification, in which we try to make the native more like us by giving her a "voice."

The charge of Spivak's essay, on the other hand, is a protest against the *two* sides of image-identification, the *two* types of freedom the subaltern has been allowed—object formation and subject constitution—which would result either in the subaltern's protection (as object) from her own kind or her achievement as a voice assimilable to the project of imperialism. That is why Spivak concludes by challenging precisely the optimistic view that the subaltern has already spoken: "The subaltern cannot speak. There is no virtue in global laundry lists with 'woman' as a pious item."[23]

Instead, a radical alternative can be conceived only when we recognize the essential *untranslatability* from the subaltern discourse to imperialist discourse. Using Jean-François Lyotard's notion of the *différend*, which she explains as "the inaccessibility of, or untranslatability from, one mode of discourse in a dispute to another,"[24] Spivak argues the impossibility of the subaltern's constitution *in life*. The subaltern cannot speak not because there are not activities in which we can locate a subaltern mode of life/culture/subjectivity, but because, as is indicated by the critique of thought and articulation given to us by Western intellectuals such as Lacan, Foucault, Barthes, Kristeva, and Derrida (Spivak's most important reference), "speaking" itself belongs to an already well-defined structure and history of domination. As she says in an interview: "If the subaltern can speak then, thank God, the subaltern is not a subaltern any more."[25]

It is only when we acknowledge the fact that the subaltern cannot speak that we can begin to plot a different kind of process of identification for the native. It follows that, within Spivak's argument, it is a *silent* gesture on the part of a young Hindu woman, Bhuvaneswari Bhaduri, who committed suicide during her menstruation so that the suicide could not be interpreted as a case of illicit pregnancy, that becomes a telling instance of subaltern writing, a writing whose message is only understood retrospectively.[26] As such, the "identity" of the native is inimitable, beyond the resemblance of the image. The type of identification offered by her silent space is what may be called symbolic identification. In the words of Slavoj Žižek:

> in imaginary identification we imitate the other at the level of resemblance—we identify ourselves with the image of the other inasmuch as we are 'like him', while in symbolic identification we identify ourselves with the other precisely at a point at which he is inimitable, at the point which eludes resemblance.[27]

Local Resurrections, New Histories

As an issue of postcoloniality, the problem of the native is also the problem of modernity and modernity's relation to "endangered authenticities."[28] The question to ask is not whether we can return the native to her authentic origin, but what our fascination with the native means in terms of the irreversibility of modernity.

There are many commendable accounts of how the native in the non-Western world has been used by the West as a means to promote and develop its own intellectual contours.[29] According to these accounts, modernism, especially the modernism that we associate with the art of Modigliani, Picasso, Gauguin, the novels of Gustave Flaubert, Marcel Proust, D. H. Lawrence, James Joyce, Henry Miller, and so forth, was possible only because these "first world" artists with famous names incorporated into their "creativity" the culture and artwork of the peoples of the non-West. But while

Western artists continue to receive attention specifically categorized in time, place, and name, the treatment of the works of non-
Western peoples continues to partake of systemic patterns of
exploitation and distortion.

Apart from the general attribution of "anonymity" to native artists, "native works" have been bifurcated either as timeless (in
which case they would go into art museums) or as historical (in
which case they would go into ethnographic museums). While most
cultural critics today are alert to the pitfalls of the "timeless art"
argument, many are still mired in efforts to invoke "history," "contexts," and "specificities" as ways to resurrect the native. In doing
so, are they restoring to the native what has been stolen from her?
Or are they in fact avoiding the genuine problem of the native's
status as object by providing *something* that is more manageable
and comforting—namely, a phantom history in which natives appear as our equals and our images, in our shapes and our forms?
Nancy Armstrong summarizes our predicament this way:

> The new wave of culture criticism still assumes that we must either
> be a subject who partakes in the power of gazing or else be an object
> that is by implication the object of a pornographic gaze. The strategy
> of identifying people according to "subject positions" in a vast and
> intricate differential system of interests and needs is perhaps the
> most effective way we now have of avoiding the problem incurred
> whenever we classify political interests by means of bodies inscribed
> with signs of race, class, and gender. But even the "subject" of the
> critical term "subject position" tends to dissolve too readily back into
> a popular and sentimental version of the bourgeois self. By defini-
> tion, this self grants priority to an embodied subject over the body
> as an object. To insist on being "subjects" as opposed to "objects" is
> to assume that we must have certain powers of observation, classi-
> fication, and definition in order to exist; these powers make "us"
> human. According to the logic governing such thinking as it was
> formulated in the nineteenth century, only certain kinds of subjects
> are really subjects; to be human, anyone must be one of "us."[30]

As we challenge a dominant discourse by "resurrecting" the victimized voice/self of the native with our readings—and such is the
impulse behind many "new historical" accounts—we step, far too
quickly, into the otherwise silent and invisible place of the native
and turn ourselves into living agents/witnesses for her. This process,

in which *we* become visible, also neutralizes the untranslatability of the native's experience and the history of that untranslatability. The hasty supply of original "contexts" and "specificities" easily becomes complicitous with the dominant discourse, which achieves hegemony precisely by its capacity to convert, recode, make transparent, and thus represent even those experiences that resist it with a stubborn opacity. The danger of historical contextualization turning into cultural corporations is what leads Clifford to say:

> I do not argue, as some critics have, that non-Western objects are properly understood only with reference to their original milieux. Ethnographic contextualizations are as problematic as aesthetic ones, as susceptible to purified, ahistorical treatment.[31]

The problem of modernity, then, is not simply an "amalgamating" of "disparate experience"[32] but rather the confrontation between what are now called the "first" and "third" worlds in the form of the *différend*, that is, the untranslatability of "third world" experiences into the "first world." This is because, in order for her experience to become translatable, the "native" cannot simply "speak" but must also provide the justice/justification for her speech, a justice/justification that has been destroyed in the encounter with the imperialist.[33] The native's victimization consists in the fact that the active evidence—the original witness—of her victimization may no longer exist in any intelligible, coherent shape. Rather than saying that the native has already spoken because the dominant hegemonic discourse is split/hybrid/different from itself, and rather than restoring her to her "authentic" context, we should argue that it is the native's silence which is the most important clue to her displacement. That silence is at once the *evidence* of imperialist oppression (the naked body, the defiled image) and what, in the absence of the original witness to that oppression, must act in its place by *performing* or *feigning* as the pre-imperialist gaze.

A Brown Man's Eye for a White Man's Eye

As part of my argument, I read an anti-imperialist text whose intentions are both antipornographic (anti-the-bad-"image"-thing) and restorative. Despite such intentions, this text is, I believe, an example of how cultural criticism can further engender exploitation of the native, who is crossed out not once (by the imperialist forces of domination), nor twice (by the cultural processes of subjection), but three times—the third time by the anti-imperialist critic himself.

In his book *The Colonial Harem*,[34] Malek Alloula focuses on picture postcards of Algerian women produced and sent home by the French during the early decades of the twentieth century. Alloula's point is a simple one, namely, that these native women have been used as a means to represent a European phantasm of the Oriental female. The mundane postcard therefore supports, through its pornographic gaze at the female native, the larger French colonial project in Algeria. Alloula describes his own undertaking as an attempt "to return this immense postcard to its sender" (p. 5).

There is no return to any origin which is not already a construction and therefore a kind of writing. Here Alloula writes by explicitly identifying with the naked or half-naked women: "What I read on these cards does not leave me indifferent. It demonstrates to me, were that still necessary, the desolate poverty of *a gaze that I myself*, as an Algerian, *must have been the object of* at some moment in my personal history" (p. 5, my emphasis). This claim of identification with the women as image and as object notwithstanding, the male critic remains invisible himself. If the picture postcards are the kind of *evidence-and-witness* of the oppression of the native that I have been talking about, then what happens in Alloula's text is an attempt to fill in the space left open by the silent women by a self-appointed gesture of witnessing, which turns into a second gaze at the "images" of French colonialism. The Algerian women are exhibited as objects not only by the French but also by Alloula's discourse. Even though the male critic sympathizes with the natives, his status as invisible writing subject is essentially *different from*, not identical with, the status of the pictures in front of us.

The anti-imperialist charge of Alloula's discourse would have us believe that the French gaze at these women is pornographic while his is not. This is so because he distinguishes between erotism and pornography, calling the picture postcards a "suberotism" (which is the book title in French and the title of the last chapter). In her introduction to the book, Barbara Harlow supports the point of Alloula's project by citing Spivak's statement, "brown women saved

by white men from brown men."[35] In effect, however, because Alloula is intent on capturing the essence of the colonizer's discourse
as a way to retaliate against his enemy, his own discourse coincides
much more closely with the enemy's than with the women's. What
emerges finally is not an identification between the critic and the
images of the women, as he wishes, but an identification between
the critic and the gaze of the colonialist-photographer *over the
images of the women*, which become bearers of multiple exploita-
tions. Because Alloula's identification is with the gaze of the colonialist-photographer, the women remain frozen in their poses.[36]
The real question raised by Alloula's text is therefore not "Can
brown women be saved from brown men by white men?" but "Can
brown women be saved from white men by brown men?"

Alloula writes: "A reading of the sort that I propose to undertake
would be entirely superfluous if there existed photographic traces
of the gaze of the colonized upon the colonizer" (p. 5). The problem
of a statement like this lies in the way it hierarchizes the possibilities of native discourse: Had there been photographs that reciproc-
ate in a symmetrical fashion the exploitative gaze of the colonizer,
he says, he would not have to write his book. His book is second
best. The desire for revenge—to do to the enemy *exactly* what the
enemy did to him, so that colonizer and colonized would meet eye
to eye—is the fantasy of envy and violence that has been running
throughout masculinist anti-imperialist discourse since Fanon. This
fantasy, as I have already suggested, is Oedipal in structure.

To make his project what he intended it to be—a *symbolic* identification, as defined by Žižek, with the native women not only as
images but also as oppressed victims with their own stories—Alloula would need to follow either one of two alternatives. The first
of these would require, in a manner characteristic of the post-structuralist distrust of anything that seems "spontaneous" or "self-evident," a careful reading of the materiality of the images.[37] Such a
reading would show that what is assumed to be pornographic is not
necessarily so, but is more often a projection onto the images of
the photographer's (or viewer's) own repression.[38] As it stands, however, Alloula's "reading" only understands the images in terms of
content rather than as a signifying process which bears alternative
clues of reading that may well undo its supposed messages. Alloula
bases his reading on very traditional assumptions of the visual as

the naked, by equating photography with a "scopic desire" to unveil what is "inside" the women's clothes, etc. Thus he not only confirms Jameson's notion that "the visual is essentially pornographic" but unwittingly provides a demonstration of how this is so in his own antipornographic writing.

On the other hand, if the problem with post-structuralist analysis is that it too happily dissolves the pornographic obviousness of the images and thus misses their abusive structuration, then a second alternative would have been for Alloula to exclude images from his book. Alloula's entire message could have been delivered verbally. Instead, the images of the Algerian women are exposed a second time and made to stand as a transparent medium, a homoerotic link connecting the brown man to the white man, connecting "third world" nationalism to "first world" imperialism. What results is neither a dismantling of the pornographic apparatus of imperialist domination nor a restoration of the native to her "authentic" history but a perfect symmetry between the imperialist and anti-imperialist gazes, which cross over the images of native women as silent objects.

The Native in the Age of Discursive Reproduction

Modernity is ambivalent in its very origin. In trying to become "new" and "novel"—a kind of primary moment—it must incessantly deal with its connection with what *precedes* it—what was primary to it—in the form of a destruction. As Paul de Man writes, "modernity exists in the form of a desire to wipe out whatever came earlier, in the hope of reaching at last a point that could be called a true present, a point of origin that marks a new departure."[39] If the impetus of modernity is a criticism of the past, then much of our cultural criticism is still modernist.

Many accounts of modernity view the world retrospectively, in sadness. The world is thought of as a vast collection, a museum of lives which has been more or less stabilized for/by our gaze. To an anthropologist like Lévi-Strauss in the 1940s, a city like New York "anticipates humanity's entropic future and gathers up its diverse pasts in decontextualized, collectible forms."[40] The cosmopolitanizing of humanity also signals the vanishing of human diversity, an event the modern anthropologist laments. Isn't there much similarity between the nostalgic culture-collecting of a Lévi-Strauss and what is being undertaken in the name of "new historicism," which always argues for preserving the "specifics" of particular cultures? Despite the liberalist political outlook of many of its practitioners, the new historical enterprise often strikes one as being in agreement with Francis Fukuyama's pronouncement about "the end of history":

> In the post-historical period there will be neither art nor philosophy, just the perpetual caretaking of the museum of human history. I can feel in myself, and see in others around me, a powerful nostalgia for the time when history existed.[41]

Why are we so fascinated with "history" and with the "native" in "modern" times? What do we gain from our labor on these "endangered authenticities" which are presumed to be from a different time and a different place? What can be said about the juxtaposition of "us" (our discourse) and "them"? What kind of *surplus value* is created by this juxtaposition?

These questions are also questions about the irreversibility of modernity. In the absence of that original witness of the native's destruction, and in the untranslatability of the native's discourse into imperialist discourse, natives, like commodities, become knowable only through routes that diverge from their original "homes." Judging from the interest invested by contemporary cultural studies in the "displaced native," we may say that the native is precisely caught up in the twin process of what Arjun Appadurai calls "commoditization by diversion" and "the aesthetics of decontextualization," a process in which

> value . . . is accelerated or enhanced by placing objects and things in unlikely contexts. . . . Such diversion is . . . an instrument . . . of the (potential) intensification of commoditization by the enhancement of value attendant upon its diversion. This enhancement of value through the diversion of commodities from their customary circuits underlies the plunder of enemy valuables in warfare, the purchase and display of "primitive" utilitarian objects, the framing of "found" objects, the making of collections of any sort. In all these

examples, diversions of things combine the aesthetic impulse, the entrepreneurial link, and the touch of the morally shocking.[42]

Appadurai, whose intention is to argue that "commodities, like persons, have social lives,"[43] refrains from including human beings in his account of commodities. By centering the politics of commoditization on *things* in exchange, he anthropomorphizes things but avoids blurring the line between things and people, and thus preserves the safe boundaries of an old, respectable humanism. However, the most critical implication of his theory begins precisely where he stops. Where Appadurai would not go on, we must, and say that *persons, like things, have commodified lives*: The commoditization of "ethnic specimens" is *already* part of the conceptualization of "the social life of things" indicated in the title of his volume. The forces of commoditization, as part and parcel of the "process" of modernity, do not distinguish between things and people.

To elaborate this, let us turn for a moment to the texts of that great modernist, Walter Benjamin. I have in mind "Eduard Fuchs: Collector and Historian,"[44] "The Work of Art in the Age of Mechanical Reproduction," and "Theses on the Philosophy of History."[45] Together these texts offer a writing of the native that has yet to be fully recognized.

Benjamin was himself a passionate collector of books, art, and other objects.[46] As an allegorist, Benjamin's writing is often remarkable for the way it juxtaposes dissimilar things, allowing them to illuminate one another suddenly and unexpectedly. Such is the way he reads the "modernity" of the collector and the making of literature by a poet like Baudelaire. Like the process of "commoditization by diversion" described by Appadurai, Baudelaire's poetry specializes in wresting things from their original contexts. Following Benjamin's allegorical method, I juxtapose his description of Baudelaire with anthropologist Sally Price's description of modernist art collecting:

> Tearing things out of the context of their usual interrelations—which is quite normal where commodities are being exhibited—is a procedure very characteristic of Baudelaire.[47]

> Once rescued from their homes among the termites and the elements, the objects come into the protective custody of Western

owners, something like orphans from a Third-World war, where they are kept cool, dry, and dusted, and where they are loved and appreciated.[48]

Such a juxtaposition makes way for a reading of Benjamin's theses of *history* against the background of primitive art in civilized places (to allude to the title of Price's book). What emerges in this reading is not so much the violence of Benjamin's messianism as the affinity and comparableness between that violence and the violence of modernist collecting. Think, for instance, of the notion of "a fight for the history of the oppressed." If we refuse, for the time being, the common moralistic reading of this notion (a reading which emphasizes the salvational aspect of Benjamin's writings and which dominates Benjamin scholarship) and instead insert "the oppressed" into the collection of things that fascinate Benjamin, we see that "the oppressed" shares a similar status with a host of other cultural objects—books, antiques, art, toys, and prostitutes. The language of fighting, plundering, stealing, and abducting is uniformly the language of "wresting objects from native settings."[49] The violent concept that is often quoted by Benjamin lovers as a way to read against "progress"—the concept of blasting open the continuum of history[50]—is as much a precise description of imperialism's relentless destruction of local cultures as it is a "politically correct" metaphor for redeeming the history of "the oppressed."

By underlining the mutual implication of Benjamin's discourse and the discourse of imperialism, my aim is not that of attacking the "ambiguous" or "problematic" moral stance of Benjamin the writer. Rather, it is to point out the ever-changing but ever-present complicity between our critical articulation and the political environment at which that articulation is directed. Because of this, whenever the oppressed, the native, the subaltern, and so forth are used to represent the point of "authenticity" for our critical discourse, they become at the same time the place of myth-making and an escape from the impure nature of political realities. In the same way that "native imprints" suggest "primitivism" in modernist art, we turn, increasingly with fascination, to the oppressed to locate a "genuine" critical origin.

Consider now Benjamin's argument in the essay with which we

are all familiar, "The Work of Art in the Age of Mechanical Reproduction." The usual understanding of this essay is that Benjamin is describing a process in which the technology of mechanical reproduction has accelerated to such a degree that it is no longer relevant to think of the "original" of any artwork. The age of mechanical reproduction is an age in which the aura of art—its ties to a particular place, culture, or ritual—is in decline. Benjamin is at once nostalgic about the aura and enchanted by its loss. While the aura represents art's close relation with the community that generates it, the loss of the aura is the sign of art's emancipation into mass culture, a new collective culture of "collectibles."

For our present purposes, we can rethink the aura of an art object as that "historical specificity" which makes it unique to a particular place at a particular time. The vast machines of modernist production and reproduction now make this "historical specificity" a thing of the past and a concept in demise. Instead of the authentic, mysterious work with its irreproducible aura, we have technologically reproduced "copies" which need not have the original as a referent in the market of mass culture. The original, marked by some unique difference that sets it apart from the mass-produced copies, becomes now a special prize of collectors with exquisite but old-fashioned "taste."

Benjamin's notion of the aura and its decline partakes of the contradictions inherent to modernist processes of displacement and identification. The displaced object is both a sign of violence and of "progress." Purloined aggressively from its original place, this displaced object becomes infinitely reproducible in the cosmopolitan space. Displacement constitutes identity, but as such it is the identity of the ever-shifting. Benjamin shows how the new reproductive technology such as film brings the object within close proximity to the viewer and at the same time allows the viewer to experiment with different viewing positions. From the perspective of the 1990s, the irony of Benjamin's 1936 essay is that while he associated the new perceptive possibilities brought by mechanical reproduction with Communist cultural production, he was actually describing the modes of receptivity that have become standard fare for audiences in the capitalist world.[51]

Such contradictions help in some way to explain the double-

edged process in which we find ourselves whenever we try to re-
suscitate the "ethnic specimen" or "native cultures." Once again,
we need to extend Benjamin's conceptualization, a conceptualization that is ostensibly only about objects—works of art and their
mechanical reproduction—to human beings. Once we do that, we
see that in our fascination with the "authentic native," we are actually engaged in a search for the equivalent of the aura even while
our search processes themselves take us farther and farther away
from that "original" point of identification. Although we act like
good Communists who dream of finding and serving the "real people," we actually live and work like dirty capitalists accustomed to
switching channels constantly. As we keep switching channels and
browsing through different "local" cultures, we produce an infinite
number of "natives," all with predictably automaton-like features
that do not so much de-universalize Western hegemony as they con-
firm its protean capacity for infinite displacement. The "authentic"
native, like the aura in a kind of *mise-en-abîme*, keeps receding
from our grasp. Meanwhile our machinery churns out inauthentic
and imperfect natives who are always already copies. The most radical message offered to us by Benjamin's texts is that the commodified aspects of mass reproduction, often described with
existentialist angst as alienated labor, are actually a displacement
structural to the modernist handling of history, in which the problematic of the authentic native now returns with a vengeance. We
could rewrite the title of Benjamin's essay as "The Native in the
Age of Discursive Reproduction."

In his lecture at the Annual Conference of the Semiotic Society
of America in the fall of 1990, J. Hillis Miller returns to Benjamin's
remarkable essay as part of a discussion about cultural studies in
the age of digital reproduction.[52] One of the scandalous points
Miller makes is that Benjamin's formulation of communism and fascism in terms of the "politicization of art" and the "aestheticization
of politics" is actually a reversible one.[53] Therein lies its danger.
What Miller means is that what begins as a mobilization for political
change based on an interest in/respect for the cultural difference of
our others (the politicization of art) can easily grow into its ugly
opposite. That is to say, the promotion of a type of politics that is
based on the need to distinguish between "differences" may conse-

quently lead, as in the case of the Nazis, to an oppression that springs from the transformation of "difference" into "superiority." Any pride that "we" are stronger, healthier, and more beautiful can become, in effect, the aestheticization of politics.

Accordingly, it is ironic that in much of the work we do in cultural studies today, we resort to cultural/ethnic/local "difference" not as an open-ended process but as a preordained fact. The irony is that such a valorization of cultural difference occurs at a time when difference-as-aura-of-the-original has long been problematized by the very availability—and increasing indispensability—of our reproductive apparatuses. Following the drift of Benjamin's argument, Miller writes:

> this celebration of cultural specificity has occurred at a time when that specificity is being drastically altered by technological and other changes that are leading to internationalization of art and of culture generally. The work of cultural studies inevitably participates in that uprooting. . . . [A]rchival work . . . is another form of the digital reproduction that puts everything on the same plane of instant availability. . . . By a paradox familiar to anthropologists, the effort of understanding, preservation, and celebration participates in the drastic alteration of the cultures it would preserve. The more cultural studies try to save and empower local cultures the more they may endanger them.[54]

For Miller, to hang on to the "local" as the absolutely different— that is, absolutely identical with itself—means to attempt to hang on to a rigid stratification of the world in the age of digital reproduction:

> if the politicizing of art is only the specular image of the aestheticizing of politics, can the former as exemplified in cultural studies be exempt from the terrible possibilities of the aestheticizing of politics? . . . [T]he more cultural studies works for the celebration, preservation, and empowerment of subordinated cultures the more it may aid in the replication of just those political orders it would contest. . . . Are not cultural studies caught in a form of the penchant of all national aestheticisms and aesthetic nationalisms toward war?[55]

The Native as other and Other

So far my argument has demonstrated a few things. I present the place of the native as that of the image and the silent object, which is often equated with a kind of "lack" in a pejorative sense. After Fanon, we tend to fill this lack with a type of discourse that posits envy and violence as the necessary structure of the native's subjectivity. Corresponding to this is the wave of "new history" which wants to resurrect the native by restoring her to her original context. But new historicism, as a modernist collecting of culture specimens, inevitably comes up against its own aporia, namely that the possibility of *gathering* "endangered authenticities" is also the possibility of dispensing with the authentic altogether. This is indicated by the collage of Benjamin's critical items—history, collecting, and the mechanical reproduction of art—in which the aura is experienced only in ruin. We are left with the question of how cultural difference can be imagined without being collapsed into the neutrality of a globalist technocracy (as the possibilities of mechanical reproduction imply) and without being frozen into the lifeless "image" of the other that we encounter in Alloula's book.

Alloula's book is disturbing because its use of the image, albeit a problematic one, nonetheless confronts us with the reality of a *relation* which is neither innocuous nor avoidable. This is the relation between technological reproduction and cultural displacement. If technological reproduction is inevitable, is not cultural displacement also? If cultural displacement is conceived derogatorily, must technological reproduction be condemned moralistically then? Does the necessity of the first make the second a necessary virtue, or does the problematic nature of the second render the first equally problematic? This nexus of questions becomes most poignant when the representation of the "native" is not only in the form of a visual other but explicitly in the form of a pornographic image produced by the technology of photography. Should the criticism of this kind of image lead to (1) the criticism of the visual image itself (if, as Jameson says, the visual is essentially pornographic); (2) an alternative form of conceiving of "otherness" that is completely free of the image; and (3) a subsequent construction of the "native" as "truth" rather than "falsehood"?

While we have no simple answer to these questions, we know that "false" images are going to remain with us whether or not we like it. That is not simply because they are willfully planted there by individuals desiring to corrupt the world; rather, it is because the image itself is traditionally always regarded with suspicion, as a site of duplicity if not of direct degeneration. Is there a way in which we can reimagine our relation to the "pornographic" image of the native?

Ever since Jean-Jacques Rousseau, the native has been imagined as a kind of total other—a utopian image whose imaginary self-sufficiency is used as a stage for the incomplete (or "antagonistic")[56] nature of human society. Rousseau's savage is "self-sufficient" because he possesses *nothing* and is in that sense indifferent and independent. The true difference between the savage and civil man is that man is completable only through others; that is, his identity is always obtained through otherness: "the savage lives within himself; social man lives always outside himself; he knows how to live only in the opinion of others, it is, so to speak, from their judgement alone that he derives the sense of his own experience."[57]

Rousseau's formulation of the native is interesting not simply because of its idealism. To be sure, this idealism continues to be picked up by intellectuals such as Kristeva, Barthes, Serres, and others, who (mis)apply it to *specific other cultures*. In doing so, they limit and thus demolish the most important aspect of Rousseau's text, which is that the idealized native is, literally, topographically *nowhere*. No cruise ship ever takes us to see a self-sufficient "native," nor are the remains of any such person to be found at any archeological site.

Rousseau's savage is, then, not simply a cultural "other," but, in Lacanian language, the Other (big Other) that is before "separation," before the emergence of the *objet petit a*, the name for those subjectivized, privatized, and missing parts of the whole.[58] Why is this important? Because it enables us to imagine the native in a way that has been foreclosed by the Manichaean aesthetics[59] in which she is always already cast—as the white man's other, as the degraded and falsified image, as the subject constituted solely by her envy and violence, *and* as the "identity" that can never free itself of any of this "pornography." My invocation of the big Other is hence not an attempt to depoliticize the realities of displaced identities in the post-imperialist world; rather, it is an attempt to broaden that politics to include more *general* questions of exploitation, resistance, and survival by using the historical experience of the "native" as its shifting ground.

A moment in Homi Bhabha's reading of Fanon suggests a similar attempt at a more extended politics, when he points out how Fanon, writing in times of political urgency, has limited it to the colonial situation:

> At times Fanon attempts too close a correspondence between the *mise-en-scène* of unconscious fantasy and the phantoms of racist fear and hate that stalk the colonial scene; he turns too hastily from the ambivalences of identification to the antagonistic identities of political alienation and cultural discrimination; he is too quick to name the Other, to personalize its presence in the language of colonial racism—"the real Other for the white man is and will continue to be the black man. And conversely." These attempts, in Fanon's words, to restore the dream to its proper political time and cultural space can, at times, blunt the edge of Fanon's brilliant illustrations of the complexity of psychic projections in the pathological colonial relation.[60]

While not giving up the politically urgent sense in which Fanon wrote, Bhabha indicates that the criticism of the history of colonialism via the problematic of the native's (the black man's) identification can in fact lead to an understanding of the larger problems of otherness that do not necessarily emerge exclusively in anticolonial discourse. This openness, which is not as expediently committed to a particular "position" as most self-declared political discourses are, is to be differentiated from the kind of idealization of another *culture* in the form of a totality that is absolutely different (and indifferent) to our own. This openness is not an attempt to recuperate an originary, primordial space before the sign. Rather, it is a total sign, the Other, the *entire* function of which is to contest the limits of the conventional (arbitrary) sign itself.[61] We may call this big Other the big Difference.

How does the big Other work? It works by combating the construction of the native as the straightforward or direct "other" of the colonizer. Instead, it adds to this "image" of the native the ability to look, so that the native is "gaze" as well. But this is not the gaze of the native-as-subject, nor the gaze of the anti-imperialist critic like Alloula; rather it is a simulation of the gaze that witnessed the native's oppression prior to her becoming image. (For instance, it is the video camera that records policemen beating their black victim, Rodney King, with clubs in Los Angeles, as he "resists arrest" by pleading for his life.) The big Other thus functions to supplement the identification of the native-as-image in the form of *evidence-cum-witness* that I have been talking about.[62]

In other words, the agency of the native cannot simply be imagined in terms of a resistance against the image—that is, *after* the image has been formed—nor in terms of a subjectivity that existed *before*, beneath, inside, or outside the image. It needs to be rethought as that which bears witness to its own demolition—in a form which is at once image and gaze, but a gaze that exceeds the moment of colonization.

What I am suggesting is a mode of understanding the native in which the native's existence—i.e., an existence before becoming "native"—precedes the arrival of the colonizer. Contrary to the model of Western hegemony in which the colonizer is seen as a primary, active "gaze" subjugating the native as passive "object," I want to argue that it is actually the colonizer who feels looked at by the native's gaze. This gaze, which is neither a threat nor a retaliation, makes the colonizer "conscious" of himself, leading to his need to turn this gaze around and look at himself, henceforth "reflected" in the native-object. It is the self-reflection of the colonizer that produces the colonizer as subject (potent gaze, source of meaning and action) and the native as his image, with all the pejorative meanings of "lack" attached to the word "image." Hegel's story of human "self-consciousness" is then not what he supposed it to be—a story about Western Man's highest achievement—but a story about the disturbing effect of Western Man's encounter with those others Hegel considered primitive. Western Man henceforth became "self-conscious," that is, uneasy and uncomfortable, in his "own" environment.

Because this "originary" *witnessing* is, temporally speaking, lost forever, the native's defiled image must *act* both as "image" (history of her degradation) and as that witnessing gaze. In the silence of the native-as-object—a silence not immediately distinguishable

from her ascribed silence/passivity—the indifference of the "originary" witness appears again—in simulation. Like the silent picture
postcards reproduced by Alloula, this simulated gaze is *between* the
image and the gaze of the colonizer. Where the colonizer undresses
her, the native's nakedness stares back at him both as the defiled
image of his creation *and* as the indifferent gaze that says, "there
was nothing—no secret—to be unveiled underneath my clothes.
That secret is your phantasm."

The Native Is Not the Non-Duped

I conclude by returning to the issue with which I began, the issue
of authenticity. As anthropologist Brian Spooner writes:

> In seeking authenticity people are able to use commodities to express
> themselves and fix points of security and order in an amorphous
> modern society. But the evolving relationship between the search
> for personal authenticity inside and the search for authenticity in
> carefully selected things outside has received relatively little atten-
> tion.[63]

My argument *for* the native's status as an indifferent defiled image is really an attempt to get at the root of the problem of the
image, in which our cultural studies is deeply involved whenever it
deals with "the other." Because the image, in which the other is
often cast, is always distrusted as illusion, deception, and falsehood,
attempts to salvage the other often turn into attempts to uphold the
other as the non-duped—the site of authenticity and true knowledge. Critics who do this also imply that, having absorbed the pri-
mal wisdoms, they are the non-duped themselves.

In a recent essay, "How the Non-Duped Err," Žižek describes
the paradox of deception. Žižek, as Jonathan Elmer writes, "con-
curs with Lacan that '*les non-dupes errent*,' that those who think
they are undeceived are the fools."[64] In his work, he often refers to
the classic topos in Lacan, the topos that only human beings can
"deceive by feigning to deceive," or deceive by telling the truth.[65]
That this can happen depends on the fact that we all assume that
there is always something else under the mask. One deep-rooted

example is that under the mask of civilization we are "savages": the savage/primitive/native is then the "truth" that is outside/under the symbolic order. The cultural critic who holds on to such a notion of the native is, by analogy, a psychotic subject:

> the psychotic subject's distrust of the big Other, his *idée fixe* that the big Other (embodied in his intersubjective community) is trying to deceive him, is always and necessarily supported by an unshakable belief in a consistent Other, an Other without gaps, an "Other of the Other" . . . a non-deceived agent holding the reins. His mistake does not consist in his radical disbelief, in his conviction that there is a universal deception—here he is quite right, the symbolic order is ultimately the order of a fundamental deception—his mistake lies on the contrary in his being too easy of belief and supposing the existence of a hidden agency manipulating this deception, trying to dupe him. . . .[66]

For us working in anti-imperialist discourse, this "hidden agency manipulating . . . deception" would be precisely "imperialism," "colonialism," "capitalism," and so forth. According to Žižek, our identification with the native in the form of a radical *disbelief* in the defiled images produced by these symbolic orders would not be wrong. What is problematic is our attempt to point to them as if they were one consistent manipulator that is trying to fool us consistently. Our fascination with the native, the oppressed, the savage, and all such figures is therefore a desire to hold on to an unchanging certainty somewhere outside our own "fake" experience. It is a desire for being "non-duped," which is a not-too-innocent desire to seize control.

To insist on the native as an indifferent defiled image is then to return to the native a capacity for distrusting and resisting the symbolic orders that "fool" her while not letting go of the "illusion" which has structured her survival. To imagine the coexistence of defilement and indifference *in* the native-object is not to neutralize the massive destructions committed under such orders as imperialism and capitalism. Rather, it is to invent a dimension beyond the deadlock between native and colonizer in which the native can only be the colonizer's defiled image and the anti-imperialist critic can only be psychotic. My argument is: yes, "natives" are represented as defiled images—that is the fact of our history. But must we represent them a second time by turning history "upside down," this time giving them the sanctified status of the "non-duped"? Defilement and sanctification belong to the same symbolic order.

So where have all the "natives" gone? They have gone . . . between the defiled image and the indifferent gaze. The native is not the defiled image and not not the defiled image. And she stares indifferently, mocking our imprisonment within imagistic resemblance and our self-deception as the non-duped.

III

POSTMODERN AUTOMATONS[1]

Modernism and Postmodernism: Restating the Problem of "Displacement"

If everyone can agree with Fredric Jameson that the unity of the "new impulse" of postmodernism "is given not in itself but in the very modernism it seeks to displace,"[2] exactly how modernism is displaced still remains an issue. In this chapter I follow an understanding of "modernism" that is embedded in and inseparable from the globalized and popularized usages of terms such as "modernity" and "modernization," which pertain to the increasing technologization of culture. I examine this technologization in terms of the technologies of visuality. In the twentieth century, the preoccupation with the "visual"—in a field like psychoanalysis, for instance—and the perfection of technologies of visuality such as photography and film take us beyond the merely physical dimension of vision. The visual as such, as a kind of dominant discourse of modernity, reveals epistemological problems that are inherent in social relations and their reproduction. Such problems inform the very ways social difference—be it in terms of class, gender, or race—is constructed. In this sense, the more narrow understanding of modernism as the sum total of artistic innovations that erupted in Europe and North America in the spirit of a massive cultural awakening—an emancipation from the habits of perception of the past—needs to be bracketed within an understanding of modernity as a force of cultural expansionism whose foundations are not only emancipatory but also Eurocentric and patriarchal. The displacement of "modernism" in what we now call the postmodern era must be addressed with such foundations in mind.

Generally speaking, there is, I think, a confusion over the status of modernism as theoretical determinant and modernism as social effect. The disparagement of modernism that we hear in "first world" circles—a disparagement that stems from the argument of modernism as "mythical," as "narrative," or as what continues the progressive goals of the European Enlightenment—regards modernism more or less as a set of beliefs, a particular mode of cognition, or a type of subjectivity. The rewriting of history by way of the postmodern would hence follow such lines to say: such and such were the governing *ideas* that characterize modernism which have been proven to be grand illusions in the postmodern era, and so on. If "modernity" is incomplete, then, postmodernism supplements it by shaking up its foundations. Therefore, if one of the key characteristics of modernism is the clear demarcation of cognitive boundaries—a demarcation that occurs with the perceptual hegemony of physical vision in the modern period—then postmodernism is full of talk about boundaries dissolving, so that that which sees and that which is seen, that which is active and that which is passive, etc., become interchangeable positions. The profusion of discourse and the illusion that every discourse has become permissible make it possible to associate postmodernism with a certain abandonment, such as is suggested in the title of a recent anthology edited by Andrew Ross, *Universal Abandon?*[3]

Once we view the modernism-postmodernism problematic not in terms of a succession of ideas and concepts only, but as the staggering of legacies and symptoms at their different stages of articulation, then the "displacement" of modernism by postmodernism becomes a complex matter and can vary according to the objectives for which that displacement is argued. For instance, for the cultures outside the Berlin-Paris-London-New York axis, it is not exactly certain that modernism has exhausted its currency or, therefore, its imperialistic efficacy. Because these "other" cultures did not dominate the generation of modernism theoretically or cognitively, "displacement" needs to be posed on very different terms.

On the one hand, modernism is, for these other cultures, always a displaced phenomenon, the sign of an alien imprint on indigenous traditions. In Asia and Africa, modernism is not a set of beliefs but rather a foreign body whose physicality must be described as a Derridean "always already"—whose omnipresence, in other words, must be responded to as a given whether one likes it or not. On the other hand, the displacement of modernism in postmodernity as it is currently argued in the West, in the writings of Jean-François Lyotard, Jürgen Habermas, Jameson, and so on, does not seem right either, for modernism is still around as ideological legacy, as habit, and as a familiar, even coherent, way of seeing. If the "first world" has rejected modernism, such rejection is not so easy for the world which is still living through it as cultural trauma and devastation. In the words of Masao Mioshi and H. D. Harootunian:

> The black hole that is formed by the rejection of modernism is also apt to obliterate the trace of historical Western expansionism that was at least cofunctional, if not instrumental, in producing epistemological hegemonism. Thus a paradox: as postmodernism seeks to remedy the modernist error of Western, male, bourgeois domination, it simultaneously vacates the ground on which alone the contours of modernism can be seen. Furthermore, colonialism and imperialism are ongoing enterprises, and in distinguishing late post-industrial capitalism from earlier liberal capitalism and by tolerating the former while condemning the latter, postmodernism ends up by consenting to the first world economic domination that persists in exploiting the wretched of the earth.[4]

In the "third world," the displacement of modernism is not simply a matter of criticizing modernism as theory, philosophy, or ideas of cognition; rather, it is the emergence of an entirely different problematic, a displacement of a displacement that is in excess of what is still presented as the binarism of modernism-postmodernism. It is in the light of this double or multiple displacement that a feminist intervention, in alliance with other marginalized groups, can be plotted in the postmodern scene. If what is excluded by the myth-making logic of modernism articulates its "existence" in what looks like a radically permissive postmodern era where anything goes, postmodernism (call it a periodizing concept, a cultural dominant, if you will, after Jameson) is only a belated articulation of what the West's "others" have lived all along.[5]

Because, vis-à-vis the dominant modern culture of the West, feminism shares the status with other marginalized discourses as a kind of "other" whose power has been the result of historical struggle, the relationship between feminism and postmodernism has not been an easy one. Even though feminists partake in the postmodernist ontological project of dismantling claims of cultural authority that are housed in specific representations, feminism's rootedness in overt political struggles against the subordination of women makes it very difficult to accept the kind of postmodern "universal abandon" in Ross's title. For some, the destabilization of conceptual boundaries and concrete beliefs becomes the sign of danger that directly threatens their commitment to an agenda of social progress based on the self and reason.[6] While I do not agree with the espousal of humanistic thinking as such for feminist goals, I think the distrust of postmodern "abandon" can be seen as a strategic resistance against the dismantling of feminism's "critical regionalism" (to use a term from postmodern architectural criticism)[7] and its local politics.

In the collection *Universal Abandon?*, Nancy Frazer and Linda Nicholson voice this understanding of the conflict between postmodernism and feminism in terms of philosophy and social criticism. While they criticize the essentialist moves feminists have had to make to stage the primacy of gender in social struggles, they are equally distrustful of the abstract philosophical frameworks in which theorists of postmodernism often begin their inquiry. Lyotard's "suspicion of the large," for instance, leads him to reject "the project of social theory *tout court*"; and yet "despite his strictures against large, totalizing stories, he narrates a fairly tall tale about a large-scale social trend."[8]

The conflicts as to what constitutes *the social* amount to one of the most significant contentions between postmodernism and feminism. *Post-structuralism* plays a role in both's relation to the social. For those interested in postmodernism, the decentering of the logos and the untenability of structuralism as a mode of cognition provide the means of undoing modernism's large architectonic claims. Once such claims and their hierarchical power are undone, the meaning of the "social" bursts open. It is no longer possible to assume a transparent and universal frame of reality. Instead, "tropes" and "reality" become versions of each other,[9] while aporias and allegories play an increasingly important role in the most "natural" acts of reading. And yet, precisely because the subversive

thrust of post-structuralism consists in its refusal to name its own
politics (since naming as such, in the context of political hegemony,
belongs to the tactics of doctrinaire official culture) even as it deconstructs the language of established power from within, it does
not provide postmodernism with a well-defined agenda nor with a
clear object of criticism other than "the prison house of language."
Instead, the persistently negative critique of dominant culture in
total terms produces a vicious circle that repeats itself as what
Baudrillard calls "implosion"—the "reduction of difference to
absolute indifference, equivalence, interchangeability."[10] Since positions are now infinitely interchangeable, many feel that postmodernism may be little more than a "recompensatory 'I'm OK,
you're OK' inclusion or a leveling attribution of subversive 'marginality' to all."[11]

The difficulty feminists have with postmodernism is thus clear.
Although feminists share postmodernism's post-structuralist tendencies in dismantling universalist claims, which for them are more
specifically defined as the claims of the white male subject, they
do not see their struggle against patriarchy as quite over. The social
for feminists is therefore always marked by a clear horizon of the
inequality between men and women; the social, because it is mediated by gender with its ideological manipulations of biology as
well as symbolic representations, is never quite "implosive" in the
Baudrillardian sense. With this fundamental rejection of indifference by an insistence on the cultural effects of sexual and gendered
difference,[12] feminists always begin, as the non-Western world must
begin, with the legacy of the constellation of modernism *and* something more. While for the non-Western world that something is
imperialism, for feminists it is patriarchy. They must begin, as Frazer and Nicholson put it, with "the nature of the social object one
wished to criticize" rather than with the condition of philosophy.
This object is "the oppression of women in its 'endless variety and
monotonous similarity.' "[13]

Visuality, or the Social Object "Ridden with Error"[14]

One of the chief sources of the oppression of women lies in the
way they have been consigned to visuality. This consignment is the
result of an epistemological mechanism which produces social dif-

ference by a formal distribution of positions and which modernism magnifies with the availability of technology such as cinema. To approach visuality as the object of criticism, we cannot therefore simply attack the *fact* that women have been reduced to objects of the "male gaze," since that reifies the problem by reifying its most superficial manifestation.[15]

If we take visuality to be, precisely, the nature of the social object that feminism should undertake to criticize, then it is incumbent upon us to analyze the epistemological foundation that supports it. It is, indeed, a foundation in the sense that the production of the West's "others" depends on a logic of visuality that bifurcates "subjects" and "objects" into the incompatible positions of intellectuality and spectacularity.

To illustrate my point, I will turn briefly to Chaplin's *Modern Times*, a film which demonstrates by its use of cinematic technology the modernist production of the space of the other.

There are, of course, many ways to talk about this film, but what makes it so fascinating to watch (and this is a point that can be generalized to include other silent movies) is the way it exaggerates and deconstructs pre-filmic materials, in particular the human body. What becomes clear in the film is how a perception of the spectacular cannot be separated from technology, which turns the human body into the site of experimentation and mass production. No audience would forget, for instance, the scenes in which the Chaplin character, an assembly line worker, is so accustomed to working with his lug wrenches that he automatically applies his twisting motions to everything that meets his eyes. This *automatizing* of the human body fulfills *in a mechanized manner* a typical description about a debased popular form, melodrama, that its characters are characters "who can be guaranteed to think, speak and act exactly as you would expect."[16] Cinema, then, allows us to realize in an unprecedented way the mediated, i.e., technologized, nature of "melodramatic sentiments." The typical features of melodramatic expression—exaggeration, emotionalism, and Manichaeanism—can thus be redefined as the eruption of the machine in what is presumed to be spontaneous. Gestures and emotions are "enlarged" sentimentally the way reality is "enlarged" by the camera lens.

In Chaplin's assembly line worker, visuality works toward an automatization of an oppressed figure whose bodily movements become excessive and comical. Being "automatized" means being subjected to social exploitation whose origins are beyond one's individual grasp, but it also means becoming a spectacle whose "aesthetic" power increases with one's increasing awkwardness and helplessness. The production of the "other" is in this sense both the production of class and aesthetic/cognitive difference. The camera brings this out excellently with mechanically repeated motions.

What these moments in *Modern Times* help foreground in a densely meaningful way is the relationship between the excess of spectacle and the excess of response that Freud explores in his discussion of the comic in *Jokes and Their Relation to the Unconscious*. Freud's question is: why do we laugh in the face of the comic? Similarly, in *Modern Times*, how is it that the automatizing of "the other" in the ways we have described becomes the source of our pleasure?

Early on in his essay, Freud indicates that the problem of the comic exists "quite apart from any communication."[17] For him the chief interest of the comic lies in *quantitative* terms. The comic is the "ideational mimetics" that involves "somatic enervation." The expenditure of energy that occurs constitutes the origin of culture in the form of a differentiation or division of labor:

> The comic effect apparently depends . . . on the difference [*Differenz*] between the two cathectic expenditures—one's own and the other person's—as estimated by "empathy"—and not on which of the two the difference favors. But this peculiarity, which at first sight confuses our judgement, vanishes when we bear in mind that a restriction of our muscular work and an increase of our intellectual work fit in with the course of our personal development toward a higher level of civilization. By raising our intellectual expenditure we can achieve the same result with a diminished expenditure on our movements. Evidence of this cultural success is provided by our machines.[18]

Although Freud's statements are ostensibly about the comic, what they reveal is the hierarchical structuring of energies which are distributed between "spectacle" and "spectator" in the intellectual endeavors which form the basis of culture. If the comic as such makes apparent a human being's dependence on bodily needs and social situations, then it also means that the moment of visualization coincides, in effect, with an inevitable dehumanization in the form of a physically automatized object, which is *produced as spectacular excess*. Freud's ironic remark that this is "cultural success" which is evidenced by our machines suggests that this process of dehumanization is accelerated by the accelerated sophistication of intellectual culture itself.

In *Modern Times*, the "increase of intellectual work" does not involve psychology in the popular sense of an interiorization of dramatic action. Rather, it involves a confrontation with the cruelties of industrial exploitation through our laughter, the response that Freud defines as the discharge of that unutilized surplus of energy left over from the difference between the two "cathectic expenditures." If the body of the assembly line worker is seen in what Freud calls its "muscular expenditure," it is also seen in a way that was not possible before mass production, including the mass production that is the filmic moment. The "human body" as such is already a *working body automatized*, in the sense that it becomes in the new age an automaton on which social injustice as well as processes of mechanization "take on a life of their own," so to speak. Thus, the moment the "human body" is "released" into the field of vision is also the moment when it is made excessive and dehumanized. This excess is the *mise-en-scène* of modernity *par excellence*.

If Freud's reading captures formally the capacity and the limit of the camera's eye, this formalism is itself a symptom of the modern history to which it tries to respond. This is the history of the eruption of "mass culture" as the site both of increasingly mechanized labor and of unprecedentedly multiplied and globally dispersed subjectivities. As Freud analyzes the comic as a spectacle and in quantifiable terms, he is reading human "subjectivity" the way a camera captures "life." The automatized mobility of the spectacularized "other" happens within a frame of scopophilia.

That this scopophilia is masculinist becomes clear when we turn to another one of Freud's texts, "The Uncanny."[19] In this essay, Freud wants to talk about emotions that pertain to inexplicable patterns of psychic repetition. Central to his argument is his reading of E. T. A. Hoffmann's tale "The Sandman," in which the student Nathaniel falls in love with a doll, Olympia. For Freud, the interest of the story does not so much lie in this heterosexual "romance" as it does in the Sandman and the "father series" in which Nathaniel's tragic fate is written.

But Freud's emphatically masculinist reading—i.e., a reading that produces a cultural and psychic *density* for the male subject— becomes itself a way of magnifying the visual object status in which woman is cast. Hoffmann's tale, of course, provides material for Freud's camera eye by highlighting two elements in Nathaniel's fall for Olympia. One: that he first sees her from afar, whereby her beauty, blurred and indistinct, takes on a mesmerizing aura. Two: when they finally meet, the collapse of the physical distance which gives rise to his pleasure at first is now replaced by another equally gratifying sensation—her mechanistic response to everything he says in the form of "Ah, ah!" The combination of these two ele- ments—visuality and automatization—leads to Freud's reading: "Olympia . . . the automatic doll, can be nothing else than a per- sonification of Nathaniel's feminine attitude towards his father in his infancy. . . . Olympia is, as it were, a dissociated complex of Nathaniel's which confronts him as a person. . . . "[20]

Freud's two arguments, the comic and the uncanny, are argu- ments about mass culture even though they are not stated explicitly as such. The two arguments intersect at the notion of the automa- tized other, which takes the form either of the ridiculous, the lower class, or of woman. The meaning of woman here is inseparable from the meaning of intellectual class struggle by virtue of the fact that woman is "produced" the way the lower class in Chaplin is pro- duced. The sight of woman is no less mechanized than the sight of the comic, and both embody the critical, indeed repressed, rela- tionship between modernist scopophilia and the compulsive and re- petitive "others" which confront Modern Man.

As the ruin of modernism, mass culture is the automatized site of the others, the site of automatized others, the site of automatons. Automatization as such is the "social object" which defines the criti- cal field for feminism. But it is not an object which exists in any pure form; rather, its impurity as cultural construct with historical weight means that feminists need constantly to seize it and steer it in a different direction from other types of politics which can lay equal claim to it. The struggles here are among (1) the perpetu- ation of masculinist modernism, (2) *feminized* postmodernism, and (3) *feminist* postmodernism. To understand this, let us discuss the term "abandon" in Ross's title.

"Abandon" belongs to that corpus of concepts which are explicitly or implicitly associated with the devaluation of women since the eighteenth century. If the certainty of a masculinist culture can only be erected by policing the behavior of men's conventional sexual other, women, then any suggestion of women's "misbehavior" amounts to a threat to the dominant culture's foundational support. Traditionally, any departure from the virtues demanded of females becomes the occasion both for male moralistic pedagogy (which asserts social control) and for male romantic musings (which celebrate acts of social transgression). The notion of "abandon" belongs to an economy in which male hegemony relies on the "loose woman" and its cognates of "looseness-as-woman" and "woman-as-looseness" for a projection of that which is subversive, improper, marginal, unspeakable, and so forth. Teresa de Lauretis has called this the "violence of rhetoric" and criticized the masculinism which informs Nietzsche's and Derrida's appropriation of the feminine for their deconstruction of established power.[21] What Nietzsche and Derrida accomplish in philosophy, others accomplish through the notions of mass culture. This historical inscription of the feminine on the notion of mass culture, Andreas Huyssen argues, is problematic primarily because of "the persistent gendering as feminine of that which is devalued."[22] The case of Emma Bovary, that "avid consumer of pulp,"[23] is paradigmatic. In Huyssen's argument, the equation of woman with mass culture is a threat to the serious purity of high modernism.

Once the implications of gender are introduced, it becomes possible to see how the twentieth-century debates about "mass" culture—what is now called postmodern culture—have been conducted over categories which bear the imprint of hierarchically defined sexual difference. For example, we can now view the classic case of Adorno and Horkheimer's devastating denunciation of American mass culture in terms of a politically astute and uncompromising masculinism. Adorno and Horkheimer define the "culture industry" as what "robs the individual of his function." This individual is the autonomous human being who holds a critically resistant relationship to the stultifying effects of undifferentiated mass culture. This critically resistant individualism is meanwhile extended to the work of art. The commitment to the possibility of autonomy and liberation is expressed negatively, in the form of an "in spite of": in spite of the deafening, blinding, and numbing powers of the mass, autonomy and liberation exist for the ones who remain sober, alert, and clear-sighted. This of course leaves open the question of how the impure nature of social history can even begin to be approached, and how social transformation can take place in a communal or collective sense.

The rigidity and pessimism of the Frankfurt School "stamp" on mass culture have been criticized on many fronts. My point in mentioning it is rather to emphasize that, precisely because Adorno and Horkheimer's argument has had such an indelible impact on our conception of the culture industry for so long, it paradoxically enables the equally problematic, "postmodern" descriptions of mass culture given by Jean Baudrillard to have great seductive powers.[24] In Baudrillard, the non-resisting activities of the reputably passive consumer now take on an "implosive" dimension. The masses, in their stubborn, somnambulent silence, in their simulated or simulating acquiescence to the media, become abandoned and "feminine" in the ruin of representation. Baudrillard's theory does not reverse Adorno and Horkheimer's view of the masses; rather, it exaggerates it and pushes it to the extreme by substituting the notion of an all-controlling "industry" with that of an all-consuming mass, a mass that, in its abandon, no longer allows for the demarcation of clear boundaries, such as between an above and a below. Huyssen writes: "Baudrillard gives the old dichotomy a new twist by applauding the femininity of the masses rather than denigrating it, but his move may be no more than yet another Nietzschean simulacrum."[25]

From Object to Strategy

Be it the repudiation of or the abandonment to the feminized mass, then, the modernism-postmodernism problematic continues the polarized thinking produced by the logic of visuality. Visuality in Freud works by displacement, which makes explicit (turns into external form) what are interiorized states called "neuroses" and "complexes." The site occupied by woman, by the lower classes, by

the masses, is that of excess; in Freud's reading their specularity—
their status as the visual—is what allows the clarification of
problems which lie outside them and which need them for their
objectification. Beyond this specularity, what can be known about
the feminized "object"?

The answer to this question is "nothing" if we insist that this
object is a pure phenomenon, a pure existence. However, if this
object is indeed a *social* object which is by nature "ridden with
error," then criticizing it from within would amount to criticizing
the social sources of its formation. Albeit in fragmented forms, such
criticisms can lead to subversions which do not merely reproduce
the existing mechanism but which offer an alternative for transformation.

For feminists working in the "first world," where relatively stable
material conditions prevail, criticism of the oppression of women
can adopt a more flamboyantly defiant tone as the affirmation of
female power *tout court*. The availability of food, living space,
mechanical and electronic forms of communication, institutionalized psychoanalytic treatment, and general personal mobility
means that "automatization" *can* turn into autonomy and independence. Hélène Cixous's challenge to Freud's reading of Hoffmann,
for instance, represents this defiant automaton-power: "what if the
doll became a woman? What if she *were* alive? What if, in looking
at her, we animated her?"[26]

These "first world" feminist questions short-circuit Freud's neurotic pessimism by rejecting, as it were, the reductionism of the
modernist logic of visuality and the polarity of masculine-human-
subject-versus-feminized-automaton it advances. It retains the notion of the automaton—the mechanical doll—but changes its fate
by giving it life with another look. This is the look of the feminist
critic. Does her power of animation take us back to the language
of God, a superior being who bestows life upon an inferior? Or is
it the power of a woman who bears the history of her own dehumanization on her as she speaks for other women? The idealism of
"first world" feminism would have us believe the latter. The mythical being of this idealism is the "cyborg," that half-machine, half-
animal creature, at once committed and transgressive, spoken of by
Donna Haraway.[27]

For those feminists who have lived outside the "first world" as "natives" of "indigenous cultures" (for such are the categories in which they are put, regardless of their level of education), the defiance of a Cixous is always dubious, suggesting not only the subversiveness of woman but also the more familiar, oppressive discursive prowess of the "first world." The "postmodern" cultural situation in which non-Western feminists now find themselves is a difficult and cynical one. Precisely because of the modernist epistemological mechanism which produces the interest in the third world, the great number of discourses that surround this "area" are now treated, one feels, as so many Olympias saying "Ah, ah!" to a Western subject demanding repeated uniform messages. For the "third world" feminist, the question is never that of asserting power as woman alone, but of showing how the concern for women is inseparable from other types of cultural oppression and negotiation. In a more pronounced, because more technologized/automatized, manner, her status as postmodern automaton is both the subject and object of her critical operations.

In this light, it is important to see that the impasse inherent in Freud's analytic insights has to do not only with visuality and the ontological polarities it entails but also with the *instrumentalism* to which such a construction of the visual field lends itself. Because Freud privileges castration as a model, he is trapped in its implications, by which the "other" that is constructed is always constructed as what completes what is missing from our "own" cognition. But the roots of "lack" lie beyond the field of vision,[28] which is why the privileging of vision as such is always the privileging of a fictive mode, a veil which remains caught in an endless repetition of its own logic.

On the other hand, Freud's analysis of the comic remains instructive because in it we find a resistance to the liberalist illusion of the autonomy and independence we can "give" the other. It shows that social knowledge (and the responsibility that this knowledge entails) is not simply a matter of empathy or identification with the "other" whose sorrows and frustrations are being made part of the spectacle. Repetition, which is now visibly recognized in the field of the other, mechanistically establishes and intensifies the distinctions between spectacular (kinetic) labor and cognitive labor, while the surplus created by their difference materializes not only in emotional (or imaginary) terms but also in economic terms. This means that *our* attempts to "explore the 'Other' point of view" and "to give it a chance to speak for itself," as the passion of many current discourses goes, must always be distinguished from the other's struggles, no matter how enthusiastically we assume the nonexistence of that distinction. "Letting the other live" with a liveliness never visible before is a kind of investment whose profits return, as it were, to those who watch. Freud puts it this way:

> In "trying to understand", therefore, in apperceiving this movement [the comic], I make a certain expenditure, and in this portion of the mental process I behave exactly as though I were putting myself in the place of the person I am observing. But at the same moment, probably, I bear in mind the aim of this movement, and my earlier experience enables me to estimate the scale of expenditure required for reaching that aim. In doing so I disregard the person whom I am observing and behave as though I myself wanted to reach the aim of the movement. These two possibilities in my imagination amount to a comparison between the observed movement and my own. If the other person's movement is exaggerated and inexpedient, my increased expenditure in order to understand it is inhibited *in statu nascendi*, as it were in the act of being mobilized . . . ; it is declared superfluous and is free for use elsewhere or perhaps for discharge by laughter. This would be the way in which, other circumstances being favorable, pleasure in a comic movement is generated—an innervatory expenditure which has become an unusable surplus when a comparison is made with a movement of one's own.[29]

The task that faces "third world" feminists is thus not simply that of "animating" the oppressed women of their cultures but of making the automatized and animated condition of their own voices the conscious point of departure in their intervention. This does not simply mean they are, as they must be, speaking across cultures and boundaries; it also means that they speak with the awareness of "cross-cultural" speech as a limit and that their very own use of the victimhood of women and "third world" cultures is both symptomatic of and inevitably complicitous with the "first world." As Gayatri Spivak says of the American university context: "the invocation of the pervasive oppression of Woman in every class and race stratum, indeed in the lowest sub-cast, cannot help but justify the institutional interests of the (female) academic."[30] Feminists' upward mobility in the institution, in other words, still follows the logic of the division of labor and of social difference depicted by Freud in his analysis of the comic. The apparent receptiveness of our curricula to the "third world," a receptiveness which makes full use of non-Western human specimens as instruments for articulation, is something we have to practice and deconstruct at once. The "third world" feminist speaks of, speaks to, and speaks as this disjuncture:

> The privileged Third World informant crosses cultures within the network made possible by socialized capital, or from the point of view of the indigenous intellectual or professional elite in actual Third World countries. Among the latter, the desire to "cross" cultures means accession, left *or* right, feminist *or* masculist, into the elite culture of the metropolis. This is done by the commodification of the particular "Third World culture" to which they belong. Here entry into consumerism and entry into "Feminism" (the proper named movement) have many things in common.[31]

By the logic of commodified culture, feminism shares with other marginalized discourses which have been given "visibility" the same type of destiny—that of reification and subordination under such terms, currently popular in the U.S. academy, as "cultural diversity." As all groups speak like automatons to the neurotic subject of the West, an increasing momentum of instrumentalism, such as is evident in anthologies about postmodernism and feminism, seeks to reabsorb the differences among them. Our educational apparatuses produce ever "meta" systems, programs, and categories in this direction. Feminism has already become one type of knowledge to be controlled expediently through traditional epistemological frameworks such as the genre of the "history of ideas."

Awareness of such facts does not allow one to defend the purity of feminism against its various *uses*. Here, the "third world" feminist, because she is used as so many types of automatons at once, occupies a space for strategic alliances.

One such alliance is worked out by foregrounding the political significance of theoretical feminist positions, even if they may have ostensibly little to do with politics in the narrower sense of political economy. The refusal, on the part of many feminists, to give up what may be designated as "feminine" areas, including the close attention to texts, can in this regard be seen as a refusal to give up the local as a base, a war front, when the cannon shots of patriarchal modernism are still heard everywhere. Although this base is also that "social object" which feminists must criticize, to abandon it altogether would mean a complete surrender to the enemy. Naomi Schor puts it this way:

> Whether or not the 'feminine' is a male construct, a product of a phallocentric culture destined to disappear, in the present order of things we cannot afford not to press its claims even as we dismantle the conceptual systems which support it.[32]

Elizabeth Weed comments:

> Schor's insistence on the need for a feminine specificity is political. It represents a recognition on the part of some feminists . . . that much of post-structural theory which is not explicitly feminist is simply blind to sexual difference or, in its desire to get beyond the opposition male/female, underestimates the full political weight of the categories.[33]

Thus the "social object" for feminist discourse in general—the oppression of women—becomes both object and agent of criticism. Vis-à-vis postmodernism, the question that feminists must ask *repeatedly* is: how do we deal with the local? Instead of the local, accounts of postmodernism usually provide us with lists that demonstrate what Lyotard says literally: "Not only can one speak of everything, one must."[34] The impossibility of dealing with the local except by letting everyone speak/everything be spoken at the same time leads to a situation in which hegemony in the Gramscian sense always remains a danger. But with this danger also arises a form of opportunity, which feminists take hold of by way of situating themselves at every point in a constellation of political forces without ever losing sight of women's historical subordination.

Pressing the claims of the local therefore does not mean essentializing one position; instead, it means using that position as a parallel for allying with others. For the "third world" feminist, especially, the local is never "one." Rather, her own "locality" as construct, difference, and automaton means that pressing its claims is always pressing the claims of a form of existence which is, by origin, coalitional.

By contrast, the postmodernist list neutralizes the critical nature of such coalitional existences. The list allows "the others" to be seen, but would not pay attention to what they say. In the American university today, the rationale of the list manifests itself in the wholehearted *enlisting* of women, blacks, Asians, etc., into employment for their "offerings" of materials from non-Western cultures. Those who have been hired under such circumstances know to what extent their histories and cultures manage to make it to significant international forums, which are by and large still controlled by topics such as "modernism" and "postmodernism." Those who want to address the local must therefore always proceed by gesturing toward the forum at large, or by what we nowadays call, following the language of the market, "packaging." One knows that as long as one deals in "first world" abstractions—what Frazer and Nicholson mean by "philosophy"—one will have an audience. As for local specificities—even though such are buzzwords for a politics of abandonment—audiences usually nod in good will and turn a deaf ear, and readers skip the pages.

It is in resistance against postmodernist enlistment, then, that various strategies for coalition between feminism and postmodernism, which all partake of a "critical regionalism," have been explored. Donna Haraway and Teresa Ebert define postmodern feminist cultural theory as "oppositional" practice;[35] Craig Owens argues the necessity to genderize the formalisms of postmodern aesthetics and to revamp the substance of postmodern thought;[36] Jane Flax speaks of "the embeddedness of feminist theory in the very social processes we are trying to critique."[37] Perhaps what is most crucial about the meeting of feminism and postmodernism is that, after the refusal to be seduced into abandonment, feminists do not put down the "pulp novel" that is postmodernism, either. Instead, they extract from the cries of abandonment the potential of social criticism that might have been lost in the implosions of simulacra. The careful rejection of postmodernist abandon as a universalist politics goes hand in hand with its insistence on the need to *detail* history, in the sense of cutting it up, so that as it gains more ground in social struggle, sexual difference becomes a way of engaging not simply with women but with other types of subjugation. The future of feminist postmodern automatons is described in this statement by Weed: "If sexual difference becomes ever more destabilized, living as a female will become an easier project, but that will result from the continued displacement of 'women,' not from its consolidation."[38]

IV

PEDAGOGY, TRUST, CHINESE INTELLECTUALS IN THE 1990s
FRAGMENTS OF A POST-CATASTROPHIC DISCOURSE

> Anyone who thinks that . . . Communist regimes . . . are exclusively the work of criminals is overlooking a basic truth: the criminal regimes were made not by criminals but by enthusiasts convinced they had discovered the only road to paradise. They defended that road so valiantly that they were forced to execute many people. Later it became clear that there was no paradise, that the enthusiasts were therefore murderers.
>
> —Milan Kundera, *The Unbearable Lightness of Being*

> . . . intellectuals attest to a passage of history of which they are in a way the waste product. The intellectual crystallizes, in the form of refuse, impulses, desires, complications, blockages that probably belong to society as a whole.
>
> —Roland Barthes, "Of What Use Is an Intellectual?" (in *The Grain of the Voice*)

King of the Children

A good place to discuss the Chinese intellectual—a well-worn topic—is always literature. There, the assumptions about culture are implicitly present but not explicitly stated. One does not find long historical discussions of how ideas evolve, but the weight of history bears upon the writing of "fiction" in such a way as to force one to reflect critically on the space in which the Chinese intellectual has had to live. This is a space without fresh air.

The Tiananmen Massacre of June 1989 brought modern Chinese history to a standstill. This is the standstill of catastrophe. If Chinese history in the past century and a half has been a series of catastrophes, the events of June 4, 1989, marked their summation in the form of a mindlessly internalized violence directed against civilians by a government which barely forty years ago had stood for hope and emancipation from the corruption of the Chinese tradition. In the continual trauma that is "modernity," the question that returns to haunt the Chinese intellectual is that of the continuity and (re)production of culture. This is a question about pedagogy. What can be taught to the younger generation? How is culture—in ruins—to be passed on, by whom, and with what means?

In the following, I explore these questions through a variety of discursive contexts, beginning with a literary text. My aims are twofold. First, I want to register the trauma of "June 4" as experienced by Chinese intellectuals not only through the carefully differentiated layers of an objective analysis but also primarily *as trauma*. To the extent that this trauma is received as something irrational, an analysis which proceeds simply by pinning it down to various points of rational understanding would fall short of capturing the enormous feeling of shock that is part of the way "June 4" will continue to be remembered. Second, I want to suggest some possibilities of discursive intervention from the perspective of the Chinese intellectuals who are now living overseas, especially in countries like the U.S. and France. This second task is virtually an imaginary mapping out of the unknown and as such is meant as a basis for collective rethinking and discussion.

Set in 1976, A Cheng's "Haizi wang" ("King of the Children," 1984) provides a good point of entry into the questions at hand. The story does not make explicit references to the Cultural Revolution, but the latter's destructive effects are felt in the threadbare state in which education is left. The narrator Lao Gan, who was a member of a production team before he was appointed to a village school, arrives at his new post to find that his more old-fashioned expectations about teaching are no longer applicable. Though he is worried about not being qualified enough himself (having only attended senior high first grade), the school authorities assign him to teaching junior high last grade. The next shock is that his students do not have the required textbook. Their "learning" up to this point has simply been copying lessons which their former teacher copied onto the blackboard from the one textbook that was available.

An important turning point comes when Lao Gan, recognizing the pointlessness of this way of teaching, overrules it. Instead of following the "copying textbook" method, he decides to teach his students how to read and write, character by character, from scratch. This change in pedagogy is suggested to him by one of the students, Wang Fu, who has been keeping a careful record of all the new words he learns by copying them down in his notebooks. Wang Fu's perseverance is evident in the way he is able to tell at any moment *how many* characters he has in his records.

From teaching his students character by character from scratch, i.e., writing as literacy, Lao Gan proceeds to teach writing as "composition." He explains these two meanings of writing this way:

> I now request . . . you must write your characters clearly. . . . The second thing: when you compose you cannot copy from editorials in the newspapers any more. I don't care what you have been copying, the point is that you can't do it any more. Without copying, what should you write? . . . You write about something—it doesn't matter what and it doesn't have to be long, but you must write honestly and clearly. Don't give me stuff like "the red flag flutters in the wind, the war drum shakes the sky." How many red flags have you seen? Whose war drum have you heard? The kind of broken drum that they beat in labor camps—how would it shake the sky? Get rid of all this. It's useless! Write about something clearly. For instance, if you write about going to school, you should write: what time you get up in the morning, what you do after that, how you walk to school, what you see on the way. . . . [1]

Lao Gan emphasizes that writing is always a matter of recording an experience after it has happened: "Recording something always happens after the event. This is an incontrovertible truth."[2] The twin mottos of his revolutionary teaching method are *qingchu* (clarity) and *laoshi* (honesty; literally, fullness or concreteness), which constitute a kind of "back to basics" approach to writing.

Toward the end of the story, Wang Fu produces a composition that is not only clear and honest but also coherent. It is called "My Father":

> My father is the strongest man in the world. In his team he carries grain-sacks like no one can. My father also eats more than anyone else in the world. At home, mother lets him eat all he wants. This is right, because father needs to work and make money for the whole family every month. But father says: "I am not as strong as Wang Fu, because he is learning how to read and write." Father is a mute, but I understand him. When someone in his team humiliates him, I understand. Therefore I must try my best to learn how to read and write, so I can speak for him. Father works very hard. Today, he is ill, but he slowly gets up and goes to work. He is unwilling to lose the money for the day. I need to go to school and cannot stand in for him now. The bright sun rises in the morning. Father walks into the mountains and into the bright sun. I think: father is strong again.[3]

This composition forms the high point of the story because it indicates the teacher's success in refreshing the habits of writing that have been deadened by official indoctrination. "Back to basics" here means that students are learning to write in such a way that words and reality correspond without falsity. The achievement of this correspondence stands for a new kind of hope amid the ruins of the Cultural Revolution. The dominant message of "King of the Children" could thus be described this way: after the blind demolition of tradition and the imposition of uniformity in thought, the younger generation should be allowed to start afresh by relearning the fundamental principles of literary creation, that is, by writing in such a way that words reflect the reality of human action correctly. Accordingly, if only one would begin at the foundations, one could, hopefully, restore meaning to the human condition in China.

The belief, at a moment of historical change, in a type of writing which is cleansed of the burdens of the past is a familiar one throughout literate world cultures. These burdens are usually apprehended as the store of perceptual inaccuracies and falsities that result from an ever-increasing rift between language and reality brought about by a conventionalized use of language. In China, the literary reforms of the May Fourth period in the early twentieth century were based primarily on the iconoclastic criticism—and the fundamental purification—of the past conceived in terms of an empty ornamental language. At that time, the urgent production of a clean, simple, and direct language—often referred to as the "vernacular," the people's language—was part of the political production of China as a modern nation. In the capitalist West, the interest in a "clean" language was present as late as Roland Barthes's little book of the 1950s, *Mythologies*. It is useful to refer to Barthes's theoretical argument briefly to underline the mutual implications of language and politics.

We turn to what Barthes calls "myth on the Left." Myth, according to Barthes, is a type of speech which hides its political meaning by naturalizing it. A tree in myth "is no longer quite a tree, it is a tree which is decorated, adapted to a certain type of consumption, laden with literary self-indulgence, revolt, images, in short with a type of social *usage* which is added to pure matter."[4] For the Barthes of the 1950s, there is one type of speech which is the opposite of myth. He describes it in a way that reminds us of the pedagogical revolution in A Cheng's story:

> If I am a woodcutter and I am led to name the tree which I am felling, whatever the form of my sentence, I 'speak the tree', I do not speak about it. This means that my language is operational, transitively linked to its object; between the tree and myself, there is nothing but my labour, that is to say, an action. This is a political language: it represents nature for me only inasmuch as I am going to transform it, it is a language thanks to which I '*act the object*'; the tree is not an image for me, it is simply the meaning of my action. But if I am not a woodcutter, I can no longer 'speak the tree', I can only speak *about* it, *on* it. . . .

> There is therefore one language which is not mythical, it is the language of man as a producer: wherever man speaks in order to transform reality and no longer to preserve it as an image, wherever he links his language to the making of things, . . . myth is impossible.[5]

What A Cheng's story tries to teach, I think, is precisely this "real language of the woodcutter." In one episode, Lao Gan asks the students to write their composition after they have chopped bamboo. The point is that they can only write about something after they have done or experienced it. However, the preconditions for the demand for a "real language" in post-Cultural Revolution China are quite different from those in the late capitalist West. In the Chinese context, the impurities the new pedagogy aims to cleanse are not the myths of media-bound bourgeois existence but those of Communist orthodoxy, which forges language into a standardized mode in the name of the Revolution. The challenge posed by A Cheng's narrative is that the Cultural Revolution—the myth on the Left—has, in the process of abolishing the "sins" of feudal/bourgeois existence, itself mythified language through propagandist usage. To demythify this language therefore means both the cleansing of its "red flags" and "war drums" *and* a return to the fundamentals of clear, expressive writing. In other words, "political language" or the language of action here seeks not only to demythify myth but also to demythify the official demythifying agenda of Chinese communism itself.

If A Cheng's story represents a much needed corrective to the Cultural Revolution, which in the attempt to raise political consciousness on a massive scale has reduced language once again to emptiness and falsehood and left Chinese culture in a state of devastation, where does this story's pedagogy leave us? This is the question which faces Chinese intellectuals in the 1990s.

The "back to basics" approach in "King of the Children" is inscribed in a form of labor which operates by cumulation. Learning character by character is like working at something piece by piece. The securing of knowledge is based on the logic of hard work and earnest persistence. One begins with nothing except one's physical will; through time and effort one acquires knowledge bit by bit until one becomes "experienced." The ultimate test of one's success is whether one can write and speak by fitting words with reality—in semiotic terms, by fitting the signifiers at one's disposal with the signified "out there." "Back to basics" as such is an idealist longing for a unity between the natural/physical world and the world of human culture. This longing characterizes much of traditional Chinese learning and the demands it puts on language and literary expression. What appears to be revolutionary pedagogy in a narrative that implicitly criticizes the Cultural Revolution hence rejoins, philosophically, the scholarly attitudes toward language and literature which the Cultural Revolution had aimed at dismantling. It is thus not surprising that, for all its desire to rid learning of what is forced and artificial, the object around which A Cheng's story revolves for its radicalism is not simple, spontaneous "nature" but the epitome of culture: the Chinese dictionary.

On a return visit to his former production team, Lao Gan asks around for a dictionary. Laidi, the woman cook, is the only person who has one. She wants to exchange the dictionary for a position of teaching music in the narrator's school. While her wish is unlikely to be fulfilled, the scene in which she offers the narrator this precious item is suffused with a phallic, fetishistic significance. Laidi catches the narrator on the road:

> "Hey, old fellow! I am so muddle-headed that I forgot what I came here for!"
> I stopped and turned around. Laidi's shadow quickly drew closer. I felt a hard object poking at my belly. I grabbed it. It's a squarish piece, held in Laidi's warm hand. She said: "This is the dictionary. Take it."[6]

This fetish of the storage of learning is thus bestowed upon the narrator as a gift of affection by a woman who is denied access to the institution of pedagogy (or what is left of it). At the end of the story, when the narrator is dismissed from the school for his radical teaching, he decides to give the dictionary to Wang Fu. He writes down "Laidi" as the donor, then signs his own name beside hers. This ending closes the narrative with a new type of genealogy: the triangle of the woman cook/singer, the man teacher, and the boy student suggests a collective reproductive unit that is no longer based on blood and heterosexuality alone. And yet, because the dominant emphasis of the story remains the passing on of knowledge based on the written word, the new genealogy with its significant inclusion of woman as an active agential force does not, to my mind, result in any serious challenge to the traditional investment in literate culture and its patrilineal mode of inheritance. The use of Wang Fu, a boy, as the recipient of that culture, his special relationship with the male teacher, and his moving composition about his own father are all elements of this patrilineal inheritance. The presence of Laidi, however unconventional, does not therefore detract from what remain the patriarchal interests of this story.[7]

Contrary to what the story seems to be saying, the act of copying itself is, I think, not a real problem. Rather, what matters to A Cheng is what and how one copies. As long as there is something correct to copy and as long as one is copying the correct way, the rejuvenation of culture is, we are led to think, possible. Hence the "back to basics" radicalism takes place not through the abolition of copying but a change in copied objects: instead of the monotonous official textbook, the students now copy the dictionary—what Wang Fu calls "the teacher of the teacher" ("*laoshi de laoshi*"). To learn means, in a way that is in keeping with a traditional Chinese pedagogical attitude that accompanies major artistic practices such as calligraphy, painting, and literary composition, to copy (or to recite) from the revered source.[8] Copying as such amounts to an empiricist and sensualist concept of reflection, that is, reflection as a mirroring rather than as production. This concept of reflection prioritizes a reality, be it in the form of nature, culture, consciousness, or action, over the materialist practices of language and discourse, which are required merely to serve as the means of transmitting and reflecting that reality.[9] Because of its deeply ideological nature, we will call this concept of reflection "reflectionism." That such reflectionism—the required subservience of language to reality—lies at the heart of what comes across as a radical resistance against Communist ideology is something profoundly disturbing. Translated into political terms, this reflectionism becomes the subservience to a higher object that characterizes the relation that Chinese intellectuals have to the authoritarian state.

A Person's Word Forms Trust: Chinese Intellectuals and the State

It is often said about Chinese intellectuals that they have the tendency to separate intellectual work from politics. What is really meant by politics here is political activism. Even then, I think this supposed separation between intellectual and political work is an imprecise way of understanding their relation. What looks like a "separation" is not simply a matter of the existential alienation felt by intellectuals nor of their practical avoidance of speaking directly about political issues. Rather, this separation is the visible but incomplete sign of a cluster of attitudes toward *the status of knowledge*—a cluster of attitudes which forms the basis of Chinese politics to this day. Before we address the question of the separation of intellectual and political work further, therefore, we need to introduce several questions in the interim. These are: What is "knowledge" for Chinese intellectuals? How is such knowledge related to the state-as-government? How does the relation between knowledge and government affect Chinese intellectuals' relation to language, the base of their operations, and vice versa?

Although Chinese intellectuals may avoid politics in the form of activist intervention, their *agency* in Chinese political life is clearly present in one chief characteristic about Chinese politics that is often mentioned—its dependence on strong leaders. This dependence on strong leaders is frequently criticized by writers interested in China's political culture. A ferocious attack comes recently from Liu Xiaobo in an essay called "Zhongguo dangdai zhishifenzi yu zhengzhi" ("Contemporary Chinese Intellectuals and Politics").[10] Liu charges that a tendency to rely on the importance of Chinese leaders' *renge* (personality, dignity) is responsible for a situation in which leaders, rather than political systems, run the Chinese state. The dichotomies between *mingzhu* and *hunjun* (enlightened versus self-indulgent rulers), between *qingguan* and *tanguan* (uncorrupt versus corrupt officials), and between *junzi* and *xiaoren* (gentleman scholar versus villain) are structural to the politics of personality. Even the severe negativity of the Cultural Revolution, in this light, is no more than a manifestation of this politics. That negativity is only superficially righteous; in fact, it is a "clever defense of Chinese despotism":[11] "The anger felt by Chinese intellectuals toward the Cultural Revolution in recent years is an error on top of an error."[12] Liu states the futility of Chinese politics this way:

> In the thousands of years of internal cruel struggles based on despotism, blood has flowed in the form of rivers and people's liveli-

hood has been destroyed, and yet these struggles have no political meaning. The big sacrifices do not lead to any change in the social system; they merely procure power for new despots.[13]

For Liu, because the origin of political meaning resides in a belief in human individuals, every major catastrophe in China generates a new form of nostalgia for the past—as benign leadership—and for precisely those values which have been previously demolished. For instance, if what was wrong with the Cultural Revolution was the despotic *rule* with which Mao Zedong secured his own power, then the negation of the Cultural Revolution should be a negation not simply of Mao himself but of the system of which Mao was a representative. Chinese intellectuals, on the contrary, continue to aim their criticisms at persons rather than the system. After one leader is de-idealized, another usually takes his place. Political activism therefore takes the form primarily of cliquishness: one is either for or against a man, in or out of a group. (We may add that reactions to the Tiananmen Massacre also followed this pattern: the good guys were Hu Yaobang and Zhao Ziyang, the bad guys were and continue to be Deng Xiaoping, Li Peng, and so on.) In a recent issue of *Time* magazine, the writer of an article on China concludes with a similar kind of disquietingly timeless message about the future of the country:

> The party and the army, in fact, are the only two viable institutions in China, and the army is in the service of the party. That leaves only one channel for positive change: a new, more enlightened Emperor who will reform the system from the top down.[14]

Liu asks:

> As a people who have experienced deep suffering (especially in modern times), why have the Chinese not really awakened? Why is it that every catastrophe produces in Chinese intellectuals such a strong nostalgia for traditional culture? The deep suffering brought about by traditional culture has not only not led the Chinese out of tradition; on the contrary, it has led them back to tradition over and over again. Isn't this precisely the vicious circle of despotism which breeds suffering which breeds despotism?[15]

How is the status of knowledge related to the issue of despotism? Let us examine the cultural basis of the belief in strong leaders. It would be erroneous to associate "strong" with physical strength. The "strong man" here is not a physically strong man but a man with a strong personality, which comes as a result of the harmony and unity between human nature and knowledge. The dedication to learning, therefore, is what traditionally lays the foundation to a form of rule which relies not on the regulatory and contractual power of law but on the moralistic conception of human qualities, a conception that is developed through the acquaintance with literary culture. The theoretical impetus behind the Cultural Revolution was, ideally, the destruction of *this* cultural basis of political power; hence the attacks on Confucianism and traditional channels of learning. But—and this is so very painful to say—in spite of its appalling consequences, the Cultural Revolution did not complete its task. Since "knowledge" and "strong man" are mutually implicated in Chinese political thinking, destroying the Confucian stronghold of "knowledge" alone led not to a new system but instead to an intensification of what in the absence of the institution of learning became a purely emotional reliance on "strong men."

Criticisms of the Chinese government from the Chinese after the Tiananmen Massacre were symptomatic of such an emotional reliance. One of the most frequently expressed reactions, for instance, was that of disbelief: We can't believe that the party would do such a thing![16] Embedded in such disbelief is the protest: "You, the Chinese authorities, share a history of deep suffering with us, the Chinese people. How can you forget? How could you do this to us?"

Such protests, more often perceived as a feeling than distinctly heard, nonetheless point to the cultural complexes that need to be criticized politically. What disbelief makes apparent is the discontinuity between personal and political actions, which is probably the most difficult thing to accept in a system which relies on *renge* as a criterion of judgment. The authorities of Deng Xiaoping's generation—were they not once among the youths who, in the first half of the twentieth century, fought wholeheartedly against the oppressiveness of tradition, feudal corruption, and foreign imperialism *on the side of the people?* The fact that they personally share the history of multifarious oppressions in modern China does not prevent them from becoming the instruments of oppression once they are "in charge of" the system, which runs them. What this means is that emotional "sharing" is a woefully insufficient basis for criticizing the systematicity of political violence. The question remains why and how the most positive values and feelings on which many modern Chinese political leaders act tend to transform into the most oppressive and destructive with the passage of time.

I now return to what I call Chinese intellectuals' agency in Chinese politics. How is the belief in strong leaders related to the "proper" realm of intellectual work? The belief in strong leaders is a kind of trust. What is the nature of this trust? The Chinese character *xin* gives us a clue here. In Chinese there is the colloquialism that refers to the making of trust: *ren yan wei xin*—"a person's word forms trust." The character *xin*, trust, is made up of "human being" on one side and "word"/"speech" on the other. The belief in the personality of leaders as a basis for rule is supported by a belief in the correspondence between the human individual and his speech. It is therefore not, as I already said, simply a belief in the physically strong man, but the strong man as the synthesis between disparate entities—such as the cosmos and humanity, and man and language—a synthesis which is traditionally grounded in textual knowledge. Trusting the political man is in essence trusting him as an integral whole, an *expressive meshing* of disjunct experiences that takes place over the "word," which, in the historical absence of transcendental religion in China, is conveniently taken to mean the *human* word. The presence of a unified, non-phonetic script further promotes this basis of trust through the reverence for the written word, a reverence which persists among both illiterate and literate Chinese people to this day.

Traditionally, the first major function of knowledge for the Chinese intellectual is that of *xiushen*, the cultivating of one's moral character, or literally, the studying, writing, compiling, and constructing of one's "self."[17] The participation in the state follows. And yet because the overriding concern is always that of a unity between man and that which is beyond man (his language, the state, the cosmos), Chinese intellectuals always work in subservience to this beyond. In a political structure, it means that even the harshest and most individualistic critics often become subordinated to the state. Oft-quoted examples of such "establishment intellectuals"[18] from premodern Chinese history include Qü Yuan of the Warring States period (475–221 B.C.) and Du Fu of the Tang Dynasty (618–907). Scholars who hold that such intellectuals form a consistent tradition argue that even controversial contemporary writers/critics from the mainland such as Bai Hua and Liu Binyan are, in this regard, traditional.[19] Being society's conscience and speaking for the people often mean a reconfirmation of the moral obsession which is part and parcel of a strong historical commitment to the authoritarian state as the "beyond" with which the human individual must merge and mesh.

If, as Liu Xiaobo asserts, the Cultural Revolution is but a climax of the vicious circle of despotism, the alternative, after the cult of the strong man is thoroughly dismantled, does *not* lie in the simple reinstatement of the other side of the Confucian moralistic political structure—knowledge—itself. (The holding on to knowledge as a way to avoid the "mess" of contemporary politics is a time-honored practice which is steeped in political reactionism. One sees this in the recent revival of interest in neo-Confucianism among sinologists in the West, for instance.) This means that the wrongs of the Cultural Revolution cannot simply be "cleansed" by cleansing the tools of pedagogy and returning them to the basics, since what is basic is already a deeply political use of language. What appears to be a radical—for some perhaps even utopian—pedagogy in "King of the Children" is therefore really a perpetuation of the belief in the power of the written word as the basis on which social responsibility can be established. The earnest cumulation and storage of characters which supposedly should enable the truthful reproduction of experience through writing is precisely the rationale behind an idealization of *mental* power, an idealization which is then projected onto the state's functioning in the person of the strong man. This idealization of mental power leads ultimately to what Liu Xiaobo criticizes as the repeated resort to nostalgia for the past being taken as an illusory new beginning. Going "back to basics" as such affirms and enacts over and over again the roots of oppression.

The Formation of Opposition

If one of the major achievements of the Chinese Communist party has been to endow a large part of the Chinese population with a political consciousness, the question becomes one of how political consciousness is to remain effective once it has been officialized. The development of the concept of opposition in China is, in this sense, out of sync with the relevance that such a concept still enjoys in many "developed" and "developing" countries. When I use this phrase "out of sync," I do not necessarily imply that Chinese politics is "backwards" in a teleological sense. Being out of sync in this instance is the sign of modern Chinese culture's apparent tenaciousness toward the governing-by-trust in the terms discussed above.

If the Chinese Communist party was, in its origins, an organizer of dispersed political masses, it has now become an armed bureaucracy which only functions as a brake on mass movements. In terms of ideology (in Althusser's sense), the party meanwhile has depended for its power on a continual appropriation of concepts and words of an oppositional nature. Its channels of propaganda have been bombarding the mainland Chinese in the past forty years with what Nadine Gordimer in a different context calls "an orthodoxy of vocabulary."[20] Words such as *pi* (criticize), *fan* (rebel, revolt), *douzheng* (struggle, combat), *gaige* (reform) are so much a part of *civil* society that they do not have the critical edge that leftist intellectuals in the liberal West, especially those in academic institutions, still attribute to them.

For Chinese intellectuals, then, how might opposition be conceived and formulated? I propose that we examine some of the arguments put forth by two officially suppressed oppositional voices: Wei Jingsheng and Fang Lizhi.

The essay which led to Wei's arrest and imprisonment in 1979 is "Yao minzhu haishi yao xin de ducai" ("Do We Want Democracy or New Dictatorship").[21] This was first published as an editorial in the periodical *Tansuo* (*Investigation*) on March 25, 1979, and also as a Democracy Wall poster in the "Beijing Spring" of 1979.

Wei's argument is a severe criticism of the authoritarianism of Mao and Deng. What emerges clearly is a politics which rejects the notion of personal trust on which Chinese leaders rule:

> For a countless number of times Chinese history clarifies this: those who want to rule despotically must first gain the people's trust by deceiving them. As the ancient saying goes: those who have the people's hearts have the world.[22]

> Should Deng Xiaoping be trusted by the people? We feel that no
> political leader as a person should have the unconditional trust of
> the people. If what he practices is policy that benefits the people,
> if he leads the people toward peace and prosperity, we should trust
> him. *What we trust is his policy and the road he wants to take.*[23]

> We can only trust those representatives who are responsible to us
> under our supervision. And such representatives must be those
> whom we have entrusted with authority and not those who are
> imposed upon us.[24]

Instead of insisting on trust as a form of unity between a "person"
and his "word," which is then projected onto the interpersonal level
as an emotional unity between a leader and his people, Wei offers
an argument on trust which is based on collective supervision and
vigilance. The point of emphasizing this collective supervision and
vigilance—what he in the early part of his essay calls *renmin
xinzhong de fating*, the "court of law in the people's hearts"—is
precisely to introduce an alternative form of power, which is to be
based on the people's speech and which would check and regulate
the personal authoritarianism enjoyed by Chinese leaders. This alternative form of power, as I will argue below, is that of *discourse*.
The trust that Wei suggests is hence a contract rather than a meta-
physics, a provisional, conditional consent arrived at through negotiation rather than an idealist meshing between a person and his
word.

While Wei argues for a democratic pluralist pragmatism in which
a political leader's actions are to be "trusted" only if they include
the people's speech, Fang Lizhi, the astrophysicist who has
emerged in recent years as the strongest and most undaunted
spokesperson for human rights in China, claims complete independence of science and knowledge from the political realm. In the
words of Orville Schell: "Fang's speeches, putting into words what
many of his colleagues thought but dared not utter in public, were
like detonations beneath the whole edifice of Party thought control."[25] In early 1989, Fang wrote to Deng for the release of Wei
and other political prisoners. This act was immediately supported
by Chinese intellectuals in the mainland and overseas.[26]

Two speeches quoted by Schell give us an idea of the way Fang
defends the independence of knowledge:

. . . To liberate oneself from the slavery of governmental and other
nonintellectual authorities, one need only view knowledge as an independent organism. But this is not so in China. Our universities
produce tools, not educated men. . . . Our graduates cannot think
for themselves. They are quite happy to be the docile instruments
of someone else's purposes. China's intelligentsia has still not
cleansed itself of this tendency. . . . Knowledge should be independent of power. It must never submit, for knowledge loses its value
as soon as it bows to power. . . .

I have heard grumbling about my political ideas, and that is fine.
But I simply will not accept any interference in my scientific research. . . . Democracy will have no protection until the entire scientific community is filled with this spirit. The products of scientific
knowledge should be appraised by scientific standards. We should
not be swayed by the winds of power. Only then can we modernize,
and only then will we have real democracy.[27]

To the reader in the West whose ears are accustomed not only to
democratic structures but also to the permitted criticism of those
structures, these words might come across as hackneyed and ideological. In the U.S., where intellectuals are increasingly forced to
recognize the political assumptions (about race, class, sexuality, and
so forth) that are imbedded even in the most objective accounts of
knowledge, and where the current brouhaha about "cultural pluralism" is in part an insistence on the impossibility of divorcing knowledge from the social and political milieu in which it is produced,
Fang is likely to appear as intelligent but naïve. On the one hand,
he seems progressively "democratic" in his defense of the independence of knowledge; on the other hand, it is precisely this defense
that marks him as being out of step with the changes in attitudes
toward intellectual production in Western democracies. Fang's defense of knowledge and Wei's defense of popular participation in
politics are, *from the perspective of the liberal West*, ideologically
incompatible positions. One would need to unlearn what might indeed be the liberal Western ability to see the differences between
these positions in order to understand something more crucial—the
oppressiveness of the contemporary Chinese political situation,
against the authoritarianism of which Fang and Wei's arguments
become, in a way that is unthinkable to many in the West, allies.

In spite of their differences, Fang's discourse is, like Wei's, a radical one in the context of what I have already referred to as contemporary China's "out-of-sync-ness." In that context, Fang's argument for the independence of knowledge shares with Wei's the urgent demand for the liberation of the Chinese people's life activities (be these acts of participation in political affairs or the pursuit of knowledge) from their bondage to the metaphysical notion of trust and the abuse that such trust entails. In the case of the pursuit of knowledge, the differences between the Chinese situation and the American situation, in which certain flexibilities are so taken for granted that they are no longer recognized as such, are tremendous. As John Israel puts it in a comparison between Chinese and American intellectuals:

> Anti-establishment intellectuals in China have less to gain and more to lose than their American counterparts. Though an American Marxist may be denied the chairmanship of a political science department in the suburbs of the nation's capital, professional competence offers a certain degree of protection in a pluralistic society. In China, intellectuals become political critics at their own risk.[28]

> For senior scientists and technical experts and even some social and humanistic scientists, professional autonomy is not to be scorned. There is an overwhelming feeling of satisfaction in simply being allowed to do one's own thing in one's own field. How many would imperil this long-denied privilege to join a crusade of critical intellectuals in pursuit of broader freedom—a high-risk enterprise in which few have more than marginal interests?[29]

That Fang not only was expelled from the Chinese Communist party and dismissed from his job as vice-president of the University of Science and Technology but, more recently, after the Tiananmen Massacre, had the title "medium-young scientist with outstanding contribution" and his status as scientific researcher removed from him by the Chinese Academy of Science attests to the current impossibility of and hence the absolute necessity for such a dislodgement of knowledge from political power in China. Paradoxically, in spite of their different ideological bases, Wei and Fang's discourses can be described as complementary parts of a concerted effort by

contemporary Chinese intellectuals to revamp the basis—historically formed through the relationship between literate culture and
the state—of their own existence.

It is true that, currently, Chinese intellectuals tend only to follow
the impetus of Fang's argument. Their tendency to avoid "politics"
is an obvious reaction against the continual meshing of knowledge
and political power and the danger this has for them as individuals.
Even democracy leaders in exile like Yan Jiaqi insist that they are
not dealing with politics but simply with the issue of human rights.
Nonetheless, this apparent separation of knowledge and politics is,
as I said, merely a partial sign of what is really at stake. As long as
Chinese intellectuals continue to invest knowledge with the moralistic structures of trust, they are still continuing to perpetuate traditional political thinking *whether or not they actively participate in
political affairs*. This last point is crucial. Grasping it would mean
that Chinese intellectuals need to recognize their own endowed
agency, activist or non-activist, in politics. It would also mean that
Fang's argument for the independence of knowledge must be com-
plemented by Wei's argument for popular political participation.

The alternative to political authoritarianism is not to refrain from
knowledge or politics but rather to use knowledge (whose independence needs to be secured on Fang's terms) to strive for and keep
alive modes of popular intervention in official political power (in
the ways proposed by Wei). As long as Chinese intellectuals harbor
the illusion that what they do can be "apolitical," the authoritarianism which throughout Chinese history has put intellectual work at
the mercy of official political power will never be checked. In this
light, even the undoubtedly ideological humanism in Fang's defense
of the "independence of knowledge" is itself a form of political intervention, because it represents a major opposition against the
officializing of knowledge that either makes it subservient to the
state or reduces it to ineffective metaphysical inquiry of a "scholarly" nature. "Independence" as such is not an ontological autonomy
but a freedom from political determination, and as such it is a radical challenge to the basic "legal" conditions that currently secure
the stability of the Chinese state. Such freedom is the basis for what
one could call a system of "dual power," in which "state power and
popular power complement each other, but also check each
other."[30]

From Trust to Discourse: Imagining Utopia

In the words of Lu Yuan, an eyewitness to the events in Beijing in the spring of 1989:

> The party leadership, in reacting as if the participants were self-conscious revolutionaries and in immediately taking counterrevolutionary measures, has actually radicalized the movement, so that it may move on to pressing for change in the nature of the party-state and not just for the limiting of its social control.[31]

To the extent that Wei and Fang, two of the strongest voices that amount to a major opposition which mobilized the masses in 1989, are currently prisoners in China—Wei, reputedly already in a state of dementia after over ten years of torture and imprisonment in Qinghai, and Fang, supposedly residing in the American Embassy since June 1989[32]—a change in the nature of the party-state is not possible in the foreseeable future. Aware of problems they will never solve on their own, including the continual arrests and secret trials of protesters, major national concerns such as an unstable economy, the state control of reproduction and hence of women's bodies, the depletion of ecological resources, and massive quotidian psychological frustrations, Chinese intellectuals in the 1990s face the question of what they in their limited capacity can do to build a viable opposition that would in due course topple the current system.

The first step they need to take in that direction is to ask themselves: What does it mean to be "Chinese"? This is a question about nationalism, in which Chinese people, like all peoples of the post-imperialist third world, are politically, emotionally, and idealistically caught. The historical China difference, however, has to do with the fact that mainland Chinese nationalism is explicitly intertwined with communism. Unlike the Central and Eastern European countries, where changes in official political structures in the post-1945 period were imposed by the external intervention of a power that was traditionally an enemy, and where, therefore, the recent overthrow of authoritarian regimes could go hand in hand with a sense of patriotic triumph, such "patriotism" will be difficult for the

Chinese after 1989. In China, precisely because communism was internally generated and, in the twenties, thirties, and forties, viewed by progressive intellectuals as the way out of a long tortuous history of feudalism, the discrediting of Communist rule is a total catastrophe, throwing into sudden uncertainty all the other investments that have accompanied the idealization of communism as the state rationale.

But with the bankruptcy of patriotic trust in the governing authorities also arises the possibility for a different kind of utopia. Here, hope cannot begin with the "back to basics" approach we find in A Cheng. Rather, it resides in the perpetual modifying of "being Chinese" as a cultural identity which can no longer be confined to national boundaries alone. The discrediting of Communist rule, in other words, ought in the long run to discredit also an ideology of nationalism which forecloses the articulation of political differences by an imposed centralized culture. Because in China, communism, nationalism, and the state centralization of culture through the dissemination of standardized histories have reinforced one another in a unique way in the past forty years, the disenchantment with one of these categories must, in a way that would be much more rigorous than what is happening in Central and Eastern Europe, involve a disenchantment with and criticism of the others as well. The difficulty of reinvesting in nationalism and hence the accelerated awareness of the need to go beyond it will be one of the most "culturally specific" elements that distinguish Chinese intellectuals' post-catastrophic discourse in the years to come.

Before any structural changes are introduced at the level of the party-state, changes need to be introduced, however imperceptibly, at the "social" level. And because there is no space for such a "social" opposition to be developed within China right now, the Chinese population in diaspora whose claims to cultural identity are rooted in "being Chinese" are the ones who must consolidate the groundwork for future change. Future change as such is, of course, imaginary. Its possibility is that of providing an alternative to what is currently being severely dismantled and demolished. This possibility is "utopian" in the sense defined by Ernesto Laclau and Chantal Mouffe: " . . . 'utopia,' . . . the possibility of negating an order *beyond* the point that we are able to threaten it."[33]

What might such a "possibility" look like?

One of the things that Chinese intellectuals can strive for to-gether in their work is a loosening of the positivity of the sign "Chinese." To do that, they need to give up their ingrained sense of self-importance and instead realize that they are "vanguards" only in the sense of a waste product as described by Roland Barthes in the passage quoted at the beginning of this chapter. Chinese intellectuals are in the forefront of the culture because, as Barthes says, they crystallize "in the form of refuse, impulses, desires, complications, blockages that probably belong to society as a whole." Among such refuse, impulses, desires, complications, and blockages, the clinging to an unquestioned ideal of being "Chinese," together with its hierarchized ways of thinking about the rest of the world, ought to be the first to be removed. This does not mean abandoning the history of the sign "Chinese" but rather using it as a base for an alliance with other types of work that are not done exclusively in China-related areas. Why is this necessary? It is so because only in such alliances can the traditional cultural tendency to sinicize the world—to mesh disparate things and to internalize them politically—be disrupted. Such a tendency derives from the strong investments in the special links between language, knowledge, and the state that I argue in this chapter. As long as "Chinese" remains a fixed center of identity, Chinese intellectuals will be perpetuating the political centrism which lies at the heart of the violence that has surfaced time and again in the modern period.

Instead of reinstating the legitimacy of traditional knowledge as a counter-political force, Chinese intellectuals need to turn *elsewhere* to form a new locus of contestation. For instance, why not sinology as the logical site of resistance for Chinese intellectuals in diaspora? As the patron field of China studies, sinology has inherited, for its operational premise, all the tendencies to internalize and centralize "Chinese culture" from the political structure of the Chinese state. Even if we were to leave aside the by now familiar issues of Orientalism of which sinology is a part—issues that have to do with the reification of non-Western cultures as objects of study which goes hand in hand with an indifference to those cultures' living members[34]—the ideological affinities between sinology and the Chinese state have yet to be properly scrutinized and challenged.

An alternative path for Chinese intellectuals overseas, who can participate more freely in discussions that take place as a result of global mass movements, is a critical use of the interventional nature of discourse, of discourse as intervention. Conventionally, terms such as "discourse" and "articulation" are grounded in expressive and cognitive theories of language, which reaffirm language as the expression or articulation of human individuals. What is relevant to the contemporary Chinese situation, however, is something other than such expressive and cognitive notions of discourse.

In current critical theories, we find formulations of an alternative notion of discourse in the writings of Mikhail Bakhtin and more recently in the work of Laclau and Mouffe. As is well known, Bakhtin's notion of "dialogue" points to the dialogic nature of each apparently "independent" utterance and hence the communal basis of language even when it is only spoken by individual speakers. The "dialogic" as such removes language from the common belief that it (language) exists separately from the consciousness of autonomous human beings who simply use it as a communicative tool. Instead, "consciousness"—that which is often assumed to be primary to and independent of language—is constituted dialogically—that is, discursively and interdiscursively.[35] In a way comparable to Bakhtin's "dialogic," Laclau and Mouffe's formulations of discourse also shift the emphasis from discourse as cognition and expression to discourse as social practice:

> a discursive structure is not a merely 'cognitive' or 'contemplative' entity; it is an *articulatory practice* which constitutes and organizes social relations.[36]

> articulation is now a discursive practice which does not have a plane of constitution prior to, or outside, the dispersion of the articulated elements.[37]

Such formulations of discourse, because they emphasize how discourse is constituted by participatory efforts from different social relations, are useful for contemporary Chinese intellectuals because they provide a theoretical means to undo that tendency to bind "person" and "word" which forms the basis of "trust" in current Chinese politics. While "trust" is founded on the meshing of the "strong man" and his "word," with the implied belief in the character of man, "discourse" emphasizes, in the same way that Wei's argument does, the "court of law in the people's hearts"—in other words, the communal regulatory power arrived at through negotiation and consensus. The independence of knowledge emphasized by Fang can, in this light, be understood as the independence, in practice, of partial articulatory/discursive units (or nodal points), which in their interrelations constitute an open-ended social field:

> *The practice of articulation . . . consists in the construction of nodal points which partially fix meaning; and the partial character of this fixation proceeds from the openness of the social, a result, in its turn, of the constant overflowing of every discourse by the infinitude of the field of discursivity.*[38]

Defined in these terms, away from the moralistic conceptions of trust, discourse is that badly needed collective intervention which would allow the possibility of a viable opposition. This possibility is *the* utopia toward which Chinese intellectuals must work.

The imposed exile from China, to which many now cannot return, effects a discontinuity, a rupture, which may in due course give rise to the emergence of a critical mass. This critical mass will address "China" without the privilege of the land. The denial of the illusion of one's existence on "Chinese soil" may in due course force Chinese intellectuals to use the rhetoric of patriotism and nationalism differently. Meanwhile, the physical distance from China means, temporarily at least, legal and political protection from official Chinese persecution and thus a chance for securing the horizontalization of discourses among various spheres of culture that would, one hopes, eventually replace the current verticalization toward central power.

For Chinese intellectuals to deal with contemporary Chinese history as the specific constitution of a people's democratic struggle, it will become increasingly necessary to move outside "Chinese" territory, geographical and cultural. Such "moving outside" is the moving outside of the exiled dissenter, the refugee, the survivor of catastrophe. It is at the same time a self-conscious moving into the global space in which discursive plurality inevitably modifies and defines specific cultural identity rather than the other way around. The ineluctability of this "global space" is evident in the standstill of history that was the Tiananmen Massacre. The mass demonstrations that began with the mourning of a dead national leader, Hu Yaobang, acquired momentum not only from intellectual circles but also from workers and different Chinese social groups elsewhere in the world, notably Hong Kong and Taiwan. The "national Chinese" issues, including the demands for the freedom of speech and for the end to bureaucratic corruption, became the partial or local "nodal points" into which the global media plugged with their own agendas. The various interpretative discourses that follow the massacre shuttle back and forth between "local" and "global" articulations in ways that clearly indicate their mutual implication. Although these discourses proceed *as if* a stabilized understanding by way of either the "local" or the "global" were possible, the sense that they are, in spite of their intentions, moving beyond such stability is undoubtedly felt. For instance, many Chinese people said afterwards that had "the world" not been present, the final massacre might not have happened. Others now say that the blood that was shed in Beijing led to the blossoming of flowers in Eastern Europe in late 1989.[39] Still others say that, while in the past the Chinese believed that socialism would save China, now "only China can save socialism."[40]

Even though these discourses attempt to approach political agency in a partialized—in this case nationalized—manner, their allusions to the presence of other forces in the interpretation of the "Chinese" event nonetheless points to a "totality" that insists itself on the "local" struggle. Totality does not refer to a closed "whole"; rather, it refers to an interdiscursive space in which the articulation of the local struggle already requires the articulation of its implicatedness in other struggles, and vice versa. This interdiscursive space is "total" not in the sense of something finished (to which nothing more can be added). Instead, the meaning of "totality" is precisely otherness—a local struggle is "total" because of its dependence on what is other than itself through the activity of equivalential articulation. To this extent, we begin to comprehend the point of a passage like this from Laclau and Mouffe:

> The strengthening of specific democratic struggles requires, there-
> fore, the expansion of chains of equivalence which extend to other
> struggles. The equivalential articulation between anti-racism, anti-
> sexism and anti-capitalism, for example, requires a hegemonic con-

struction which, in certain circumstances, may be the condition for
the consolidation of each one of these struggles. The logic of equivalence, then, taken to its ultimate consequences, would imply the
dissolution of the autonomy of the spaces in which each one of these
struggles is constituted; not necessarily because any of them become
subordinated to others, but because they have all become, strictly
speaking, equivalent symbols of a unique and indivisible struggle.[41]

This "indivisible struggle" is not the kind of universalism that
subsumes individual histories; rather, it is the constellation of specific historical forces in their indivisible or *irreducible relations
with one another*. These relations establish but do not exhaustively
constitute the identity of any particular struggle. It is thus in terms
of lack—that is, the lack of exhaustive/complete constitution of single cultural identities—that the utopia of opposition is formed.

The Chinese government's response to the Tiananmen Massacre
was exactly opposite to this utopia. Throughout the period around
June 4, 1989, while the world watched in sensationalized anticipa-
tion, the Chinese authorities attempted to prevent the demonstrators' struggle for political pluralism from becoming global through
repeated emphases on what they considered to be a strictly "Chinese internal affair." This attempt to restrict the interdiscursivity
between the "local" struggle and the mobilizations by global forces
was ultimately sealed in blood by militaristic violence. Afterward,
in order to "mop up" the traces of violence, it became necessary to
tighten surveillance of the mental condition of Chinese citizens:
since June 4, 1989, censorship of Western and pro-Western publications has been reinforced, and mass media "reeducation" campaigns
have been in full swing. Around June 4, 1990, Tiananmen Square
was closed off to prevent any resurgence of demonstrations that
would commemorate the massacre a year before, and Chinese citizens were reminded of their history of *oppression by foreigners*
that began with the Opium War of 1839. In its desire to unify the
"Chinese nation," the Chinese government thus continues to fanta-
size its own brutality retroactively in the form of a Chinese nationalist struggle, in which "Western imperialists" alone are the real
enemy.

The Chinese government's absolute moves demand a politics of
opposition that is equally absolute in its determination to abandon

the ongoing structures of violence. Living after catastrophe for Chinese intellectuals is living with the awareness that their "Chinese" identity is an illusion. It is an illusion not because they cannot return to China. Rather, it is because "Chinese-ness," to which they intuitively cling, is always an other, which at specific moments also becomes the source of oppression and catastrophe which they will try to survive. This survival means they must continue to question the very constitution and centrality of their cultural identity—to displace, in other words, the *zhong* ("center") in *zhongguo* ("central kingdom").[42]

(See **Glossary** for Chinese names, terms, and passages.)

V

AGAINST THE LURES OF DIASPORA

MINORITY DISCOURSE, CHINESE WOMEN, AND INTELLECTUAL HEGEMONY

Modern Chinese Literature as "Minority Discourse"

The questions I would like to address in this chapter can be stated very simply: Why is it so difficult to bring up the topic of women in the field of Chinese studies? What can the critical spotlight received by "Chinese women" tell us about the discursive politics in play? These questions are not only questions about women and Chinese studies. They have to do with the problematic of the post-colonial discursive space in which many "third world" intellectuals who choose to live in the "first world" function. Within that space, these intellectuals are not only "natives" but spokespersons for "natives" in the "third world." Currently, the prosperity of that space is closely tied up with the vast changes taking place in Western academic institutions, notably in North America, where many intellectuals "of color" are serving as providers of knowledge about their nations and cultures. The way these intellectuals function is therefore inseparable from their status as cultural workers/brokers in diaspora, which may be a result of graduate studies, research, visiting or permanent appointments, immigration, and, in some cases, exile or political asylum. In this chapter I want to use the increasing interest in "women" in the field of Chinese studies as a way to focus the problems of the "third world" intellectual in diaspora. The implications of these problems go far beyond narrow institutional designators such as "women's studies" and "area studies" in which the study of "third world women" is most commonly lodged.

Superficial developments in the humanities across the U.S. indicate the opposite of the first of my opening questions. Following the legitimation of feminist interests in the West, receptivity to women's issues in other parts of the world seems unprecedentedly great at present. In the Asian field, it is not difficult to find research projects, dissertations, books, and conferences devoted to women. For the first time in Asian history, perhaps, we can identify a visible group of scholars, largely women, whose work centers on women. And yet the spotlight on "women" in our field seems also to make the shape and sound of the enemy more pronounced than ever.

I use "enemy" to refer not to an individual but to the attitude that "women" is still not a legitimate scholarly concern. Depending on the occasion, this enemy uses a number of different but related tactics. The first tactic may be described as habitual myopia: "You don't exist because I don't see you." The second is conscience-clearing genitalism:[1] "Women? Well, of course! . . . But I am not a woman myself, so I will keep my mouth shut." The third is scholarly dismissal: "Yes, women's issues are interesting, but they are separate and the feminist approach is too narrow to merit serious study." The fourth is strategic ghettoization: since "women" are all talking about the same thing over and over again, give them a place in every conference all in one corner, let them have their say, and let's get on with our business. These tactics of the enemy—and it is important for us to think of the enemy in terms of a dominant symbolic rather than in terms of individuals, that is, a corpus of attitudes, expressions, discourses, and the *value* espoused in them—are not limited to the China field. They are descriptive of the problems characteristic of the study of non-hegemonic subjects in general.

Leaving aside the issue of women for the time being, I would like to argue that the notion of modern Chinese literature as we know it today depends, implicitly, on the notion of a "minority discourse" in the postcolonial era. As two critics define it, "minority discourse is, in the first instance, the product of damage, of damage more or less systematically inflicted on cultures produced as minorities by the dominant culture."[2] Modern Chinese literature is, in this respect, not different from other postcolonial national literatures; its problems are symptomatic of the histories of non-Western cultures' struggles for cultural as well as national autonomy in the aftermath of Western imperialism. Because postcolonial literatures are linked to the hegemonic discourse of the West as such, they are, in spite of the typical nativist argument for their continuity with the indigenous traditions,[3] always effectively viewed as a kind of minority discourse whose existence has been victimized and whose articulation has been suppressed.

While the "world" significance of modern Chinese literature derives from its status as minority discourse, it is precisely this minority status that makes it so difficult for modern Chinese literature to be legitimized as "world" literature, while other *national* literatures, notably English, French, and Russian, have had much wider claims to an international modernity in spite of their historical and geographical specificity. In spite—and because—of the current clamor for "minority discourses," there is no lack of voices supporting the opposite viewpoint. The debates in the U.S. on the issue of canonicity, for instance, are driven by the urge to perpetuate what has been established as the "universals" of "cultural literacy." In fact, the more frequently "minor" voices are heard, the greater is the need expressed by the likes of Allan Bloom and E. D. Hirsch, Jr. for maintaining a canon, so that a Western notion of humanity can remain as the norm.[4] We understand from the Gulf War that it is by resorting to the rhetoric of preserving universals— love, knowledge, justice, tradition, civilization, and so forth, argued both in George Bush's "new world order" and Saddam Hussein's pan-Arabism—that political power sustains its ideological hold on the populace. The rhetoric of universals, in other words, is what ensures the ghettoized existence of the other, be it in the form of a different culture, religion, race, or sex. As all of us know, the battle against the ideology embedded in the rhetoric of universals is also one faced by those working on "women" in the China field.

The proposal I want to make, however, is that, for the investigators of "Chinese women," this battle *cannot* simply be fought by a recourse to "minority discourse," or to Chinese women as the suppressed and victimized other. I will explain by discussing the precarious relation between "minority discourse" and "women" in the China field, with special emphasis on the difficult and challenging role of Chinese women intellectuals today.

Consider one of the primary tasks faced by Chinese intellectuals in the twentieth century—that of establishing, in the throes of imperialism, a national literature. If the desire to establish a national literature is a desire for a kind of universal justice—a justice in the eyes of which Chinese literature and culture would become legitimate internationally rather than simply "Chinese"—how is this desire pursued? While there are many efforts to demonstrate modern Chinese literature's continuity with past literary achievements, what distinguishes modern Chinese writings is an investment in suffering, an investment that aims at exposing social injustice. This investment in—or cathexis to—suffering runs through Chinese cultural production from the beginning of the twentieth century to the present—from the upsurge of interest in romantic love in popular Mandarin Duck and Butterfly stories of the 1910s, to the pro-science and pro-democracy attempts at national self-strengthening in May Fourth writings, to the focuses on class struggle in the literature of the 1930s and 1940s, to the official Communist practice of "speaking bitterness" (*suku*), by which peasants were encouraged by cadres of the liberation forces to voice their sufferings at mass meetings in the 1950s and 1960s, and to the outcries of pain and betrayal in the "literature of the wounded" (*shanghen wenxue*) of the post-Cultural Revolution period. In other words, the attempt to establish a *national* literature in the postcolonial era requires a critical edge other than the belief in a magnificent past. For twentieth-century Chinese intellectuals, this critical edge has been *class consciousness*. In orthodox Marxist terms, "class" is that contradiction between the surplus of capital on the one hand and labor on the other. The surplus of capital leads to a situation in which those who do the least work enjoy the most privilege, while those who work continue to have the products of their labor taken or "alienated" from them. The category of "class" thus supplies a means of analyzing social injustice in economic terms, as the unequal distribution of wealth between the rich and the poor.[5] In the Chinese context, in which intellectual work was formerly part of the hegemony of the state, "class consciousness" is inseparable from *cultural* revolution, a revolution that seeks to overthrow not only the economic but specifically the ideological dominance of the ruling classes. Thus even in the crudest usage by the Chinese Communists, "alienated labor" carries ideological as well as economic implications.

The historian Arif Dirlik refers to the use of class for nation-building as the practice of the "proletarian nation." Commenting on a passage from *The Crisis of the Arab Intellectual* by Abdallah Laroui (who derived much of his historicism from Joseph Levenson's work on China), Dirlik writes:

> [The new China is] the "proletarian" nation of revolutionary intellectuals (Li Dazhao, Sun Yat-sen, Mao Zedong come to mind immediately). If it does not bring the proletariat (or the oppressed classes) into the forefront of history, it at least makes them into a central component of the national struggle—as a referent against which the fate of ideas and values must be judged.[6]

We cannot understand modern Chinese literature without understanding the ways in which nationhood and class are intertwined in literary discourse. The use of "class consciousness" as a way to build a national culture is one of the most important signs of Chinese literature's modernity, a modernity that is, as May Fourth and subsequent writings show, self-consciously revolutionary. If modern Chinese literature emerges as an "other," a "minor" literature in the global scene, it also emerges by putting the spotlight on its oppressed classes, among which women occupy one but not the only place.

In its investment in suffering, in social oppression, and in the victimization and silencing of the unprivileged, modern Chinese literature partakes of the many issues of "minority discourse" that surface with urgency in the field of cultural studies/cultural criticism in North America today. Central to such issues is the question "can the subaltern speak?" as we find it in Gayatri Spivak's essay of the same title.[7] In this regard, the history of modern Chinese literature can be seen as a paradigm for contemporary cultural studies, simply because the most "written" figure in this history is none other than the subaltern, whose "speech" has been coming to us through fiction, poetry, political debates, historical writings, journalistic representations, as well as radio plays, films, operas, and regional cultural practices. In a fashion paralleling the theorizations of "minority discourse" that emphasize the production of postcolonial subjects whose speeches and/or writings disrupt the hegemonic discourse of the imperialist, modern Chinese literature specializes, one might argue, in producing figures of minority whose overall effect has been an ongoing protest against the cultural violence they experience at physical, familial, institutional, and national levels. At the same time, the conscious representation of the "minor" as such also leads to a situation in which it is locked in opposition to the "hegemonic" in a permanent bind. The "minor" cannot rid itself of its "minority" status because it is that status that gives it its only legitimacy;[8] support for the "minor," however sincere, always becomes support for the center. In Communist China, one could go as far as saying that "class consciousness," as it becomes an ideological weapon of the state, offers a "critical edge" only insofar as it permanently regenerates the reality of social injustice rather than its dissolution.

How is this so? Let me explain by relating "class consciousness" to the conceptualization of social change *through language*. Among Marxist critics working in the West, the advocacy of "class consciousness" is often closely related to a specific theory of language. For instance, speaking of the "subaltern," Gayatri Spivak says:

> The subaltern is all that is not elite, but the trouble with those kinds of names is that if you have any kind of political interest you name it in the hope that the name will disappear. That's what class consciousness is in the interest of: the class disappearing. What politically we want to see is that the name would not be possible.[9]

The theory of language offered here is that the act of articulating something moves and changes it, and therefore may cause it to disappear. In China, however, the relation between language and reality has been very differently conceived because of the lingering force of Confucius's concept of *zhengming*—the rectification of names. The Confucian attitude toward language is expressed in a well-known passage in *Lunyü (The Analects)*:

> If names be not correct, language is not in accordance with the truth of things. If language be not in accordance with the truth of things,

affairs cannot be carried on to success. . . .

Therefore a superior man considers it necessary that the names he uses may be spoken *appropriately*, and also that what he speaks may be carried out *appropriately*. What the superior man requires is just that in his words there may be nothing incorrect.[10]

For Confucius as for the majority of Chinese people, naming is the opposite of what Spivak suggests. Instead of causing the reality to disappear, naming is the way to make a certain reality "proper," that is, to make it real. That is why it is so important to have the right name and the right language.

To use the words of Slavoj Žižek, we may say that Confucius understood "the radical contingency of naming, the fact that naming itself retroactively constitutes its reference." It is "the name itself, the signifier, which supports the identity of the object."[11] "In other words," Žižek writes, "the only possible definition of an object in its identity is that this is the object which is always designated by the same signifier—tied to the same signifier. It is the signifier which constitutes the kernel of the object's 'identity.' "[12] Strictly speaking, there is nothing false or misleading about Confucius's theory of language. As a process, *zhengming* demonstrates the practical politics involved in any claim to visibility and existence— namely, that such a claim must be at the same time a claim to/in language. Hence, even though—in fact, precisely because—it is *no more than a claim*, language is the absolutely essential means of access to power. In their struggles to be seen and heard, minority groups all prove the truth of Confucius's theory: Before "dismantling" and "decentering" power in the way taught by deconstructionists, they argue, they must first "have" power and be named, that is, recognized, so.

The act of naming, then, is not intrinsically essentialist or hierarchical. It is the social relationships in which names are inserted that may lead to essentialist, hierarchical, and thus detrimental consequences.[13] Historically, the problem with Confucius's teaching was that it was used to address civil servants in their service to the state. A very astute understanding of language was thus instrumentalized in organizing political hierarchy and consolidating centralized state power, with all the reactionary implications that followed. *Zhengming* became a weapon that ensured the immovability of an already established political hegemony and in that sense a paradigmatic case, in Derrida's terms, of *logocentric* governance.

By extension, we understand why, in their mobilization of "class consciousness," the Chinese Communists have actually been following the Confucian model of language as it is inherited in Chinese politics in spite of their overt "ideological" contempt for the Master. The raising of "class consciousness" as official "reeducational" policy during the two decades following 1949 did not so much lead to the disappearance of class as it did to a reification/rectification of the name "class" as the absolute reality to which every citizen had to submit in order to clear their "conscience." Hence, in pursuit of the ideal of the "proletarian nation," strengthening national culture became equal to hounding down the class enemy, even though "class enemy" was *simply a name*. In a discussion of the contemporary Chinese political situation by way of Jacques Lacan's notion of *jouissance*, Kwai-cheung Lo writes:

> The "class enemy" in the Chinese Cultural Revolution is, in a sense, a fetish structuring the jouissance. The whole country is summoned to ferret out the class enemy, to uncover the hidden counterrevolutionaries. The class enemy is everywhere, in every nook and corner of our social life, but it is also nowhere, invisible and arcane. It is clear that the class enemy is jouissance, which is an impossibility but can produce traumatic effects. It is also the *objet petit a*, a pure void which keeps symbolic order working and sets the Cultural Revolution in motion. The paradoxical character of the class enemy is that it always returns to the same place, exerts effects on the reality of the subject, and it is itself a nothing, a negativity. Thus, in the end, when we have looked in every corner to ferret out the class enemy, we then have to uncover the enemy in our heart. The Cultural Revolution turns out to be a Stalinist trial. Everyone must examine their whole life, their entire past, down to the smallest detail, to search for the hidden fault and, finally, confess themselves as sinners. . . .
>
> When the people are asked to confess, to "open their hearts to" [*jiaoxin*] the party, and they look deep into their hearts, what they find is not a subject who is unable to express the signified, but a void, a lack which has to be filled out by the object, the sin, the incarnation of impossible enjoyment, jouissance. . . . [14]

In their obsession with the name "class enemy," the "rectification" of which led to the madness of the Cultural Revolution, the Chinese Communists thus proved themselves to be loyal disciples of Confucius's teaching about state control.

Perhaps the greatest and most useful lesson modern Chinese culture has to offer the world is the pitfall of building a nation—"the People's Republic of China"—on a theory of social change—"class consciousness"—in the illusion that the hope offered by that theory—the disappearance of class itself—can actually materialize in human society. Chinese communism was the dream of materializing that theory by officializing a concept of language and literature in which the minorities, the oppressed, and the exploited are to be vindicated. But when the force of "class consciousness" is elevated to official ideology rather than kept strictly as an analytical instrument (as it was in the texts of Marx), it also becomes mechanical and indistinguishable from other ideological strongholds of governmental power.[15] To date, the mainland government is still trying to keep this rhetoric of "class consciousness" alive after its latest abuse of the peaceful seekers of democratic reforms. When a government that was originally founded on the ideal of social justice dwindles to the level of open injustice and continual deception of its people, as the Chinese government does today, we must seek strategies that are alternative to a continual investment in minority, in suffering, and in victimization.

Masculinist Positions in the China Field: Women to the West, Fathers to Chinese Women

The clarified relation between "nation" and "class" in twentieth-century China allows one to ask: How do women intervene? How can we articulate women's *difference* without having that difference turned into a cultural ghettoization of women while the enemy remains intact? How can women "speak"?

Current trends in contemporary cultural studies, while being always supportive of categories of difference, also tend to reinscribe those categories in the form of fixed identities. As in *zhengming*, categories such as "race," "class," and "gender" were originally named in order to point out what has been left out of mainstream categorizations and thus what still remains to be named, seen, and heard. "Names" of "difference" as such are meant as ways for the marginalized to have some access to the center. And yet, one feels that these categories of difference are often used in such a way as to stabilize, rather than challenge, a preestablished method of examining "cultural diversity," whereby "difference" becomes a sheer matter of adding new names in an ever-expanding pluralistic horizon. If categories such as "race," "class," and "gender" are to remain useful means of critical intervention, they must not be lined up with one another in a predictable refrain and attached to all investigations alike as packaging. Instead, as terms of intervention, they must be used to analyze, decode, and criticize one another, so that, for instance, "gender" is not only "gender" but what has been muted in orthodox discussions of class, while "class" is often what notions such as "woman" or even "sexual difference" tend to downplay in order to forge a gendered politics. How do we conceive of gender within class and distinguish class within gender? How is it that scholars, including Asianists, seem more ready to accept "gender" when it is spoken of *generally* across the disciplines, while to bring it up in the interpretation of specific texts within a particular field such as Chinese studies, one still runs the risk of being considered unscholarly and non-objective?

A valid point made by Dirlik is that in order to destroy culturalist hegemony, it is not enough to concentrate on unequal relations between nations (such as those between the "first" and the "third" worlds). What is of similar importance is an investigation of the unequal relations *within* societies. In the context of China, the narrative of "class" as a way to address the unequal relations within society has proved itself inadequate because of its official abuse, an abuse which takes the form of an armed appropriation—a turning into property and propriety—of a particular language, the language of the oppressed or what we have been calling "minority discourse." That is to say, if the past forty years of Chinese political history has been a failed revolution, it is in part because the revolution has been a secret cohabitation between Confucius and the Communists, between *zhengming* and a theory of language in which "naming" is, ideally, the first step to changing social reality. In this cohabitation, Confucius, saturated with practices of bureaucratic hierarchy, remains on top.

After June 4, 1989, it is unlikely that the Chinese intellectuals who have begun careers in the West will "return" to China. In their diaspora, Chinese intellectuals will emerge as a group whose distinction from the "objects" they use for their research will be more and more pronounced. Geographic, linguistic, and political differences are going to turn internationalized Chinese women intellectuals, for instance, into a privileged class vis-à-vis the women in China. As we continue to use Chinese women's writings and lives as the "raw material" for our research in the West, the relationship between us as intellectuals overseas and them "at home" will increasingly take on the coloration of a kind of "master discourse/native informant" relationship. The inequality of this relationship should now be emphasized as that inequality *within* a social group that Dirlik mentions. While intellectuals are rewarded for their work in the West, voices of the oppressed continue to be unheard and intellectual work continues to be persecuted in China. There is very little we can do overseas to change the political situation "back there." The attention bestowed upon Chinese events by the world media is arbitrary. In early 1991, for instance, as global attention was directed toward the Gulf War, the Chinese government's trial and sentencing of the June 4 protesters went largely unnoticed. Whether we like it or not, our position with regard to China is one of waiting and hoping.

As "minority discourse" becomes a hot topic in cultural studies in the West, some overseas Chinese intellectuals are now choosing to speak and write from a "minor" position. While enjoying the privilege of living in the West, they cling, in their discourse, to the status of the neglected "other." While this espousal of minority status may not be stated as such, it is most often detected in discourses which moralistically criticize "the West" in the name of "real" "Chinese" difference or otherness. Depending on the political interest of the person, "Chinese difference" (by which is usually meant Chinese identity) may take the form of a reactionary confirmation of traditional, humanistic attitudes toward "culture" and "knowledge," or it may assume a liberalist guise by reading Chinese culture in terms of the Bakhtinian "dialogic" and "carnivalesque." In some cases, while being fashionably skeptical of "Western theory," these intellectuals nonetheless revere Fredric Jameson's ethnocentric notion that all "third world" texts are necessarily to be read as "national allegories"[16] and proceed to read Chinese culture accordingly. However, to "nationalize" "third world" cultural productions "allegorically" this way is also to "other" them uniformly with a logic of production that originates in the West. What is being forgotten here is how "first world" production comprises not only the production of tangible goods but also intangible value. The latter, as I will argue in the following pages, is exported as ideological exploitation, which plays a far more crucial role in structuring the lives of peoples in the non-West. Without a discussion of "value" as such, the notion that all "third world" peoples are necessarily engaged in national struggles and that all "third world" texts are "national allegories" is quite preposterous.[17] In Jameson's model, "third world" intellectuals are, regardless of their class and gender, made to speak uniformly as minors and women to the West. Following Jameson, many contemporary Chinese intellectuals' desire to play the role of the other confirms what Nancy Armstrong, writing about the historicization of sexuality in the British novel, says: "the modern individual was first and foremost a woman."[18]

Vis-à-vis the "insiders" of the China field, on the other hand, these intellectuals' strategy is decidedly different. There, faced with new types of research and new interests such as women's issues, their attitude becomes, once again, patriarchal and mainstream; women's issues do not interest them the way *their own minority* in relation to "the West" does. Faced with women, their attitude resembles that of right-wingers in the American academy. They defend tradition, sinocentrism, and heritage, and denounce feminist scholarship as unscholarly. It is as if, dealing with the "insiders," they no longer remember the political significance of the "minority discourse" which they speak only when it is opportune for them to do so. They are minors and women when faced with "foreigners"; they are fathers when faced with "insiders," especially women.

To return, then, to the question of why it is so difficult to bring up the topic of women in the field of Chinese studies. It is difficult not because women's issues are insignificant—there has been interest in "woman" and "the new woman" in Chinese writings since before the 1910s. Quite to the contrary, it is because "woman," like the "minor," offers such an indispensable position *in discourse*, traditional and modern, that feminists have difficulty claiming "her." One question that traditionalists in the field often ask feminists is: "But there is no lack of femininity in classical Chinese literature! Why are you saying that the feminine has been suppressed?" A look at Chinese literary history would suggest that these traditionalists are, literally, right: *Chinese literary history has been a history of men who want to become women.* In the past, male authors adopted women's voices and wrote in "feminine" styles; in the modern period, male authors are fascinated by women as a new kind of literary as well as social "content." We may therefore argue that it is in the sense of men preempting women's place as the minor (vis-à-vis both tradition and the West) and claiming that place for themselves that "the Chinese woman," to use Mao Zedong's words to André Malraux, "doesn't yet exist."[19] Chinese women are, in terms of the structure of discourse, a kind of minor of the minor, the other to the woman that is Chinese man.

Throughout the twentieth century, it is the continual creation of alternative *official minor positions* that continually puts off a direct attack on the subjugation of women. To defend the "Chinese culture," pairs of oppositions are always set up: tradition and modernity, China and the West, China and Japan, the Communists and the Nationalists, the feudal landlords and the people, the rich and the poor, and so forth. The place of a minor discourse—as that which must struggle to speak—is therefore always already filled as long as there is always a new political target to fight against. The common view that women's issues always seem to be subsumed under the "larger" historical issues of the nation, the people, and so forth is therefore true but also a reversal of what happens in the process of discourse construction. For in order for us to construct a "large" historical issue, a position of the victim/minor must always already be present. In terms of language, this means that for a (new) signifier to emerge as a positive presence, there must always be a lack/negative supporting it. The producer of the new signifier, however, always occupies (or "identifies with") the space of the lack/negative (since it is empty) in order to articulate. This goes to show why, for instance, among all the "Chinese people," it is the peasants, the ones who are most illiterate, most removed from the intellectuals, and therefore most "lacking" in terms of the dominant symbolic, who most compel progressive Chinese intellectuals' fantasy.[20] Chinese women, on the other hand, are always said to be as powerful as Chinese men: We keep hearing that they "hold up half the sky." If minority discourse is, like all discourse, not simply a fight for the content of oppression it is ostensibly about but also a fight for the ownership—the propriety, the property—of speaking (that is, for *zhengming*), then Chinese women are precluded from that ownership because it has always been assumed by others in the name of the people, the oppressed classes, and the nation.

Precisely because the truly minor is the voiceless, it can be seized upon and spoken for. As Spivak says, "If the subaltern can speak . . . the subaltern is not a subaltern any more."[21] The Chinese Communist government serves a good example of an agency speaking for "minorities" in order to mobilize an entire nation. As such, its governance is in accordance with a notion of marginality "which implicitly valorizes the center."[22] For intellectuals working on "women" in the China field, therefore, the first critical task is to break alliance with this kind of official sponsorship of "minority discourse." Instead, they need to use their work on Chinese women to deconstruct the paternalistic social consequences resulting from a hegemonic practice of *zhengming* itself.

The Dissolute Woman and the Female Saint

In a recent interview with the press in Hong Kong, the Taiwanese feminist Xü Xiaodan, well known for her use of nudity in political campaigns, described her ambition in the following way: "I will enter Congress in the image of a dissolute woman; I will love the people with the soul of a female saint."[23] What is remarkable about Xü Xiaodan's statements is the introduction of a feminist practice that refuses conformity with the Chinese "elite." The meaning of the term "elite" varies from society to society,[24] and I use it here to designate those among the Chinese who have had the privilege of being highly educated and whose views of female sexuality remain in accordance with the Confucian and neo-Confucian notions of female chastity. The point, however, is not for Chinese intellectuals to exclude/excuse themselves from the "elite" but rather to break up the traditional alliance between education and Confucian standards of female sexuality.

While being well educated herself, Xü Xiaodan challenges the traditional morality that demands Chinese women to be chaste, self-sacrificing, and thus virtuous. Her politics is different from the sentimental sponsorship of "the oppressed" that we often encounter in "minority discourse." For if traditional morality organizes female sexuality by upholding the female saint and condemning the dissolute woman, Xü Xiaodan does not simply criticize that morality by speaking up as the "minor"—the dissolute woman—only. Instead she shows that it is by straddling the positive and the negative, the clear distinction between which is absolutely essential for traditional morality's functioning, that she speaks and acts as a feminist. Instead of speaking from the position of "minority," then, she offers a model which by its very impure nature defies the epistemic violence underlying the perpetual dependence of the "minor" on the center. Women's sexuality, hitherto strictly organized according to the difference between the female saint and the dissolute woman, returns to a freedom which is not an arbitrary freedom to act as one wishes but rather a freedom *from* the mutual reinforcement between education and morality, which are welded together by stratifying female sexuality.

Where the notion of "class" allows us the negative capacity to criticize "privilege" but never identify with it, the notion of gender can operate both from and against privilege, allowing us the possibility of both identification and opposition. This means that we can, as we must, attack social injustice without losing sight of the fact that even as "women" speaking for other "women" within the same gender, for instance, we speak from a privileged position. While an orthodox "class consciousness" would have us repress the self-reflexive knowledge of the speaking intellectual's social position as such (since to reflect on one's own privileged voice would be to destroy the illusion that one is speaking purely for universal justice), gender, insofar as it shows the organization of female sexuality in ways that are related but not restricted to class, makes it easier (though not necessary) to reflect on the difference between the speaking subject and the spoken object. This is because that difference (between the privileged and unprivileged) has not been prescribed as the definitive object of attack as it is in "class consciousness." Paradoxically, therefore, it is because "class consciousness" has chosen "social injustice" as its target and its content that it cannot reflect on the form of its own possibly privileged, unjust utterances. Self-reflection of this kind leads only to paralysis, as we see in many examples of May Fourth literature.

Lu Xun's literary texts, I think, best illustrate this point. The question that his stories often imply is: How can intellectuals pretend to be speaking for the oppressed classes since, precisely, we have a voice while they don't? Don't speaking and writing already mark our social privilege and permanently separate us from them?

If it is true that "our" speech takes its "raw materials" from the suffering of the oppressed, it is also true that it takes its capital from the scholarly tradition, from the machineries of literacy and education, which are affordable only to a privileged few.

On the other hand, because its target and content is the inequality between the sexes, an issue which is not limited to a narrow definition of class difference (in which having privilege equals "bad" and not having privilege equals "good"), "gender" has room for enabling reflection on the inequality inherent in the construction of discourse, i.e., the difference that separates those who speak and those who are spoken of/for. Precisely because its content is not necessarily economic (in the narrow sense described above), the discourse of gender *can* know its own economic privilege. Knowing its own form as such does not, unlike in the case of a practice of "class consciousness" that must remain blind to itself, annul its project.

In the field of China studies, gender and women's issues are likely to emerge as the predominant critical paradigm in the years to come. This will be so *not only* because of Chinese women's traditionally "minor" status. Rather, it will be because, even while they may choose, from time to time, to forsake the claims of their "femininity," *intellectual* Chinese women who speak of "Chinese women" will, I hope, not forget their own social position. While they do not lose sight of the oppression of women, these intellectuals should admit rather than repress the inequality inherent in discourse and the difference between them and their "objects." They should articulate women's issues both as "dissolute women" and as "female saints," but never as either one only. If the relative freedom in intellectual work that the Chinese living in the liberal West enjoy is a privilege, Chinese intellectuals must use this privilege as truthfully and as tactically as they can—not merely to speak as exotic minors, but to fight the crippling effects of Western imperialism and Chinese paternalism at once.

Postscript: The Lures of Diaspora

At the two conferences where the bulk of this chapter was presented,[25] there were questions as to whether what I am doing is not a kind of essentialist "identity politics" in which, once again, the "authenticity" of a particular group is privileged. These questions demand a detailed response.

If we describe the postcolonial space in Hegelian terms, we can say that it is a space in which the object (women, minorities, other peoples) encounters its Notion (criterion for testing object), or in which the "being-in-itself" encounters the "being-for-an-other." In this encounter, "consciousness" undergoes a transformation, so that it is no longer only consciousness of the object but also consciousness of itself, of its own knowledge. What consciousness previously took to be the object *in-itself*, Hegel writes, is not an *in-itself* but an in-itself (an object) *for consciousness*. Hence "consciousness" has, in truth, *two* objects—object and knowledge of object—which do not mutually correspond but which are related in a movement Hegel calls experience:

> Since consciousness thus finds that its knowledge does not correspond to its object, the object itself does not stand the test; in other words, the criterion for testing is altered when that for which it was to have been the criterion fails to pass the test; and the testing is not only a testing of what we know, but also a testing of the criterion of what knowing is.
> . . . *Inasmuch as the new true object issues from it,* this *dialectical* movement which consciousness exercises on itself and which affects both its knowledge and its object, is precisely what is called *experience [Erfahrung].*[26]

Supplementing Hegel, we may say that this *dialectics of experience* finds one of its most compelling personifications in the "third world" intellectual in diaspora. While their cultures once existed for Western historians and anthropologists as objects of inquiry within well-defined geographical domains, the growing presence of these intellectuals in "first world" intellectual circles fundamentally disrupts the production of knowledge—what Edward Said calls Orientalism—that has hitherto proceeded by hiding the agenda of the inquirers and naturalizing the "objects" as givens. To paraphrase Hegel, "first world" inquirers must now cope with the fact that their "objects" no longer correspond to their "consciousness." "Third world" intellectuals, on their part, acquire and affirm their own "consciousness" only to find, continually, that it is a "consciousness" laden with the history of their objecthood. This history confronts

them all the more acutely once they live in the "first world," where
they discover that, regardless of personal circumstances, they are
beheld as "the other."

The explosive nature of this dialectics of experience deals the
death blow to older forms of protest that were bound to native territorial and cultural propriety. *For "third world" intellectuals espe-*
cially, this means that the recourse to alterity—the other culture,
nation, sex, or body in another historical time and geographical
space—no longer suffices as a means of intervention simply because alterity as such is still the old pure "object" (the being-in-itself) that has not been dialectically grasped. Such recourse to
alterity is repeatedly trapped within the lures of a "self"-image—a
nativism—that is, precisely, imperialism's other.

In naming "Chinese women intellectuals," thus, my intention is
not to establish them as a more authentic group of investigators
whose claim to "women" in the Chinese field would exclude that of
other investigators. Naming here is, first and foremost, a way to
avoid repeating the well-worn discursive paradigm of Orientalism,
in which the peoples of the non-West are taken factographically as
"objects" without consciousness while the historical privileges of
speaking subjects—in particular the privilege of "having" consciousness—remain unarticulated.

Second, naming is also a way of *not giving in* to the charms of
an alterity in which so many of the West's "others" are now called
upon to speak. Naming is not so much an act of consolidating power
as it is an act of making explicit the historical predicament of investigating "China" and "Chinese women," especially as it pertains
to those who are ethnically Chinese and/or sexually women.

Third, it follows that naming the investigators amid the current
"multicultural" interest in "women" in non-Western fields is also a
means of accentuating the otherwise *muted* fact of intellectual
women's privilege as intellectuals and thus (particularly in the Chinese context) as members of the elite. While this privilege is, at
this point, hardly acknowledged in the masculinist explorations of
modernity, nationhood, and literature, because masculinist explorations are themselves preoccupied with their own minority and
womanhood vis-à-vis the West, it is peremptory that women investigators, especially Chinese women investigators investigating the
history of Chinese women's social subordination, handle the mode

of their speech—which historically straddles the elite and the sub-altern—with deliberate care. In naming them as such, therefore, my point is to place on them the burden of a kind of critical aware-ness that has yet to be articulated in their field. The weight of each of the terms under which they work—Chinese, women, intellec-tual—means that their alliances with other discursive groups, as well as their self-reflection on their own positions, must always be astute. Both practices, allying with others and reflecting on oneself, are by necessity more demanding than a blanket dismissal of names and identities as "essentialist."[27] Such a dismissal is often the result of an ahistorical espousal of "difference" and "femininity" as is found in some influential theories which, by equating the feminine with the negative and the unrepresentable, dismiss all processes of iden-tification as positivistic. (A good case in point is the work of Julia Kristeva, which is popular with many feminist critics despite Kristeva's unwillingness to name "woman"[28] and to name herself "feminist.") The question on which to insist, however, is not "to name or not to name" but: What is to be gained or lost in naming what and whom, and by whom?

What I am arguing can also be stated in a different way: What are we doing talking about modern Chinese literature and Chinese women in the North American academy in the 1990s? As such activities of speaking and writing are tied less to the oppressed women in Chinese communities "back home" than to our own in-tellectual careers in the West, we need to unmask ourselves through a scrupulous declaration of self-interest. Such declaration does not clean our hands, but it prevents the continuance of a ten-dency, rather strong among "third world" intellectuals in diaspora as well as researchers of non-Western cultures in "first world" na-tions, to sentimentalize precisely those day-to-day realities from which they are distanced.

The diasporic postcolonial space is, as I already indicate, neither the space of the native intellectual protesting against the intrusive presence of foreign imperialists in the indigenous territory nor the space of the postcolonial critic working against the lasting effects of cultural domination in the home country (now an independent "na-tion") after the phase of territorial imperialism. In the case of China, it is necessary to remember that "Chinese" territory, with the exceptions of Taiwan from 1895 to 1945, Hong Kong from 1842

to 1997, and Macau (occupied by the Portuguese since the mid-six-
teenth century) from 1887 to 1997, was never completely "colonized" over a long period by any one foreign power, even though
the cultural effects of imperialism are as strong as in other formerly
colonized countries in Asia, Africa, and Latin America. One could
perhaps say that such cultural effects of foreign dominance are, in
fact, *stronger*: they are most explicit, paradoxically, when one sees
how the mainland Chinese can hold on to the illusion—born of
modern Western imperialism but itself no less imperialistic—of a
"native land," a *zuguo*, that was never entirely captured and that
therefore remains glorious to this day.

The space of "third world" intellectuals in diaspora is a space that
is removed from the "ground" of earlier struggles that were still tied
to the "native land." Physical alienation, however, can mean precisely the intensification and aestheticization of the values of "minority" positions that had developed in the earlier struggles and that
have now, in "third world" intellectuals' actual circumstances in the
West, become defunct. The unself-reflexive sponsorship of "third
world" culture, including "third world" women's culture, becomes
a mask that conceals the hegemony of these intellectuals over those
who are stuck at home.

For "third world" intellectuals, the lures of diaspora consist in
this masked hegemony. As in the case of what I call masculinist
positions in the China field, their resort to "minority discourse,"
including the discourse of class and gender struggles, veils their
own fatherhood over the "ethnics" at home even while it continues
to legitimize them as "ethnics" and "minorities" in the West. In their
hands, minority discourse and class struggle, especially when they
take the name of another nation, another culture, another sex, or
another body, turn into signifiers whose major function is that of
discursive exchange for the intellectuals' self-profit. Like "the people," "real people," "the populace," "the peasants," "the poor," "the
homeless," and all such names, these signifiers *work* insofar as they
gesture toward another place (the lack in discourse-construction)
that is "authentic" but that cannot be admitted into the circuit of
exchange.

What happens eventually is that this "third world" that is produced, circulated, and purchased by "third world" intellectuals in
the cosmopolitan diasporic space will be exported "back home" in

the form of values—intangible goods—in such a way as to obstruct the development of the native industry. To be sure, one can perhaps no longer even speak of a "native industry" as such in the multinational corporate postmodernity, but it remains for these intellectuals to face up to their truthful relation to those "objects of study" behind which they can easily hide—as voyeurs, as "fellow victims," and as self-appointed custodians.

Hence the necessity to read and write against the lures of diaspora: Any attempt to deal with "women" or the "oppressed classes" in the "third world" that does not at the same time come to terms with the historical conditions of its own articulation is bound to repeat the exploitativeness that used to and still characterizes most "exchanges" between "West" and "East." Such attempts will also be expediently assimilated within the plenitude of the hegemonic establishment, with all the rewards that that entails. No one can do without some such rewards. What one can do without is the illusion that, through privileged speech, one is helping to save the wretched of the earth.[29]

(See **Glossary** for Chinese names, terms, and passages.)

VI

THE POLITICS AND PEDAGOGY OF ASIAN LITERATURES IN AMERICAN UNIVERSITIES

The major role currently played by feminism in the field of Asian studies consists of work done on Asian women, dead and living, as cases of social historical study; investigations of feminine themes, tropes, and subjectivities in literature; and growing interest in Asian women writers. As in the case of fields traditionally dominated by scholarly criteria that are indifferent to the issues of gender, feminism is essential in Asian studies as a means of combat against entrenched habits of reading guarded by specialists. However, feminism's most significant contribution to the academic institution does not lie in an exclusive focus on women's problems. Rather, it lies in the way it alerts us, through women's experience of social subordination, to the barbarism and mutilation that go on in other spheres of knowledge production. As feminism consolidates its place in the reinterpretation of knowledge in all (especially Western) fields, there persist other types of problems which feminists need to recognize and confront—by forsaking the argument for the rights of women as their primary goal.

The following chapter, originally written for a panel of the same title at the 1989 MLA Annual Convention in Washington, D.C., deals with a specific problem in the institu-

tional arrangement called "area studies"—the teaching of Asian literatures.

Even though feminism owes much of its current institutional power to the transdisciplinary character of gender, neither the emphasis on women nor transdisciplinarity itself is necessarily the most adequate means of intervening in the politics of institutional marginalization and exploitation. Many Asia specialists (male and female) would now accede to giving women their voices in scholarship while continuing to de-emphasize the crucial relation between language and knowledge by marginalizing the language-intensive work of literature teachers. Similarly, because the production of knowledge in "area studies" is stabilized—or pre-stabilized—by the notion of fixed geographical areas, the claims of "transdisciplinarity" and "multi-discursivity" often become simply another way of emboldening the tendency, adhered to among many social scientists, toward information retrieval based on unproblematized models of linguistic "communication."

The question I want to raise in regard to the topic "feminism and the institution"[1] is therefore not whether we can or cannot locate interest in women's issues in the Asian field. (The answer to that is, increasingly, yes.) Rather: What do the problems which obstruct the teaching of Asian literatures tell us about the seemingly wider and more ready acceptance of feminism in American universities? If this is a reflection of how feminism itself has become "normalized," then feminists need to ask what other kinds of institutional marginalization continue in the course of their own empowerment. Because such marginalization is systemic, we may not recognize it until it is too late.

Take for instance the policy, now implemented in some universities, of a mandatory second language requirement for undergraduates. Superficially, a policy like this is aimed against the monolingualism and parochialism typical of many American undergraduate curricula. And yet, precisely the emphasis on a second language can mean a death blow to the teaching of literature in a field such as Asian studies. In Asian departments where the duty of language teaching often already falls upon the shoulders of literature teachers, increased second language requirements would simply sap literature teachers of whatever energy and time they would otherwise have to concentrate on literature. While the managers of Asian departments may congratulate themselves on increased enrollments, these departments are fast being transformed into mere language-training units. The teachers of "literature" would, of course, continue to be employed for the "transmission of knowledge about foreign cultures," but in effect they would be serving as the support staff for training business, military, and technical professionals even in a university setting, while the interventions they can offer in ideological struggles through the teaching of literature become nullified.

Against the politics of this kind of institutional exploitation, and hopefully addressing (albeit indirectly) similar concerns of "fellow travelers" in other fields, this essay is intended as an argument for the teaching of Asian literatures as a multiply critical event in the American university today.

Peter Wang's "A Great Wall" (1986) is a film about a Chinese-American family's visit to their "original" home, Beijing, and the contradictory emotions involved in this experience. The father, who spent his youth in China, is now a well-established computer expert in Silicon Valley, California. Although he enjoys his occasional bowl of Chinese-style noodles and dislikes the idea of his American-born son marrying anyone but a Chinese, he and his family are well acclimatized to the American way of life. The visit "home" is, in its small and subtle ways, traumatic, woven with memories of childhood in a China that is no longer there. While the son, Paul, finds everything in his "native" land exotic if somewhat boring, his Chinese counterpart, a local young man who is studying for his university entrance examination, is greatly fascinated with everything American: he drinks Coca-Cola, loves Pavarotti, and shows off his English to his girlfriend by reciting the Gettysburg Address. One of the highlights of the film shows the two young men competing at ping-pong. Despite his more powerful physique, Paul loses by forgetting the rules several times. The film ends with the Chinese-American family returning to California, where the father now practices *qi gong* daily. In his new peace of mind, we are given a sense of Chinese cultural triumph.

The responses to this film among my friends are fascinatingly dissimilar. A Chinese person thought that this film pandered to the taste of *kweilo* (Cantonese for "foreign devils"). A European couple, who completely missed the fact that the Chinese youth won the ping-pong match, found the film aesthetically offensive because it polarizes America and China in terms of technological supremacy and backwardness. An American liked the film because it showed people living on the fault line between cultures and trying to hold them together—"Real people are hyphenated people," he said. What interests me about these responses is the strong if lopsided conviction with which each type of view is expressed. It soon became clear that this was one of those texts which are thought-provoking not so much because of intrinsic merit as because of the way they trigger divergent and even opposed views from their audiences. These views, heavy with historical resonances, turn a rather stereotypical story into the battleground for contending—perhaps mutually uncomprehending—claims as to how an Asian-American "homecoming" experience should be aesthetically produced.

Though casually expressed, my friends' critical views already contain what are in fact formulations of nativism, aesthetic formalism, and cultural pluralism, which epitomize problems that characterize the teaching of non-Western literatures and that are increasingly felt by the teachers of Asian literatures in American universities. Chief among these, felt by Asianists as a group, is the by and large ghettoized status of their existence. While some see the general lack of exchange between scholars of Asian and Western literatures in terms of a "mutual parochialism,"[2] many feel, with good reasons, that the greatest problem for students of Asian literatures is that of Western cultural hegemony. For, even when studies of a comparative nature are undertaken, the terms of reference are often provided by the West, "so that we have had considerations of symbolism in Chinese poetry, in which, for example, the Chinese phenomena were described in terms of their congruence, or divergence, from French and German ones."[3] In other words, vis-à-vis European literatures, Asian literatures share with other non-West-

ern literatures the task of a Gramscian "counter-hegemonic ideological production." The distinctive labeling of "Asian" is the sign
of an allied insurgency among marginalized cultures within the establishment of the American university itself.

Marginalization within Asian Studies

Meanwhile, teachers of Asian literatures need to combat the politics which confines them to the simple "West" vs. "Asia" dichotomy.
Like all classifications, "Asian literatures" is elusive, having more
institutional usefulness for those who do not know what these literatures are and need to set them aside *en bloc* in a separate category
than for those who are concerned with its specific problems. For
those of us who have worked with Asian literatures, it is well known
that in American universities, the standard representatives have for
a long time been China and Japan in East Asia, India in South Asia,
and Persia and Arabia in the Middle East. The categories provided
by the *Journal of the Association for Asian Studies* usually list "Asia
General," "China," "Japan," then "South Asia," and sometimes
"Southeast Asia" and "Inner Asia." In recent years, interest in the
Korean and Vietnamese languages and literatures has emerged in
some institutions, but as in the case of fields in which the surfacing
of minority issues serves to reveal all the more clearly the homog-
enizing tendencies of extant categories, China, Japan, and India
remain the most heavily researched among Asian cultures in the
West. In order to address the politics of teaching Asian literatures
in American universities, therefore, it is necessary to insist on their
non-monolithic nature, even when we must from time to time talk
of "Asian literatures" as if they were one single entity.

The politics of teaching Asian literatures is by no means restricted to the struggle between Asia and the West, or between
Asianists and scholars of Western topics. To see this, we need to
clarify what we mean when we speak about "marginalization." How
are Asian literatures marginalized? The answer to this question requires us to distinguish between different forms of marginalization
within Asian literatures and Asian studies as they are currently institutionalized.

Among Asian classicists, culture is often still viewed as a kind of general literacy which comes before such things as periodization and specialization. According to this view, if one has spent enough time with the classics spanning a few major dynasties, one would also be qualified to deal with anything that comes afterward. The reverse, however, is not true: if one has worked only with modern literature, one is a kind of illiterate who does not possess the depth of knowledge and breadth of experience which a classical education offers. This notion of a general literacy that one acquires not as a skill but as an *upbringing* in standard written texts and well-aged artistic practices (such as *qin qi shu hua*, or music, chess, calligraphy, and painting, for the Chinese) acts as a way to define the limits of centralized culture, even if the practitioners of that culture are dilettantes only. The farther one is removed from this *centralized literacy*, the more dubious is one's claim to the culture. When I told a senior Chinese classicist that I was going to a conference on contemporary Hong Kong literature, for instance, the response I got was: "Oh, is there such a thing?"

While this kind of elitism vis-à-vis modern and contemporary culture is a universal phenomenon, my point here is that in those areas which have only a marginal status within the American university to begin with, the elitism which stresses the importance of non-Western cultures by way of a hierarchical evaluation of their "excellence" or "superiority" actually collaborates with the minimalization of those non-Western cultures. Such "nativist" elitism is as frequently, if not more frequently, espoused by non-native area specialists as it is by the "natives" themselves. It leads to a situation in which the Asian classical literatures, precisely because of their arcaneness, are highly respected areas of scholarly cultivation. The general literacy that was a hallmark of culturedness in the past now becomes a "specialty" with a national designation in the contemporary West. Here, although one can speak of marginalization, since specialization in these areas requires not only the gift of mastering foreign languages and years of patient learning but also a commitment to spiritual ideals which may be at odds with the contemporary world, this is a marginalization fully in keeping with the notion of culture as high culture. It is also in keeping with the hierarchical class, ethnic, and gender distinctions that follow from such a notion. Since it puts Asian cultures on a par with all great civilizations of the world, this kind of specialization is often privileged over the study of texts whose production is much more obviously inscribed in the politics of post-imperial (after-the-emperors) and post-imperialist ("Westernized" or "modernized") Asia.[4]

The *alliance* of nativist elitism and institutional Orientalism produces hegemonic paradigms of thinking and method that have as powerful an impact in determining the objects worthy of study as military, economic, and religious aggressivity did in producing accounts of "Asia" in the past. The tendency within Asian studies to belittle *modern* literature is often justified in terms of "quality," even though the criteria used are seldom scrutinized. It is interesting to see how the reasons for the marginalization of Asian literatures vis-à-vis European literatures, a fact about which Asian classicists feel indignant, are equally applicable to *the marginalization of modern Asian literatures within Asian studies*. Once we shift the comparison between "European" and "Asian" to a comparison between classical Asian and modern Asian texts, we realize that similar patterns of incomprehension, discrimination, or sheer indifference appear in relation to the latter group. As the terms of reference remain "classical," modern Asian literatures are often criticized for not being "literary," and when they are considered literary, they are often judged to be tainted by hybridization. This type of evaluation in which one sphere of specialization becomes the norm and criterion for all other spheres therefore does not only account for the marginalization of Asian literatures in general but also especially for *the doubly marginalized nature of modern Asian literatures*, since they are not merely unknown to nonspecialists but are dismissed by specialists of Asian cultures as well. That this takes place within the parameters of what I earlier refer to as an area of Gramscian counter-hegemonic ideological production is in part the result of a persistent Orientalist politics. While it permits the preservation of "culture" in classics, this politics discourages and disables the pursuit of literature as an ongoing historical discourse whose major concern may not be that of classical aesthetic excellence. In a discussion of East-West literary relations, Edward Said describes it this way:

> Sanskrit was a language that stood for a very high cultural value in Europe, but it was a dead language, far removed from the backwardness of modern Indians. The romantic imagination of European writ-

ers and scholars was saturated with Orientalism, but their Orientalism was gained at the expense of any sympathy they might have felt for the benighted natives they ruled. One of the faint lines of thought running through early nineteenth-century Orientalist scholarship . . . is that Orientalist enthusiasm is often fueled by apathetic ignorance not only of the ancient Orient but especially of the modern Oriental.[5]

Said's argument enables us to see the manner in which Orientalism continues to inform the institutionalization of *scholarship* on Asia in America. The conservation of the classics, the programmatic insistence on archival, archeological, and textual research, and the careful distinction made between scholarship and politics are all part of this ongoing Orientalism. In this light, the specialization of the indologist, the sinologist, or the japanologist does not necessarily help correct the marginalization of Asian literatures in the world context but in all likelihood serves to continue that marginalization by giving us an Asia which, apart from cheap laborers and multitudinous consumers, also continues to produce *ancient* culture.

The Culture of Illiteracy

Of course, modern Asia, too, is amply investigated. It simply does not produce "literature." Take the study of China, for example. While sinologists specializing in premodern texts feel disdain toward modern and contemporary Chinese literature, modern China as a text is heavily populated with the views of historians, anthropologists, political scientists, economists, and so on. Such a division is never simply the division between ancient and modern China, but a struggle for social control among the disciplines, each of which has a competing claim to discursive authority in the formation of the modern nation-state.

The issue of language is a critical one here. Everyone is familiar with the demands made by the teacher of literature on students' knowledge of the language they are using. But the insistence on linguistic aptitude means different things in different pedagogical situations. Whereas it is still typical of specialists in French and German literature to assume that knowledge of French and German amounts to something of a global cultural imperative, it is not possible for the teacher of Asian literatures to insist on such knowledge of her languages even as she is teaching them. To secure enrollments for classes in an Asian literature, one needs to make sure that the students are, on the one hand, attracted to the culture and, on the other, not so daunted by the language that they would stop trying after a short period of time. The rare combination of interest and effort means that very few students venture beyond a superficial reading of the literatures, whether taught in translation or in the original, and those who do usually become intellectually so invested that their scholastic achievements blind them to the racist and sexist ideologies that are ingrained in the instruments of pedagogy themselves.

Unlike the teacher of French and German, the Asian literature teacher would almost guarantee her own inaudibility if she were to insist on using the original language in a public setting. The problem she faces can be stated this way: Does she sacrifice the specificities of the language in order to generalize, so that she can put Asian literatures in a "cross-cultural" framework, or does she continue to teach untranslated texts with expertise—and remain ghettoized?

One of the results of this dilemma, for instance, is that whenever Asianists publish in non-Asian journals, they have to provide long plot summaries and simplified accounts of their stories/histories at the expense of their arguments. Some publications never go beyond the plot summary stage, and often, simply because of the relatively unrepresented nature of their subject matter, they become acceptable to journals which are eager to beef up their "interdisciplinary" and "cross-cultural" profiles. The reduction to plot summary—that is, transparent communicability—and to sensational details—that is, fetishized exoticism—describes the space accorded to Asian literatures in the American university at large.

One might ask at this point: How indeed can we discuss literature beyond the plot summary? Hasn't *all* literature already been reduced to this status, a status which Asian literatures, by virtue of being multiply marginalized, urgently magnify? Ironically, one way in which literature's specificities can be dismissed is precisely that of "interdisciplinarity" itself. A student I know once applied to an excellent "interdisciplinary" program on the West Coast and was rejected on the grounds that his project was "too literary." This student was proposing to work on a little-known Asian literature as part of a critique of cultural imperialism. An incident like this is worth bringing to the attention of all because it is an example of how, because theoretical development in North America has reached such an advanced stage that awareness of cultural diversity means it is no longer adequate for us simply to focus on "literature," someone from the "third world" with a project about a "third world" literature becomes old-fashioned and, from the "first world's" "critical" point of view, politically incorrect. This means that either such a literature remains unknown in its foreignness or, if it is known, it is known only in the universalist language of "interdisciplinarity," "cross-cultural plurality," etc., in which it becomes a localized embellishment of the general narrative.

What the foregoing argument shows is that, at the same time that an idealist appeal to ancient culture as a way to legitimize the understanding of modernity corroborates the marginalization of the Asian field, the current environment in which the non-West is "allowed to speak" by affirmative pedagogical attitudes/policies in support of "cultural pluralism" can be equally detrimental to the realization of a genuinely critical project. The current upsurge of interest in non-Western cultures owes its origins to the broader political context in which the American university is only a part. The widening of our curriculum to include such things as the "third world" and minorities, and the extension of job opportunities to African American, Hispanic, and Asian scholars are part of an ongoing program of instrumentalizing language and culture. Indeed, we can say that the current "cultural studies" programs in institutions of higher education are homological entities to the "literacy campaigns" that are aimed at the lower strata of American society. While the poor need to learn how to read and write, the educated need to read and write *other cultures*. The universalist ambitions by way of terms such as "culture" and "discourse" belong therefore to a market economy in which "culture remains a force but largely of social control, a gratuitous image drawn over the face of instrumentality."[6]

At this juncture, the relationship between the teaching of language and the teaching of literature becomes less a hierarchical than a parallel one. It is, of course, still true that teachers of language usually occupy a lower status than teachers of literature. The fact that writing programs are usually staffed by graduate students in need of financial support attests to that—the logic has been that our subservients take care of the "dirty work" of training writing skills while we perform the more lofty task of thinking literarily. However, this situation is quickly changing precisely because of the widening of the curriculum to include such items as "third world studies." What face teachers of "third world" literatures are demands of instrumentality similar to those that are produced by the lucrative professional disciplines on the teachers of language. When students of economics, business administration, and computer science fill up Japanese language class-lists, the teacher of Japanese *literature* becomes equally useful as a transmitter of fragmented pieces of Japanese culture and history, enabling such students to have claims to knowledge about Japan while they carry on their high-tech and business vocations. Thus a paradoxical situation arises: as we broaden our curriculum and make it "easier" for Asian languages and literatures to be "represented" in teaching, a more restricted, much more superficial kind of knowledge about such cultures is produced which students now use to fulfill "requirements" of multiculturalism. The result of such restrictions and superficialities is what Wlad Godzich calls the "new culture of illiteracy, in which the student is trained to use language for the reception and conveyance of information in only one sphere of human activity: that of his or her future field of employment." Once we substitute the terms "literature" and "culture" for the term "language" in Godzich's statements, the dire circumstances under which teachers of literature, especially minority literatures, work are clearly evident:

> . . . whereas one would have expected that a crisis of literacy would have called for a greater appreciation of the multiplicity of functions that language performs, the foremost of which is the ability to code and to transcode experience and to provide cultural directions for its interpretation, handling, and elaboration, one finds instead a further instrumentalization of language, where the latter is shattered into a multiplicity of autonomous, unrelated languages, with the competence to be acquired restricted to just one of these.[7]

The Question of Literature in "Cultural Studies"

If the rationale for cultural studies programs across the U.S. begins with the apprehension of the insufficiencies of models of learning "culture" that are based on the nation-state (which appear in the form of departments of national languages and literatures in the humanities), the question remains as to what is to be done after the traditional boundaries of knowledge-production have been overthrown.

In a way, that question was answered much earlier in the non-Western fields, simply because "culture" in these fields, by virtue of being cut up historically through the imposition of Western languages and modes of living, had already been delivered into the hands of Western social scientists. The anthropologists, archeologists, sociologists, economists, and historians were dividing Asia and Africa among them long before the humanists realized that they, too, must join the "scramble for concessions"—to use a description of the West's invasion of China in the nineteenth century—and stake a claim for "culture." This, I think, is where the institutional mushrooming of "cultural studies" gets its momentum. What happens to literature in a field like Asian studies?

Because modern Asia is not "literary" any more, the close and patient attention that classicists devote to literary texts simply evaporates. Instead, works of modern literature become mere research documents for the historian or political scientist. While there is nothing wrong with the use of literature as social documentation, what is alarming is the way such uses redirect the focus of the field of Asian studies to one of information production, thus making "interpretation," the critical coding and transcoding of experience which Godzich mentions, a more or less "subjective" (privatized) and hence dispensable activity. It is in the light of this cognitive hegemony of information that Said writes:

> The one issue that urgently requires study is, for the humanist no less than for the social scientist, the status of *information* as a component of knowledge: its sociopolitical status, its contemporary fate, its economy. . . . What happens to information and knowledge,

> . . . when IBM and AT&T—two of the world's largest corpora-
> tions—claim that what they do is put "knowledge" to work "for the
> people"? What is the role of humanistic knowledge and information
> if they are not to be unknowing (many ironies there) partners in
> commodity production and marketing, so much so that what human-
> ists do may in the end turn out to be a quasi-religious concealment
> of this peculiarly unhumanistic process? A true secular politics of
> interpretation sidesteps this question at its peril.[8]

What Said's passage makes clear is the primary role played by
information nowadays in the organization of knowledge both in the
humanities and the social sciences. For those of us in literature,
this passage serves to highlight one of the most devastating aspects
of literature's marginalization within cultural studies. This is the
methodological subordination of literature to other disciplinary con-
trols in such a way that the instrumentalist, reflectionist assumptions about language and representation, which literature
challenges as part of its critical project, remain entirely unex-
amined. Instead, such assumptions often accompany the use of
literature—now for many simply one type of discourse among others—and become normative ways of reading. If information is,
strictly speaking, "*a* component of knowledge" as Said puts it, the
problem we face is that of information replacing knowledge altogether. Often, not only does literature's potential in subverting the
increasing trend toward *informationalization* remain unrealized,
but literature itself becomes an instrument in that process of informationalization and a subordinate part to the world historical record.

The informationalization of literature produces the illusion that
there is no real need to pay attention to literature and to the work
it performs upon its readers. Here, the marginalization of *modern*
Asian literature is especially acute. What is marginalized as a result
of the institutional desire for information is the experience of *cultural modernity* in modern Asian texts that is not immediately reducible to models of "communication." While the ancient texts still
possess cultural capital and are allowed to retain their opacity (formal difficulty) as exotica, the modern texts are, in spite of their
density, conceptually streamlined with writings in the other disciplines for the overall (i.e., not specialized) knowledge about Asia.

Caught between the past as culture and the present as realpolitik, and between classicists who view them as "not really Asian" and other Asianists who fail to see their formal specificities, modern Asian literatures are thus consigned to an impossible struggle for survival in American academic institutions where funding is predisposed toward the fact-and-profit-yielding disciplines.

While many universities still pursue the study of Asian literatures in specially designated language and literature departments, many others now adopt a different kind of organizational structure—what is called an "area studies program," in which scholars whose research bears upon, say, an Asian topic convene for the collaborative administration of Asian studies. What could be the logic justifying this kind of coercive coexistence apart from its convenience for administrators? The university here acts as an agent for disseminating a quickly changing view of culture as something to which students can have *access* regardless of the differences in their disciplinary backgrounds and the conflicts involved. Access is promised by the nominal designation of an area as an information target field. Traditionally marginalized areas such as East Asia, South Asia, or Eastern Europe are among the first to be identified in the form of such a target field.

The consequences of departmentalizing a group of literary critics, historians, sociologists, geographers, statisticians, and so forth can, of course, be positive at one level. Such a group may serve to bridge the gaps in our knowledge about one another.[9] Yet why must such bridging take place over one geographical area? The radical critical implications of each of the disciplines brought together in this way must always be subsumed, through a kind of pseudo-intellectual division of labor, under the notion of an "area" whose conceptual stability contributes toward the successful institutionalization of knowledge.

When scholars are departmentalized simply because they are all "doing" "China," "Japan," or "India," what actually happens is the predication of so-called "interdisciplinarity" on the model of the colonial territory and the nation-state. In the twentieth century, the colonized countries of the "third world," caught between the bankruptcy of traditional social organization and the need to assert self-determination in the throes of imperialism, are forced to adopt the model of the nation-state, complete with the ideological dead-ends that that model entails. It is therefore not an accident that, in the massive trends of reconceptualizing the disciplines in the U.S., it is precisely the cultures of such countries that are among the first to be put into "area studies" programs, at the same time that the dominant literary culture, English, continues to hold its autonomy. To the extent that it would seem absurd to most to insert English into some such program as "Western European studies" or "North American studies," we understand the magnitude of discriminatory politics involved. (Let us not forget that "discrimination" here applies to *U.S. culture* as well. In the wake of anti-imperialism, whereupon former British colonies like India, Canada, and Australia rightly insist upon the uniqueness of their own cultural/literary productions, it is the national literature of the U.S.'s former colonizer that continues to be taught with dignity in most English departments in the American university, while the indigenous literature and culture remain, with little respectability until recent years, "ghettoized" in the field called "American studies"!)

In the case of Asian studies, the most immediate concern for the teacher of literature is the increasing risk posed to the teaching of modern literature under these circumstances. Such a risk cannot simply be measured by the number of courses one can or cannot put in the curriculum. It has much more to do with the reenactment of the discourse of imperialism in pedagogy itself. In my own experience, for instance, the language and literature teachers in one such area studies department are often accused by the social scientists of being "unproductive" and deserving of the low esteem they receive. This kind of rhetoric is institutionally effective because, by a show of objective rationality, it erases its own implication in the history of Western cultural hegemony in the name of quantifiable scholarship. As the teachers of language and literature are often native speakers while the teachers of the social sciences often are not, the tensions involved in the marginalizing of literature quickly take on a racial or ethnic coloration, and the charges of "unproductivity" precisely replicate, in an academic context, the implications of the classic claim of the "white man's burden."

The problem of "productivity" is in many ways faced by all teachers of literature. Literature teachers are, in the *thematics* of contemporary culture, "unproductive" since productivity is always assumed to be the productivity of the technological world. No matter how we argue for the relation between literature and society, literary people are, in the words of Gayatri Spivak, "still caught within a position where they must say: Life is brute fact and outside art; the aesthetic is free and transcends life."[10] Of course, within literature, people can spend time debating what the nature of art is, but the ideological division between art and life continues to determine how public policy is made. It follows that literature remains—in an institutional language transformed by technology—a "soft" and thus superfluous subject. Consequently:

> . . . if the study of literature is "only" about literary representation, then it must be the case that literary representations and literary activities (writing, reading, producing the "humanities," and arts and letters) are essentially ornamental, possessing at most secondary ideological characteristics. The consequence is that to deal with literature as well as the broadly defined "humanities" is to deal with the nonpolitical, although quite evidently the political realm is presumed to lie just beyond (and beyond the reach of) literary, and hence *literate*, concern.[11]

There is no better way of confirming this than by surrendering the politics of interpretation to the general discursive transparency in which the communicability and information status of knowledges become the primary goals of pedagogy. In the reverse extreme, literary people, especially those in the minor fields, can collaborate in the demise of their own practice by thinking of it as a purely formal matter. C. T. Hsia clarifies this point by criticizing those who reduce the study of Chinese fiction to fictional construct only:

> . . . students of Chinese fiction have apparently lagged behind the historians: in their objective examination of novels and stories in terms of style, point of view, and narrative method, or in their more ambitious interpretations of the same in terms of myth, archetype, and allegory, they study fiction as literature and nothing more. Apparently, they think that only Marxist critics are concerned with social reality. . . .[12]

Concern with social reality must be accompanied with a close attention to how language works—not so much in the creation of formal beauty as in the concealment of ideology. Such close attention to language is not that of appreciation but a form of vigilance. It is like constructing barricades against the enemies along small streets in a city, when large boulevards are constantly being built that will effectively wipe out the possibility of such political resistance. Spivak alludes to the urgency of our situation in these terms: "the Army, the Foreign Service, the multi-nationals themselves, and intelligence and counter-intelligence take the necessity of language-learning with the utmost seriousness. We have something to learn from our enemies."[13]

Preconditions of Reference and Criticism: Ruins and Reason

For the Asianist, the task of teaching literature is further complicated by the fact that she has to demonstrate not only the "literariness" but also the "Asian-ness" of her undertaking. Here, what is often taken for granted and pronounced as self-evident truth— "Chinese," "Japanese," "Indian," and so forth—runs up against the ruining of indigenous tradition in the aftermath of imperialism and colonialism. What is the nature of such ruining? The presence of the West does not simply put an end to native daily practices, most of which, in fact, are allowed to continue exactly as they were in the past. British policy in Hong Kong, for instance, benignly honors every major Chinese festival around the year and even abides by the rules of Chinese folklore and geomancy on significant celebratory occasions.

What are disrupted, eroded, and foreclosed are the very terms of legitimation *and* criticism—philosophical, philological, and aesthetic—on which traditional scholarship in these cultures depends. Using the example once again of Hong Kong, such demolitions of what are in fact the preconditions for cognition and the production of knowledge in a southern Chinese society take place most effectively through policies of colonial education, in which the discrimination against teachers with college degrees from China, the promotion of English as the primary medium of instruction from kindergarten or primary school on, and the reduction of Chinese literature to one subject among many that secondary school children can choose for their public examinations work smoothly in conjunction with an environment that is, like everywhere else in the "developing" world, already predisposed toward vocational and technical training. Traditional culture, having lost its power to intervene politically since the preconditions for that power have disappeared, takes on an ornamental function in the form of museum masterpieces. The kind of "specialized" dedication it requires—once the sign of a general cultural literacy—preempts it from participation in realpolitik.

In the American university today, the establishment of cultural studies and, increasingly, comparative literature programs represents, to a certain degree, an attempt to address the global crisis that follows from the loss of the critical function that traditional literary culture used to possess. Cognizant of the extent to which national cultures have been dismantled—as is most pronounced in the case of "third world" countries—the notion of "cultural studies" increasingly attempts to supply the referential as well as critical ground for the understanding of humanistic culture. The development of cultural studies in this sense is comparable, perhaps even companionable, to the development of area studies. Instead of a geographical territory, "culture" itself becomes the point of institutional stabilization. It is, after all, entirely possible to view "culture" as an "area" in which an instrumentalized communicability among the disciplines comes as first priority in the progress of knowledge.

Because the nature of their tasks tends to be predefined in the foregoing terms, teachers of Asian literatures face the problem of how to sustain the critical import of their work. It is incumbent upon them not only to disseminate knowledge about Asia but, more importantly, to demonstrate how, precisely because of the precarious status of their operations, this dissemination of knowledge is inseparable from the political intervention without which knowledge itself easily becomes *either* ornamentation *or* the military weaponry of instrumental reason.

In the struggle for the articulation of critical intervention, a familiar path taken by Asianists has been that of scholarly nativism, which sees returning to the authority of tradition as a way to understand modernity. The return to traditional authority, or to tradition as authority, inevitably clings to a notion of past culture as a pure phenomenon. The consequent romanticizing of indigenous cultures as untainted origins fits the scholarly agenda of Orientalism extremely well. But while Asia is served as a "specialty" in Western institutions, Asian peoples whose "cultures" are in the pages of research journals and archives in the West receive little representation in the form of an articulation of how they feel about being the silenced objects of Western study.

Since much of such scholarly nativism is currently espoused in the name of a respect for "cultural difference," teachers of Asian literatures must become extremely wary of how they teach cultural difference itself. Often, in an attempt to differentiate Asian from Western literatures, we belabor the former's differences in terms of elements such as—in the case of East Asia, for instance—spiritualism, resignation, worldviews that prefer peace and quiet to conflict and struggle, etc. Such standard descriptions of East Asian literatures are often made in neglect of the problems of ideology that accompany the production of literature and culture. But the portrayal of Asian literatures as apolitical is not so much an objective portrayal as it is a companion tactic to the economic and political coercion of the past and a superficial cross-cultural understanding by way of commodified (or standardized) notions of "cultural difference" in the present. Instead of political apathy, teachers of Asian literatures need to emphasize, with non-Asianists, the "dialectical and continuous crosshatching of ideology and literary language."[14] This is simply because "[n]ot just anthropologists, economists, and political scientists, but students of literature too, with their theories of discourse, rhetoric, and textual criticism, provide the necessary information and tools of analysis for the propagation of cultural and even military domination."[15] As long as students come to Asian literatures with the ideological notions of learning about the continuity of great traditions, the truth of humanity, the beauty of aesthetics, etc., we are continuing to perpetuate the general dismissal of literature's relevance as a mode of social inquiry whose methods are central to other modes of social inquiry.

Preconditions of Reference and Criticism:
Interrogations of Identity

Much like the reactions to "A Great Wall," the politics regarding Asian literatures cannot be defined purely in terms of the intrinsic value of the "cultural object" at hand. As we constantly encounter situations in which the teaching of Asia is divided among people with very different backgrounds and different claims to what having knowledge about Asia means, the problems faced by teachers of modern Asian literatures are not going to be resolved by our thinking that one day everyone will come around to appreciating how great literature is and how great Asian literatures are. Whether we like it or not, strong combative feelings that are rooted in the tensions between members of different groups with histories of ethnic, disciplinary, and institutional conflict will increasingly come into play in the daily routines of pedagogy, both in terms of decisions regarding the objects of study and in terms of the human relations governing collegiate collaboration in a university setting.

In the U.S., the kind of space which is now given to the study of minority cultures has been the result of a long struggle for civil rights. Unlike the view put across by Nathan Glazer, for whom ethnicity in America is "voluntary" in character,[16] the consciousness of ethnicity for Asian and other non-white groups is inevitable—a matter of history rather than of choice. Like Hispanics, African Americans, and Native Americans, Asians were for a long time categorized by way of the notion of "problem," which, as Vine Deloria, Jr. writes, "relegates minority existence to an adjectival status within the homogeneity of American life."[17] If this "problem" status has now acquired some visibility, since the dominant white culture itself has been undergoing fragmentation to the point at which, as Stuart Hall puts it, "the centering of marginality" has become "part of post-modern experience,"[18] it does not mean that the ideology which is inscribed in the previous acts of discrimination has disappeared once and for all. Because it is regarded as common sense, ideology always lags behind:

> Ideology in the critical sense does not signify an avowed doctrine. It is rather the loosely articulated sets of historically determined and determining notions, presuppositions, and practices, each implying the other by real (but where does one stop to get a grip on reality?) or forced logic, which goes by the name of common sense or self-evident truth or natural behavior in a certain situation.[19]

The multiple ideological stakes—cross-cultural, chronological, and disciplinary—involved in the teaching of modern Asian literatures find their expression in an issue that keeps recurring in mod-

ern Asian texts: *identity*. It is crucial for us to see that what looks
like an ontological preoccupation that has exhausted its theoretical
relevance in the West means something quite different here. Given
the demolition of the traditional terms of reference and the de-le-
gitimation of the grounds of criticism that such terms provide, and
given the untenability of a return to traditional culture in any un-
adulterated form, the very instability of cultural identity itself becomes a combative critical base. This critical base engenders a new
set of terms for the production of knowledge and for intervention
that are no longer simply cognitive or ontological but are informed
by subjectivity and experience.

In North America, where the study of Asian literatures cannot
be divorced from the knowledge of the history of Asian immigrants,
Asian "identities" are split between paradigms of distant grandeur
and recent deprivation. Even if we were to continue to use, as is
often the case in Asian studies, the language of tradition and heritage, we must ask ourselves: "which heritage and which tradition?"
On the misty lands of dragons, gods, and goddesses are superim-
posed the more recent historical memories of racially discriminated
railroad workers, laundry men and women, restaurateurs, garden-
ers, and prisoners in concentration camps. "Ancestry" is not continuous but fraught with displacements and destructions. *What
does it mean to be "Asian"?*

The self-consciousness that surfaces in modern Asian texts, be
they literary, historical, or critical, goes against the point, often
made by traditionalists, that the personal self is insignificant among
Asians. The concern with identity as such, of course, is not only
about the personal self; however, problematizing the self does become a major theoretical development through which modern Asian
texts depart from trajectories of the classics.[20] What makes the
problematizing of the self interesting is perhaps not so much the
"Westernization" of Asian literatures through a personal category;
rather, it is the emergence of a critical means of gauging modern
Asian experience in its essentially non-monolithic, often "self"-con-
tradictory, multiplicity.

The articulation of the self in modern, especially contemporary,
Asian writings suggests a new politics that is both *resistant* and *re-
demptive*.

The notion of "resistance literature" is the one Barbara Harlow
uses to study contemporary "third world" liberation movements.[21]

Examining the writings produced for resistance struggles in Palestine, Nicaragua, and South Africa, Harlow powerfully criticizes the vast negligence, in our teaching of literature in the West, of the relationship between writing and political movements. What is remarkable about her study is that, while it gives an account of resistance writers in the "third world," it also questions our habitual—ideological—assumptions about literature. Her book asks: Do these "resistant" writings not require that we redefine our concepts of literature? Should "resistance" not be regarded simply as one kind of literature but as what constitutes the basis of literature itself?

While I do not think that modern Asian literatures would be adequately understood through the notion of resistance in the radical sense that Harlow gives it, what is extremely relevant is the other, implied, part of her argument without which resistance would not be recognized. This is the redemption of materials which are otherwise lost or unknown. For the teachers of literature, who work with texts and who discuss political movements from afar, redemption is *the* practice of resistance against the obliviating moves of any dominant politics. What need to be redeemed are not the classics— our museums and libraries do that for us—but the experiences of uneasy translations between cultures, translations that are mediated by the possession and lack of power.[22]

For instance, how do we read "America" in twentieth-century Asian literatures? How does the experience with "America" translate into literary production? On the leftist American front, we are accustomed to hearing condemnations of American involvement in the Second World War, the atrocities committed in Japan, Korea, Vietnam, and so on. In Asia, in many parts a world torn by warfare, poverty, and undemocratic politics, "America" still looms large with hope because of the sheer opportunity it represents—for Chinese democracy protesters as much as for tens of thousands of Vietnamese waiting for years in refugee camps for that magical "immigrant" status. In the Asian countries which are politically stable, the translation of "America" structures everyday realities. Rock and roll, hamburgers, shopping malls, television programs, computer games, and tourism constitute the materiality of "culture" which is not so much about past grandeur or political resistance as it is about accommodation, collaboration, and complicity.

Redemption-in-translation, translation-as-redemption: such lived experiences are appropriately captured in Stuart Hall's notion of *migranthood*. In an account about identity called "Minimal Selves," Hall emphasizes his identity as a black Jamaican scholar living in England in terms of the migrant. He describes the two kinds of questions every migrant faces:

> The classic questions which every migrant faces are twofold: "Why are you here?" and "When are you going home?" No migrant ever knows the answer to the second question until asked. Only then does she or he know that, really, in the deep sense, she/he's never going back. Migration is a one way trip. There's no "home" to go back to. There never was.[23]

These statements, when *translated* into the field of Asian literatures in the American context, carry great historical import. Once the implications of migranthood are dislodged from their narrow "personal" frame and juxtaposed with the questions we have been discussing, they demand a reconceptualization of each of these terms—modern, Asian, literatures—in fundamental ways. The two questions facing Hall's migrant become: why is there the category of "Asian literatures" in American universities? When or how are these literatures "going home"?

In the realm of classical Asian literatures, as I have been trying to show, the question of origin has always been answered by going back to the ancient texts. There, at least for now, the standard practice is to give Asian literatures authority by letting them "go home" to the time and space of their ancestry. The question of origin is a much more difficult one in the modern context. Even though the classical method of tracing origins is still often used (typically, in studies of "influences"), the notion of migranthood is far more pressing and productive. The question "When are you going home?" can be responded to in the following manner: home is here, in my migranthood. This migranthood is not a negative or nostalgic way of gesturing toward the philological and philosophical density from which modern Asian literatures have been permanently dislocated. Rather, it is, precisely because of its deterritorialized mode, a form of *interference*—the "crossing of borders and obstacles," the "determined attempt to generalize exactly at those points whose generalizations seem impossible to make." Said goes on:

> One of the first interferences to be ventured, then, is a crossing from literature, which is supposed to be subjective and powerless, into those exactly parallel realms, now covered by journalism and the production of information, that employ representation but are supposed to be objective and powerful.[24]

To extend the metaphors used by Gilles Deleuze and Félix Guattari, the boundary-crossing interrogations of identity in Asian literatures are the "minor" practice within the major language of instrumentalized culture.[25] This minor practice is the first step toward the formulation of a new type of cultural reference.

As part of this preconditioning for understanding Asian literatures, the conception of "identity" changes from nationalistic to ethnic terms. Ethnicity signifies the social experience which is not completed once and for all but which is constituted by a continual, often conflictual, working-out of its grounds. Instead of the instrumentalist production and retrieval of information characteristic of much of the work currently done under the rubrics of "area studies" and "cultural studies," it is ethnicity understood in this sense of an unfinished social field that should provide the new terms of criticism as well as reference. As Hall puts it, "The slow contradictory movement from 'nationalism' to 'ethnicity' as a source of identities is part of a new politics."[26] In this new politics, the question "why are there Asian literatures in American universities?" becomes an important event. The question cannot be answered simply by conscientious demonstrations of the intrinsic "value" of Asian literatures (beauty, depth, aesthetic quality, etc.), nor simply by resorting to the debatable objectives of "cultural pluralism." Rather, it is in terms of the cultural interventions which Asian literatures, in alliance with other minor literatures, bring to American society as a politically constituted community that answers should and will be sought in the decades to come.

VII

LISTENING OTHERWISE,
MUSIC MINIATURIZED
A DIFFERENT TYPE OF QUESTION
ABOUT REVOLUTION

> *Every time I close my eyes I think of you*
> *You are like a beautiful slogan that can't be*
> *   waved away*
> *In this world of (political) criticism and*
> *   struggle*
> *We need to learn to protect ourselves*
> *Let me believe you are true, comrade lover*
>
> from the song "Comrade Lover"
> by Luo Dayou[1]

Hong Kong 1990: a place caught in postcolonial nostalgia, the simulacra of late capitalist technological advancement, the terror of Communist takeover in barely seven years, the continual influx of unwanted refugees, the continual outflow of prized citizens. Hardly a second goes by without some commercial transaction taking place. "Merchandise for emigration" becomes the mainstay of many stores, which are chronically offering "sales." Who are the oppressed of this place? There are many. They are faceless, voiceless, living in refugee camps, housing estates, rented rooms, rented beds, and other unknown corners of the over-crowded colony. Inside the packed spaces of the working city, the oppressed one most commonly encounters are the keepers of ubiquitous department stores and supermar-

> *kets—bored, unpleasant, expressionless, unhelpful salesmen*
> *and women, earning minimum wages, doing hardly any-*
> *thing day in and day out. These "sales specialists" neither*
> *make, finance, nor earn profit from the merchandise they*
> *sell. To that extent they have a similar relationship to the*
> *merchandise as the buyer/consumer—with one significant*
> *difference: once the transaction is over the buyer/consumer*
> *can leave, while the sales specialists are stuck in their job*
> *and their boredom forever. What accompanies them is the*
> *eternal Muzak in the stores, or, if they are lucky, they*
> *might be able to listen to their Walkmans secretly once in*
> *a while.*

In response to the imperative to give everyone "a voice," it is now trendy to raise the question "Who speaks?" in the investigations of oppressed peoples. Versions of this question include "Can X speak?", "What does it mean to speak?", "Who has been silenced?", "How to speak?", and so forth. These are questions of linguistics and narratology applied to issues of power. In one respect, such questions are based on the assumptions of classical—what some might call "vulgar"—Marxism: superstructure (speaking) on top, infrastructure (economic privilege) at the bottom. I want to clarify at the outset that I have no problem with vulgar Marxism as such. For all the attacks it receives, the vulgar Marxist refusal to let go of economics' strategic role in shaping social *vocal* structures continues to yield some of the most powerful (!) results of cultural criticism to date.

But while it effectively raises our consciousness in regard to the privileged positions enjoyed by those who are economically successful, the question "Who speaks?" tends to remain useless in its capacity to change existing economic power relations. This is because the posing of the question itself is already a form of privilege, mostly affordable for those who can stand apart and view the world with altruistic concern. The question that this question cannot ask, since it is the condition of its own possibility, is the more fundamental inequality between theory—the most sophisticated *speaking* instance, one might say—and the oppressed.

Like anthropologists, medical doctors, zoological researchers, and their like, theorists need "objects" to advance their careers. The current trend is for theorists in the humanities to discover objects of oppression for the construction of a guilt-tripping discourse along the lines of "Who speaks?" and thus win for themselves a kind of moral and/or rhetorical victory. Strictly speaking, we are not only living in the age of "traveling theories" and "traveling theorists," as the topic of a recent issue of a journal indicates,[2] but also of *portable oppressions* and *portable oppressed objects*. Our technology, including the technology that is the academic conference, the visual and aural aids with which we present our "objects," the field trips we take for interviewing and archeological purposes of every kind, is what makes portability, a result of mechanization whose effects far exceed the personal mobility of speaking humans, an inherent part of "voices," even though this portability is often ignored in our theorizing.

The problem with the question "Who speaks?", then, is that it is still trying to understand the world in the form of a coherent narrative grammar, with an identifiable (anthropomorphic) subject for every sentence. The emphasis of the question is always on "who." From that it follows that "Who speaks?" is a rhetorical question, with predetermined answers which however cannot change the structure of privilege against which it is aimed. Obviously, it is those who have power who speak—this is the answer this question is meant to provoke.

What if we were to attempt another type of question, one that is not centered on (1) the act of speaking and (2) the quest for a grammatical subject? How might the issue of oppression be approached? This brings us back to the scenario with which I began this chapter. In Asian cities like Hong Kong where oppression is multifarious and contradictory in nature, the question to ask, it seems to me, is rather: What are the forms of surplus? How does surplus inhabit the emotions? What is the relationship between surplus, the emotions, and the portability of oppression? *What plays?* I will lodge these questions in the realm of contemporary Chinese popular music.

The Collective and the Composite

Any attempt to construct a discourse about contemporary Chinese popular music needs to come to terms with the fact that many linguistically determined senses of "discourse" do not work. One can go so far as to say that much of this music, which often blends lurid commodified feelings such as "love" with a clichéd mockery of both capitalism and communism, is about the inability or the refusal to articulate and to talk. This is not simply because humans are, after all, animals that cannot be defined by their speech alone. It is also because inarticulateness is a way of combating the talking function of the state, the most *articulate* organ that speaks for everyone.

When you listen to the songs by mainland China's young singers such as Cui Jian, you'll find that they are lively, Westernized, and full of the kind of physical rhythmic quality that we associate with rock music. Cui Jian's music poses a familiar problem about the emotions involved in our listening—the problem of physicality. Theodor Adorno has warned us against such physicality: "The physical aspect of music . . . is not indicative of a natural state—of an essence pure and free of all ideology—but rather it accords with the retrogression of society."[3] The diatribe of retrogression is a formidable heirloom in the house of popular culture theories. But treasures of the past are most valuable when they are pawned for more pressing needs of the present. If the physicality of a particular music is indeed retrogressive, we need to ask why.

Contemporary popular Chinese music raises many issues similar to those of rock and roll in the West. Foremost among these is that of the music's critical function in regard to the dominant culture. Any consideration of popular cultural forms confronts questions like the following: If such forms provide alternative practical consciousnesses to the dominant ideology,[4] are the modes of subversion and resistance in them not infinitely reabsorbed by the dominant culture? Are such forms capable of maintaining their autonomy? Furthermore, how do we come to grips with such practical consciousnesses when that category indispensable to traditional Marxist social analysis—class—seems no longer adequate in mapping the cultural differentiations that persist beyond class distinctions? Take the example of American popular music. For many critics, the problem posed by this music is how to locate in it a genuinely oppositional function when class distinctions in the United States are more often elided than clearly defined. One might say that it is the impossibility of identifying any distinct class struggle—and with that, the impossibility of legitimizing the notion of class struggle itself for social criticism—that in part accounts for Adorno's reading of American popular music as a massive numbing. The blurring of class distinctions—as reflected in "easy listening" music—is inordinately discomforting for the sober Frankfurt School critic.[5] The disappearance of the category of class struggle, which is inherent to the old distinction between high culture and mass or commercial culture, is a point argued by Fredric Jameson.[6] Following Jameson, Katrina Irving writes: "The opposition of highbrow and lowbrow with its in-built notion of hierarchy is eliminated, and yet another site of difference around which a counter-hegemonic discourse might have been articulated is removed."[7]

It is, thus, when we focus on what still remains for many as an indispensable category in social criticism—class struggle—that contemporary Chinese popular music, despite its resonances with Western popular music, poses the greatest enigma. China is a "third world" nation, and yet where do we find the expression of class struggle in its popular cultural forms these days? Instead of exhibiting the classic "symptom" of a "third world" nation in the form of an obsession with "class," contemporary Chinese popular culture "speaks" a different language of "oppressed" emotions. In the realm of music, we find the conscious adoption of Western models of rhythm, instrumentality, recording, and modes of distribution for the production of discourses which are *non-Western in the sense of an inattentiveness to class struggle.* Many of the motifs that surface in contemporary Chinese popular music, like their counterparts in fiction, television, and film, can be described as individualist and populist—troublesome terms for Western Marxists who at one point looked to Communist China for its utopian aspirations. Such motifs are surfacing at a time when the mainland Chinese official ideology is still firmly "Communist." Therefore, while the perception of class is undoubtedly present in the subversive emotions of contemporary Chinese popular music, it is present less as an agency for struggle than as the disciplinary cliché of the dominant culture *to be struggled against.* This is precisely because "class struggle" has been lived through not merely in the form of critical talk but also in everyday experience, as official ideology and national culture. (In mainland China, "struggle" is a transitive verb, an act one performs directly on another: thus, "to struggle someone.")

Speaking of his inability to deal with the directly political, Roland

Barthes says (in an interview): "these days a discourse that is not impassioned can't be heard, quite simply. There's a decibel threshold that must be crossed for discourse to be heard."[8] Barthes's statement offers us a way of defining "dominant" culture in musical terms, not only as that which crosses a particular decibel threshold as a rule, but also as that which collectivizes and mobilizes with its particularly loud, indeed deafening, decibel level. If revolution is, among other things, a technology of sound, then its mode of implementation is that of mechanized and institutionalized recording, repetition, and amplification. As early as 1928, the Chinese writer and critic Mao Dun used the technology of sound in a discussion of "proletarian literature" to indicate the danger of the new political orthodoxy which based its moves on prescriptive slogans: "I . . . cannot believe that making oneself into a gramophone shouting 'This is the way out, come this way!' has any value or can leave one with an easy conscience. It is precisely because I do not wish to stifle my conscience and say things I do not believe . . . that I cannot make the characters in my novelette ["Pursuit"] find a way out."[9]

The past forty years of Chinese communism can be described as a history in which class struggle is used as the foundation for the official culture of a nation-state. The question "Who speaks?" underlies the most brutal of political interrogations and exterminations. The "who" that is identified through arrests, purges, and murders as the landlords, capitalists, and running dogs is replaced with the "who" that is "the people." Entwined with nationalism and patriotism, and strategically deployed by the state, "the people's speech" that supposedly results from successful class struggle forms the cadences of a sonorous music. One thinks of pieces such as the "International Song," "Dongfanghong" (The East is red), "Meiyou gongchandang meiyou xin zhongguo" (There would be no new China without the Communist party), and many others that are standardized for official celebrations to invoke patriotic sentiments. Official state culture champions an irresistible grid of emotions that can be defined by Susan Stewart's notion of "the gigantic," which "we find . . . at the origin of public and natural history."[10] Gigantic emotions are the emotions of reverence, dedication, discipline, and nostalgia, all of which have to do with the preservation of history as it ought to be remembered. Such an institution of memory is, in the words of Friedrich Kittler, "an act of sheer and external violence."[11] In a "third world" nation whose history is characterized by a struggle against imperialism as well as internal turmoil, the history that "ought to be remembered" is the history of the successful collectivization of the people for the establishment of a national community.

Many examples of contemporary Chinese popular music, however, follow a very different trajectory of sound. Here, the question about popular cultural form is not a question of its ultimate autonomy from the official culture—since that official culture is omnipresent—but how, against the single audible decibel level amplified at random with guns and tanks, popular music strikes its notes of difference. The comments of Václav Havel on rock music in Czechoslovakia before the fall of the authoritarian regime in 1989 speak germanely to the Chinese situation:

> In our former conditions, rock music acquired a special social function. And that's connected with the fact that culture and arts in general fulfill a different role in our country than they do in the Western world. Under a totalitarian regime, politics as such are eliminated and the resistance has to find substitute outlets of expression. One of those substitute channels was rock music. That's why its role here was more significant than it is where it's part of a general consumption.[12]

The *words* of one of Cui Jian's most popular songs, "Rock and Roll on the Road of the New Long March" (EMI Music Publishing Ltd., S.E. Asia, 1989), allude to one of the founding heroic events of the Chinese Communist state, the Long March to Yanan. The last few lines (which I translate from the Chinese) go as follows:

> What should I say, what should I do, in order to be the real me
> How should I play, how should I sing, in order to feel great
> I walk and think of snowy mountains and grasslands
> I walk and sing of our leader Chairman Mao
> Oh! one, two, three, four, five, six, seven.

By recalling the words, I don't mean to imply that the truth of Cui Jian's music lies in its verbal content. Rather, the disjuncturing of words from music points to the significance of the partial—of emotions as partializing rather than totalizing activities which jar with the symphonic effects of official culture.

There is, first of all, the difference between the "decadence" of the music and the "seriousness" of the subject matter to which the music alludes. Without knowing the "language," we can dance to Cui Jian's song as we would to any rock and roll tune; once we pay attention to the words, we are in the solemn presence of history, with its insistence on emotional meaning and depth. This is why Cui Jian's music so deeply antagonized the officials in the Chinese state bureaucracy that he was dismissed from his post in the Beijing Symphony Orchestra and prohibited from performing in Beijing a couple of years ago.[13] The official Chinese repudiation of his music is moralistic, aiming to reinforce a kind of obligatory cultural memory in which the founding deeds of Communist ancestors are properly honored instead of being "played with"[14]—least of all through a music imported from the capitalist West.

But as we look closely at the words themselves, we see that even the words—the medium in which solemn historical emotions can be respectably lodged—partake of the "play" with tradition. Instead of words with sonorous historical meanings, Cui Jian's lyrics read more like grammatically incoherent utterances. Even though they conjure up "historical" images, his words speak against literate and literary culture by their choppiness and superficiality. The Long March, one of the nation's best-selling stories since 1949, is a signifier for something vague and distant, and Chairman Mao a mere name to complete the rhyme. In reacting against Cui Jian's music, the Chinese authorities were therefore not clinging to solemn words as opposed to flippant music but rather to what does not exist either in the words or in the music, namely an idealized notion of official history. Therefore, while the difference between the words and the music exists in terms of their different semiotic orders, the words and music are also mutual renditions of each other insofar as they both dis-member and dis-remember official history. The words, by becoming illiterate, turn into physical sound, thus joining the music in the production of a kind of emotion that is, one might say, "beyond words."

By associating emotion with musicality and physicality, I may be reinvoking many of the oldest myths about each of these terms. It is often argued that it is the association of music with emotionality that is responsible for its relegation to the realm of the irrational, the feminine, and the simply pleasurable. At the same time, as we examine a non-Western culture such as the Chinese in the 1990s, we notice a resurfacing of precisely such notions about music and the emotions. The discoursing of the emotions here is therefore at an interesting crossroads. How do we describe the emotions of a music which is resistant to the oppression of Communist state culture, but which seems to go against the theories of music in the West which are struggling to rescue music from the mythical paradigms in which it has been cast? In other words, how do we theorize the significance of music-as-emotion at a time when it is precisely the reduction of music to emotionality that must also be critiqued?

The problem of emotionality, it would seem, is the problem of surplus in the sense that it is what exceeds the limits by which its functions can be rationally charted. Music, it is well known, has always been theorized as a pure form, as that which signifies nothing. In the words of Julia Kristeva, for instance, music's semiotics is such that "while music is a system of *differences*, it is not a system of *signs*. Its constitutive elements do not have a signified." For Kristeva, music "takes us to the limit of the system of the sign. Here is a system of differences that is not a system that *means* something, as is the case with most of the structures of verbal language."[15] Because of this "empty," translinguistic status, music suits the theorizing of surplus the best, because it provides a means of suggesting what goes *beyond*. One might say that it is the use of music's power as surplus—as that which cannot be safely contained—for a criticism of the straitjacket of orthodox state ideology that is most evident in the making of Chinese popular music today. And it is this surplus which is commonly recognized as its emotionality.

Of course, no matter how excessive the emotions are, they can always be narrativized and thus attributed a more familiar purpose. Dong Wenhua's "Xueyan de fengcai" (Blood-stained spirit) is a good example. This compelling song was first sung for Chinese soldiers fighting in the Sino-Vietnamese War of the sixties. A newer version, resung by Wang Hong, has since then appeared and met with tremendous success among the Chinese especially around and after the Tiananmen Massacre of 1989. Other versions continue to be heard on major occasions such as the fund-raising concerts and gatherings held by Chinese communities around the world for China's flood relief in the summer of 1991. The song clearly demonstrates the power of music to harmonize populist emotions. To the extent that it serves the function of patriotic unification, contemporary Chinese popular music shares with its many counterparts decidedly conventional and conservative moments as well.

In an account about rock and roll, pleasure, and power, Lawrence Grossberg argues that "The affective economy of rock and roll is neither identical to, nor limited to, the production of pleasure."[16] If there is an undeniable affinity between the emotionality and musicality, we must also add, in Grossberg's words, that "the affective investment, while asignifying, is not a pristine origin (as the concept of libido might suggest) which precedes the ideological entanglements of the articulation of . . . differences. It is a plane of effects, a circuit of empowerment."[17] What kind of empowerment? Grossberg suggests it in these terms: "In the rock and roll apparatus, you are not what you don't listen to (which is not necessarily the same as you are what you listen to)."[18]

This statement—"you are not what you don't listen to"—signifies a view of human labor that is not positive but negative, but the meaning of this negativity is the defiant message that human labor cannot be reduced to a narrowly defined political goal. In contemporary Chinese fiction, the forty years of Communist history are increasingly understood to be the alienation of human life *par excellence* through what poses as the "collective" good. The collective is now perceived as that mysterious, objectified Other against which one must struggle for one's life.[19] Such is the instinctual battle fought by the protagonist in the controversial novel *Half of Man Is Woman* by Zhang Xianliang. Working in a labor camp in the countryside where official instructions are regularly announced through loudspeakers, this man reflects on physical labor in the following terms. Describing hard labor as a "trance," he distinguishes between hard labor as such and the officially assigned "job": "A job is for someone else. Labour is your own."[20] This insistence on the difference between the work that is performed for a public sphere with its clearly organized goals and the work that is one's own is not an insistence on "privacy" or private property but rather a resistance against the coercive regimentation of emotions that is carried out under the massive collectivization of human lives in the Chinese Communist state. Contrary to orthodox Socialist beliefs, the protest made in contemporary Chinese popular culture is that such collectivization of human lives is what produces the deepest alienation ever, because it turns human labor into the useful job that we are performing for that "other" known as the collective, the country, the people, and so forth. In his book *Noise*, Jacques Attali makes a point similar to that of Zhang Xianliang's protagonist when he comments on political economy in these terms:

> Political economy wants to believe, and make others believe, that it is only possible to rearrange the organization of production, that the exteriority of man from his labor is a function of property and is eliminated if one eliminates the master of production. It is necessary to go much further than that. Alienation is not born of production and exchange, nor of property, but of usage: the moment labor has a goal, an aim, a program set out in advance in a code—even if this is by the producer's choice—the producer becomes a stranger to what he produces. He becomes a tool of production, itself an instrument of usage and exchange, until it is pulverized as they are.[21]

We find in the preceding passage a transgression of the classic paradigms in which we are accustomed to considering human labor. What Attali suggests is that "use" itself, instead of being the original, inalienable part of labor, is actually the most basic form of alienation, for it is already an exchange for something else—in other words, it is predicated on an other, a collective.[22]

At a time when we have become rightly alert to issues in the "third world," it is precisely the problem of "use" that has to be rethought. Something is "useful," we tend to think, because it serves a collective purpose. While on many occasions I have no objections to this kind of thinking, it is when we deal with the "third world" that we have to be particularly careful in resorting to paradigms of the collective as such. Why? Such paradigms produce stereotypical views of members of "third world" cultures, who are always seen as representatives driven solely by the cause of vindicating their own cultures. To the extent that such peoples are seen as representatives deprived of their individuality and treated as members of a collective (read "third world") culture, I think that the morally supportive narrativizing of the "third world" by way of utilitarianism, however sophisticatedly utilitarianism is argued, repeats what it tries to criticize, namely the subjection of entire peoples to conceptual paradigms of life activities that may have little relevance to such peoples' struggles for survival.

In the case of China, I read the paradigm of collectivity as part of the legacy of imperialism imposed upon a "backward" nation. Like most countries in the post-imperialist era, the alternative to ultimate destruction in the early twentieth century was, for the Chinese, to "go collective" and produce a "national culture." Collectivity as such was therefore never an ethnic empowerment without neuroses, and it is the neuroses which are now surfacing in popular cultural forms like music. At this point in time, the narrative of collectivity does little to explain the kinds of emotions that are played (upon) in contemporary Chinese music, apart from making us notice this music's negativity and, for some, nihilism. These emotions of negativity are summed up by Cui Jian's description of the Chinese on the mainland: they are "extremely angry, but have no way of expressing their anger."[23] Many of his songs, with titles such as "Nothing to My Name" ("Yi wu suo you"), "Starting Over Again" ("Cong tou zai lai"), "Solution" ("Jiejue"), "The Opportunist" ("Touji fenzi"), "Like A Knife" ("Xiang yi ba daozi"), and "The Last Gun Shot" ("Zuihou yi qiang"), suggest a deliberate turning away from the collective's thematic burdens through lightheartedness, sarcasm, physicality, brutality, and semantic vagueness.

While such emotions of negativity are not capturable in any one medium alone, in this essay I want to emphasize their special connection with music, in part to criticize the privilege enjoyed by visuality in most discussions of postmodern culture. Like popular culture elsewhere, popular culture in East Asia tends to gravitate toward the image. From large-scale concerts by stars, to contests for young singers, to the "self-service" performances of the Japanese-style "Karaoke," to the equivalents of MTV programs on Asian television, music is bound up with the fast-pace technologizing of a part of the world which relies on spectacular images for the sustenance of commodity culture. Music is always simply an accompaniment for the visual. Even when fans go to the concerts of their favorite singing stars, one feels that it is the stars' performance on stage, rather than their singing, that the fans have come to see. Music becomes a mere pretext, and singers, instead of performing with the voice, must excel more in their inventiveness with costumes, dancing, and acrobatics.

Although contemporary Chinese popular music can definitely be pursued by way of the spectacle of performance, its interest for me lies elsewhere. While the image marks the body, in music one has to invent a different language of conceptualizing the body, that is, of perceiving its existence without marking and objectifying it as such.

The body's existence is here realized through what Attali calls "composition," in which the body, instead of always living in an alienated relation to itself through the stockpiling effects of representation, is present for itself and for "the pleasure outside of meaning, usage and exchange."[24]

For this new presence of the body to emerge, the previous codes in which it was written must be destroyed. We hear in a song like "Rock and Roll on the Road of the New Long March" the physicality of such a destruction, which comes to us in the form of a composite. Often, "destructive" songs are made up of a mixture of voice, instruments, and versions of older songs, as well as previous sayings, proverbs, and idioms. Now, we may, if we are intent on reading in what I'd call the Western Marxist way, dismiss this as a form of permissive "pluralism." At the same time, this composite structure points to a kind of musical mutation, in which no single theme or event is allowed to monopolize the decibel level, so that it is precisely at the dissonance of these musical *parts*—in the form of debris—that the physicality of these songs makes itself heard. Often, therefore, "destructive" songs do not distinguish themselves from noise. From the actual coarseness of a singer's voice to the insertion of moments of "clearing the throat," from the disharmonious presence of different musical backgrounds in the same song to the adaptation of familiar folk tunes and themes for a heavily electronic music, what we hear is a mutual "plugging" between partial noises—between differences. This plugging is at the same time an unplugging of preceding codes, in which the fundamental distinction between the human voice and the musical instrument, between rehearsing and actual performing/recording, between traditional and contemporary musical forms, becomes itself *a part of playing*.

The distinction between producer and listener breaks down also. In Attali's words, "The listener is the operator." This notion of the listener-as-operator extends composition beyond the realm of music:

> Composition, then, beyond the realm of music, calls into question
> the distinction between worker and consumer, between doing and
> destroying, a fundamental division of roles in all societies in which
> usage is defined by a code; to compose is to take pleasure in the
> instruments, the tools of communication, in use-time and exchange-
> time as lived and no longer as stockpiled.[25]

An example of such composition in East Asia is the form of entertainment, very popular of late, called "Karaoke." Originating in
Japan, "Karaoke" is the singing, done either in public (Karaoke bars
and clubs) or in private (with individual machines for the home),
which breaks down the traditional distinction between performing
and listening. A person selects a song she or he likes to sing from
a collection that accompanies the Karaoke machine, then sings by
following the music and the images (with lyrics) on the video screen.
What is most interesting is that the common requirements of "good"
performance, such as the excellence of the voice, adequate training
and practice, etc., no longer matter. The entire human body, together with its noise-producing capacity, follows the machine's
sounds and images. The machine allows one to feel like—to be—an
original performer, but one is literally performing as a listener, with
all the "defects" that a performer is not supposed to have. One is
liberated from the myth of performance and does not need to "know
how" in order to sing anymore.

In the rest of this chapter I will discuss two specific aspects of
composition. First, what does it mean for composition to be read,
as Attali suggests, "as an indication of a more general mutation af-
fecting all of the economic and political networks" (p. 135)? Second,
what does it mean to say (Attali is here referring to the musical
theory of John Cage) that "music is to be produced . . . everywhere
it is possible to produce it, in whatever way it is wished, by anyone
who wants to enjoy it" (p. 137)?

Listening Otherwise

The lyrics of the "Song of the Dwarf" ("Zhuru zhi ge," Praiseplan
Ltd., Hong Kong, 1989), by the Taiwanese singer Luo Dayou (who
now bases his work in Hong Kong), go as follows:

We must hold hands, hold hands tight
Beware of the giants waving at you from far away
These history-making faces, these figures of the times
They are always carrying guns for the sake of the people
The road of the Long March is rough
Forcing their way into Tiananmen, they arrive at Beijing
The index is alluring in the market of "struggle"
Revolutionary doctrines fluctuate like stock prices
Five thousand years of despotic rule await your cleansing
Beware:
The characters who revolt against others are themselves revolted
    against
They clutch at their clothes. They need to have face.
How many lives has Mr. Marx destroyed
The glorious results of war are woven in our compatriots' blood
We dedicate the great victory to the people
Five thousand years of despotic rule await your cleansing
But who can wash the blood on your hands
We must hold hands, hold hands tight
Beware of the smile on the face of the dwarf who is approaching
These faces behind (him), these great figures—
They are always carrying guns for the sake of the people.[26]

   This song, once again, demonstrates that separation between musicality and verbality I mentioned as characteristic of many others.
In the remarkable lines "The index is alluring in the market of
'struggle'/Revolutionary doctrines fluctuate like stock prices," the
mockery of the Communist state is done by a clever combination
of the languages of revolution and the market economy, or rather,
by rewriting revolution in terms of the market economy, effecting
a demolition of the altruistic claims made by the practitioners of
the Marxist ideology, which is included as part of the 5,000-year-old
Chinese despotic tradition.
   The clashing of these two usually incompatible languages, revolution and the market, suggests a fundamental need to revamp the
bases for both. Their clashing reveals the grounding of emotions
not in "nature" but in technology. Because of the ineluctability of
technology, what clash are also the thematics of the "third world"
and the "first world." Technology is that collectivized goal to which
East Asian cultures, as part of the non-Western world that survives
in the backwash of imperialism, have no choice but to adopt. In the

case of mainland China, the successful technologizing of an entire nation through the regimentation of life activities in collective form was accomplished through the Communist revolution. In other, non-Communist Chinese communities in East Asia, notably Taiwan, Hong Kong, and Singapore, the success of technology is evident in sophisticated modes of living, inseparable from the production and consumption of commodities. The co-presence of these two meanings of technology—as the collectivized and the commodified—constitutes a unique type of ethnicity in ways that exceed the orthodox paradigms of demarcating "first world" and "third world" economic and political networks.

Contrary to the paradigms of struggle and protest—the cultural stereotypes that are being laid across "third world" peoples with uniformity, soliciting them into a *coded* narrative whether or not they are willing to participate in it—the emotions that emerge here imply a new writing of ethnicity. This writing cannot consider the "ethnic" person simply in the role of the oppressed, whom we in the West, armed with questions such as "Who speaks?", attempt to "liberate" by giving a voice, a voice that amounts to a kind of waged labor (the permit to participate in the working world with "choice" and "freedom"). The presence of technology means that the deeply historical perception of the unpredictable but oppressive nature of official culture is here conveyed through instruments that are accomplices as well as resisters to that culture. In "Queen's Road East," a song he sang with Jiang Zhiguang and produced through his company "Music Factory" in 1991, Luo Dayou turns the knowledge and memory of local political history into the makings of an accessible and entertaining music. In the lyrics, written by Lin Xi, Hong Kong's colonial past and present, signified by the image of the "friend" called "the Queen" on money coins, are juxtaposed with Hong Kong's colonial future, which is signified by "the comrades" who will stamp a new meaning on everything, even street names. In the production notes to the collection featuring the song, Luo Dayou writes about his ethnic agency in terms of a transaction with the unknown and unknowable. The historical predicament underlying this agency is spoken of almost beguilingly—as a dream:

> In the past hundred and fifty years or so, Hong Kong grew up in a state of abandonment, making her survival with compromises in the

gaps between East and West. Her history is the orbit of a dream.
. . . So the moment finally comes: the 1990s. I feel like a broker
conducting the biggest transaction between the past and the future.
Among those who live here at this time, who doesn't? . . . The short-
est distance between two points is neither a straight line nor a struggle. It is a dream. . . . Between the past and the future, we are in
the embrace of a dream, heading toward a time only it knows about. [27]

Precisely because historical injustice is the very ground on which
the struggle for survival takes place, such injustice is often alluded
to indirectly rather than confronted directly. The music of Cui Jian
and Luo Dayou is as semantically loaded with the feelings of oppression as it is electronically saturated, but the feelings of oppression impinge upon us as an inerasable, *because* invisible, referent,
like a language with an insistent syntax but no obvious semiotics/
signs with meanings. [28] The dreaminess and emotional opacity of
this music function like beautiful but illegible notes, defying us to
make sense of them while retaining their power for combat through
an amateurish crypticness and a posed abstractness. Official Chinese culture, on the other hand, does not only suppress such *emotions* in order to uphold the clear, glorious version of history; as
usual, it would also criticize the *electronics* in the name of protecting the integrity of Chinese culture against excessive Westernization. [29] Operating under the domination of a patriotic rhetoric that
cannot be turned off, [30] the counter-discourse we find in many popular songs is thus deliberately unfinished or inarticulate, by way of
a music that is lighthearted, decadent, playing to the rhythms of
expensive life-styles in forgetfulness of the wretched of the earth.
The forms of nihilism are used consciously for enervation, producing moments of positivity that restructure relations to the political
state.

On the streets of Hong Kong, Taipei, and other East Asian cities,
as one strolls along shop windows among crowds, in restaurants,
bookstores, fresh markets, streetside stalls, Chinese herbal tea-
shops—in all such public places, it is not uncommon to hear this
kind of popular music being played on the side for entertainment
by the people tending the stores. What the music contributes to
the public sphere is a kind of "easy," nonverbal culture that conditions passersby, who nonetheless never focus on it seriously. Unlike

the overwhelming presence of commodified images, popular music leads a life on the side, as a kind of distraction made possible by technology, a distraction that, moreover, is not visible.

Such listening on the streets is not merely the substitution of one kind of attention for another, the aural for the visual. Instead, because it is always played on the side, as we are doing other things, it is what I would call a "listening otherwise." Listening otherwise changes the meaning of music from its traditional association with a plenitude that escapes concrete articulation on account of its infinity to that of a part object whose field is always elsewhere. At the same time, this part object is surplus; it is not reducible or graspable in the form of an externalized image. Its *excessive partiality* requires a different kind of theorizing.[31]

"Hear There and Everywhere":[32] Music Miniaturized

What we need, in other words, is a history of listening—a history of how listening and the emotions that are involved in listening change with the apparatuses that make listening possible.[33] Traditionally, listening is, as a rule, public. For a piece of music to be heard—even under the most private circumstances—a certain public accessibility can always be assumed. Such public accessibility continues even when music becomes portable with the transistor radio and the portable cassette tape player. With the invention of headphones, on the other hand, listening enters an era of interiorization whose effect of "privacy" is made possible by the thoroughly mechanized nature of its operation. But listening through headphones is still attached to relatively large pieces of machinery, which tend to remain stationary. (We use them when we don't want to disturb others occupying *the same space*.)

The form of listening that is a decisive break from the past is that made possible by the Walkman. One critic describes the Walkman this way: "that neat little object . . . a pregnant zero, . . . the unobtrusive link in an urban strategy, a semiotic shifter, the crucial digit in a particular organization of sense."[34] Even though the popular songs I am discussing may not be consciously intended for playing on the Walkman alone, what I would argue is that the conception of the Walkman—as part of "the equipment of modern nomadism"[35]—is already written into these songs. The Walkman is implied in their composite mode of making, which corresponds to a composite mode of listening that involves multiple entries and exits, multiple turnings-on and turnings-off. If music is a kind of storage place for the emotions generated by cultural conflicts and struggles, then we can, with the new listening technology, talk about the production of such conflicts and struggles *on the human body* at the press of a button. In the age of the Walkman (or its more sophisticated affiliate, the Discman), the emotions have become portable.

In contrast to the gramophone or loudspeaker, without which the "gigantic" history of the public would not have been possible,[36] the Walkman ushers in the history of a miniaturized music. But the notion of miniature is useful here only indirectly, as a way to point to the need for us to invent another language that would more appropriately describe the partiality of music. Susan Stewart's study of the narratives of the miniature provides us with the necessary assistance. Among the most important characteristics of the miniature, according to Stewart, is that it establishes a correspondence with the things of which it is a miniature. The miniature is thus unimaginable without visuality: "the miniature is a cultural product, the product of an eye performing certain operations, manipulating, and attending in certain ways to, the physical world."[37] The miniature is the labor of multiplying and intensifying significance microscopically:

> That the world of things can open itself to reveal a secret life—indeed, to reveal a set of actions and hence a narrativity and history outside the given field of perception—is a constant daydream that the miniature presents. This is the daydream of the microscope: the daydream of life inside life, of significance multiplied infinitely *within* significance.[38]

Insofar as Walkman music is shrunken music, music reduced to the size of the little portable machine that produces it, it is a kind of miniature. But the most important feature of music's miniaturization does not lie in the smallness of the equipment which generates it. Rather, it lies in the *revolution in listening* engendered by the equipment: while the music is hidden from others because it is compacted, this hiddenness is precisely what allows me to hear it full blast. The "miniaturizing" that does not produce a visible body—however small—that corresponds with "reality" leads to a certain freedom. This is the freedom to be deaf to the loudspeakers of history, even though "deafness" is itself a simulacrum of our technologized fate. We do not return to real individual or private emotions when we use the Walkman; rather the Walkman's artificiality makes us aware of the impending presence of the collective, which summons us with the infallibility of a sleepwalker. At the same time, what the Walkman provides is the possibility of a barrier, a blockage between "me" and the world, so that, as in moments of undisturbed sleep, I can disappear as a listener playing music. The Walkman allows me, in other words, to be missing—to be a missing part of history, to which I say: "I am not there, not where you collect me." In the Walkman, the hiding place for the music-operator, we find the music that "is to be produced everywhere it is possible to produce it, by anyone who wants to enjoy it." Here, Barthes's statement that "Politics is not necessarily just talking, it can also be listening"[39] takes on a new meaning. For listening is not, as Adorno describes popular music in America, "a training course in . . . passivity";[40] rather it is a "silent" sabotage of the technology of collectivization with its own instruments.

As the machine of what we might call "automatic playing," the Walkman offers a means of self-production in an age when any emphasis on individualist positions amounts to a scandal.[41] What is scandalous is that self-production is now openly autistic. The autism of the Walkman listener irritates onlookers precisely because the onlookers find themselves reduced to the activity of looking alone.[42] For once, voyeurism yields no secrets: one can look all one wants and still nothing is to be seen. The sight of the Walkman listener, much like the sight of some of our most brilliant scientists, artists, and theorists, is one that we cannot enter even with the most piercing of glances. (The Walkman allows us for the first time to realize that our "geniuses" have always lived with earphones on.) Critics of the Walkman, like critics of mass culture in general, are condemned to a position of exteriority, from which all kinds of ineffectual moralistic attacks are fired. This position of exteriority amounts to the charge: "Look at yourself! Look how stupid you look!" But the autistic sight is the one which is free of the responsibility to look, observe, and judge. Its existence does not depend on looking, especially not on looking at oneself.

The music operator's activity frankly reveals that the "collective" is not necessarily an "other" to be idealized from afar but rather a mundane, mechanical, portable *part* of ourselves which can be tucked away in our pocket and called up at will. This "self"-production through the collective requires not so much slogans as AA batteries, and it takes place in the midst of other, perhaps equally insignificant, activities. It substitutes listening for the writing of music and demolishes the myth of creativity through a composite discoursing of the emotions. The noises and voices of production become ingredients of self-making. Deprived of their images and their bodily presence in onstage performances, even singers— "stars" and "icons"—become part of the technologically exteriorized "inner speech" of the listener. As such, the emotions of music are dehydrated, condensed, and encapsulated, so that they can be carried from place to place and played instantly—at "self-service."

VIII

MEDIA, MATTER, MIGRANTS

Truth or Dare

In June 1989 the world's attention was riveted on mainland Chinese students and workers demonstrating for democracy in Tiananmen Square. Politically progressive people now remember this as the Tiananmen Massacre, yet another instance of Western imperialism dominating a "third world" culture—this time by way of a claim to objective news-making. But there is more to be learned than how to distance ourselves from spurious claims to objectivity. What remains unarticulated is the confrontation between historical relations toward the media that are overlapping yet not entirely coincidental, a confrontation we repeatedly see in the U.S.'s dealings with foreign cultures, especially those that do not share a European origin.

Paul Virilio says that the unknown side of politics has always been speed.[1] "More than on reason," he writes, "Western history has been built on the reasons of moving forces—in other words, on the power of what animates, activates or carries, at the expense of the reality principle or even of similar realism."[2] While others call the great revolution that has occurred since the nineteenth century the Industrial Revolution or the Transportation Revolution, Virilio calls it a "dromocratic revolution" because what was invented "was not only the possibility of multiplying similar objects . . . but especially a means of fabricating speed. . . . "[3] Political power was to be increasingly invested in acceleration; politics became pro-motion. And yet, Virilio asks: "What if the aim of movement has become like that of military invasions or sports records: to go faster while

going nowhere, in other words to disappear?"[4] Would it be possible
to change speed, to set up barricades in time, to stop?

The question of speed is ultimately the question of the medium—that is, the nature and texture of the instruments and apparatuses of transmission and dissemination. In the China crisis, we
saw how the Western media, typified by CNN, displayed their
prowess not only through the quick transmission of news and the
frequency of broadcasting but also through gearing the representation of news toward one seemingly *instant* sense perception—sight.
As Sylvère Lotringer says, "What's 'moving' about speed is that it
makes things visible."[5] "News" is, by definition, what is visually
spectacular in speed, what we can catch "in the wink of an eye."

The obsession with visuality means also the obsession with a certain understanding of visuality, namely, that visuality exposes the
truth. In their attempt to deliver the truth, the Western media
worked much more in terms of a collaboration and coalescing of
the senses than in terms of their differentiation: An array of forces,
including the camera, the telephone, the fax machine, the tape re-
corder, and the newspaper, were combined to give us "the event."
All sensations merged into the sensation of seeing and the epistemological and moral imperative of watching. It was believed that
by watching—that is, by concentrating all media into that of
sight—we would be able to prevent disasters from happening. The
"view" of another culture went hand in hand with the belief that
our technologized gaze was equivalent to the gaze of God, which
should have made murder impossible. Alternatively, visuality was
believed to be scientific. The other culture was "observed" through
our electronic windows as a biological "culture" would be observed
under a scientist's microscope. Whether theological or scientific,
moreover, the media believed themselves to be transparent, impartial—nonexistent.[6]

The Chinese government's response was equally astounding.
Media in China are not as advanced as in the West—but what exactly does this mean? It means that the crude—that is, un-
disguised—aspects of mass communication reveal themselves more
readily, without losing or hiding their basic characteristic as an-
nouncement, demonstration, and propaganda. Operating on the
premise of an older notion of the political state, whereby politics is
a matter of overt exhibitionism—a show of force—the Chinese gov-

ernment completely failed to meet up with the theological and scientific imperatives of the West's visualism. For the Chinese authorities, there was nothing just, impartial, or transparent about visuality. Instead, visuality was a force, the force of an opponent in front of whom they had to demonstrate their physical potency. Sensing the intensity of the world's gaze, the Chinese government, like many of its counterparts in the non-Western world, felt it had to act—not merely to produce action but also to play-act, to perform, to fabricate. Precisely the West's wish that the Chinese government talk rather than act—that is, neutralize the physical feelings of the students' confrontation—was thwarted. Interpreting the gaze of the world's media as *daring* them to respond to their challenge, the Chinese authorities rose to the occasion by putting their best foot forward—by showing that they dared kill even their own students and workers. Hence what was intended as a form of checking, regulation, and a capturing of truth through visuality turned into its opposite. Visuality became not the policing or investigatory order that it aspired to be but a theatrical order and an exchange—not of gazes but of faces (face being analogous to honor or pride). If the West's gaze can be paraphrased as "let's keep a watch over you so that you don't act foolishly," the Chinese government's response was, "since you are watching me so closely, let me show you how I can act."[7]

The Progress toward Non-Sense

What I intend the foregoing description to show is not the equal claim that each of the two parties has to "power" but rather how, in the confusion of contending notions of visuality and the media, real bodies are slaughtered and sacrificed. In the aftermath of history-making, we attribute a "martyr" function to the bodies that were mashed into the pavement. But were these bodies not in fact the casualties of unequally competing discourse networks none of which cared about their survival even though they all used these bodies to justify their own brand of altruism—such as the "production of impartial knowledge," the "sponsorship of human rights," or the "maintenance of social order and stability"?

In his elaborate work on the history of the media, Friedrich

Kittler argues that the trend toward digitization is erasing the notion of the medium itself. When everything is computed in the form of numbers and figures, and when sense perceptions such as sight and sound are increasingly mixed up in electronic reproductions so that their traditional differentiation no longer "makes sense" to us, the notion of the medium, together with the memory and sensuality that it signifies, gradually disappears.[8]

The disappearance of sense perception nowadays applies everywhere, often in unexpected places. The replacement of vinyl records by compact discs and laser sound technology is being followed by the replacement of books by digitized data: The invention of the Electronic Book now goes hand in hand with new players such as Sony's Data Discman and Microsoft's Multimedia PC (MPC).[9] A new electronic technique called "virtual reality" is being developed to enable mental previews of not-yet-existent realities while one can still make alterations. (The technique is now used to sell kitchens in Japan.)[10] On a different note, we read about how illiteracy among the visually handicapped is on the rise because the traditional training in Braille is increasingly being replaced by tapes and other types of sound technology.[11]

When cultural theorists discuss the media, they tend to follow the same rules that dominated the West's reportage of the China crisis. By focusing on the media as communicative instruments, many discussions present the media in a unidirectional manner, as transmissional and at the same time projectal and forward-going agents. In other words, the media are imagined as a form of transparency moving forward, or a form of speed producing a transparent effect. Kittler's work is interesting in this regard because, instead of transparency and speed, it focuses on the notion of the medium instead. And yet this is not "medium" in the sense of some authentic substance prior to use, but "medium" as the coded/used materiality that is inscribed in even the most common forms of "communication," including the sense perceptions such as hearing, seeing, talking, and so on, that we assume to be "natural."

Focusing on the medium makes it possible to notice other aspects of the media. Before the nineteenth century, perceptions of communication were not preoccupied solely with transmission and thus, we might say, not with speed. Storage and recording—that is, ways of saving that enable us to relive irrevocably past time—were equally important aspects of communication: Without something being stored, nothing could be transmitted. Hence the ground-breaking success of the phonograph and the cinematograph was due to the fact that they were able to store time[12] and thus allowed the fabrication of sensuality and memory in novel ways. Theodor Adorno wrote in the 1930s that phonograph record albums, photographic albums, and postage-stamp albums were all "herbaria of artificial life that are present in the smallest space and ready to conjure up every recollection that would otherwise be mercilessly shredded between the haste and hum-drum of private life."[13]

For Adorno, who was always melancholically preoccupied with memory and its loss, the most important thing about the medium remained its ability to preserve time. Through the phonograph record, for instance, "*time* gains a new approach to music. It is not the time in which music happens, nor is it the time which music monumentalizes by means of its 'style.' It is time as evanescence, enduring in mute music." Mechanical reproduction was regarded by Adorno as the "process of petrification" by which the ephemeral and perishing life of art was rescued.[14] With the phenomenal expansion of archival capacity in the electronic age, however, time itself has turned hyperreal. When there is infinite capacity to store, time cannot be "lost" and thus need not be redeemed. Think for instance of the technology of Photo CD, which is described—in a way that echoes but also dates Adorno's description above—as "a creative way for families to store and view photograph albums." This technology replaces negatives with disks and thus eliminates once and for all the chemical errors that are an inherent part of photo-finishing. Not only does it allow us to zoom and crop images any way we want, it also gives us images that do not change or fade with time. With these eternal images, photography is no longer simply that wonderful storage technique for saving time past; rather it is what manufactures a present that will forever be new and clear, and always conveniently available.[15] Reality is now an imperfect copy of its images.

Moreover, thinking of technology by way of storage is still thinking in terms of substance in the manner of Aristotelian philosophy, in which accidents are relative and contingent to substance. For a critic like Virilio, the age of speed is the age in which the order of substance and accidents is reversed.[16] The development of our technologies since the late nineteenth century is such that accidents themselves—signs of the imbalance between substance and its transferral from one time and place to another—become structural rather than accidental. The enormous increases in speed drastically change the relations between time and space. The speediness (decreased time) that is now part of any medium of transmission alters the substance (occupied space) that is being transmitted as well as the traditional notions of storage and recording.

The universal mediatization of human life has often if not always been considered in terms of an increasing democratization. The invention of new techniques of reproduction and communication is always accompanied by the dream of a more open, more radical politics. Thus in the 1920s and 1930s, Walter Benjamin saw in the technology of film possibilities of a politics which would be open to the participation of the masses, who, because of their *distraction*, would revolutionize the premises of aesthetic production and reproduction. In distraction, the presence (the here-ness and together-ness) of the conventional human body—with its capacity for consciousness, concentration, and voluntary memory—gives way to modes of communication in which mass is overtaken by forces of speed (forces which Benjamin located in the processes of mechanical reproduction). For Benjamin writing in the early twentieth century, when there was still hope for the success of a Communist political revolution, the unconscious dimensions of reality released by the media were signs of a democratic future, in which the traditional boundaries separating producer and audience would break down.[17]

The development of our high tech in the late twentieth century continues to manufacture dreams of freedom. Our most routine machines such as the telephone, the photocopier, and the fax machine make communication instantaneous, while Walkmans, laptops, and scanners make pleasure and information portable. For academics, perhaps the most revolutionary of access technologies is hypertext, the multimedia system—if it can still be called that—of research-data acquisition and computation that will eventually eliminate our linear notions of book organization and our spatial habits of searching libraries. Since it arranges knowledge as a network and thus makes irrelevant classical hierarchical constraints such as the "Propædia" of the *Encyclopædia Britannica*, hypertext is regarded by some as the ultimate freeing of learning. Hypertext's endless, multiple entry capabilities demystify once and for all the barriers that writers and readers have collaborated in establishing in order to perpetuate that coded activity called "reading." The hypertext user will be the expert distracted person who can switch from any part of one text to any part of another text across space and time. This user will be gliding across surfaces and browsing through materials with a comprehensiveness unimaginable to the most diligent researcher. As in a dream, nothing will be lost, anything can be found, and more is to be generated. The practical behavior of the hypertext user will be like the air traveler who covers large stretches of space in little time—"in no time," we might say—while sitting in one spot. This user is no longer a reader or writer in the traditional or even post-structuralist sense[18] but a passenger-in-transit, whose sedentariness is a factor of his/her rapid motions through time and out of time.

Critics have responded to the gradual non-sense of the medium in dissimilar ways. Jean Baudrillard, for instance, consistently argues against the "sense" or logic of production, interiority, and depth in the postmodern age. Central to Baudrillard's writings is the *immateriality* of resistance against the media, whose power resides in the way they permeate every aspect of life, including resistance itself, which now shares with capital a *reversible* relation. The only way "out" is staying put, that is, "disappearing" into/with the media's non-sense itself.[19] For Baudrillard, "disappearance" is not a bad thing; it is not the "end" of something in the sense of its finality. Rather, disappearance refers to the mercurial nature of appearance, whose many "simulations" lead to the "ecstasy of communication" (to use two of his book titles).

For Virilio, however, the disappearance of "sense" and "politics" is alarming. Virilio defines the chief characteristic of "the society of disappearance" as a repression resulting from overexposure, in the following terms:

> Until the Second World War—until the concentration camps—societies were societies of incarceration, of imprisonment in the Foucauldian sense. The great transparency of the world, whether through satellites or simply tourists, brought about an overexposure of these places to observation, to the press and public opinion which

now ban concentration camps. You can't isolate anything in this world
of ubiquity and instantaneousness. Even if some camps still exist,
this overexposure of the world led to the need to surpass enclosure
and imprisonment. This required the promotion of another kind of
repression, which is disappearance. (Gangsters had already invented
it by making bodies disappear in cement.)[20]

Virilio's conclusion about "disappearance" is therefore radically
different from Baudrillard's. Virilio describes that difference this
way: "for him it's positive. For me, it's *totally* negative. I fight against
the disappearance of politics."[21]

Language against Speed, Language as Speed

Marshall McLuhan's well-known definition of the media—that
the medium is the message—follows from an understanding of this
progress toward non-sense and disappearance I outline above.
From the perspective of language, the basic medium of human
communication, McLuhan's definition sounds exactly like Russian
Formalism's definition of art—"Art is a way of experiencing the
artfulness of an object; the object is not important"[22]—or Anglo-
American New Criticism's defense of poetry in the first half of the
twentieth century, that "a poem should not mean but be." The opponents of these statements see them as instances of an outdated
and priggish "formalism" which disregards the real concerns of history. But it is possible to read "formalism" in a different light, as an
involved response to—and a fight against—speed technology. The
preoccupation with form as such is the preoccupation with the
fundamentally transformed relation between substance and transmission, between storage and communication. That transformed
relation does not simply mean a reversal of the primariness of substance and secondariness of transmission. Rather, transmission and
mediatization—forms in speed, forms in motion, forms in the process of deformation—are now structural to the conception of matter.

The best indication of the Russian Formalists' and New Critics'
involvement with speed lies in their attention to language—to language, moreover, as a way to arrest speed—even though such at-

tention is already inscribed within a new and irreversible notion of speed itself. Think, for instance, of the Formalists' argument for "roughened form" and "retardation" as the general law of art,[23] and the New Critics' emphasis on the organic unity of a work of litera-ture that was expressed in the symbol of the "well-wrought urn."[24] Such attempts were, in the language of technology, attempts at slow motion and close-up. The arguments of the Russian Formal-ists, of course, had a much greater affinity with the innovative as-pects of the new media such as film, but even the New Critics with their academic gentility and stodginess, their humanistic embrace of tradition, and their highbrow hostility toward technologized cul-ture were actually producing a theory of the medium that protested against the homogenization of substance by transmission and trans-parency that was threatening to take over all definitions of lan-guage. For instance, I. A. Richards's defense of poetry, made in sentimental and moralistic terms in contempt of mass culture and science (even though Richards was himself interested in the new science of psychology), could now be seen as a kind of desperate effort to rescue precious heavy matter—"culture"—as it is con-densed in a medium of memory and sensuality—poetry—against the imminent onslaught of instrumental mediatization of even po-etic language itself.[25]

As speed and transparency supersede communication, "litera-ture" and "art" become opaque, abbreviated, and truncated in order to stage the last vestige of resistance. Artistic rebellions are them-selves signs of the success of speed. It was not an accident that early twentieth-century artistic and linguistic experiments concen-trated their energies on spatialized, discontinuous forms rather than on their continuity, which could be subsumed under and conquered by speed. Freud's "unconscious," Proust's involuntary memory, Kafka's short stories and unfinished novels, Benjamin's aphorisms, Brecht's epic theater with its self-conscious gestures and tableaux (that prevented the continuity between character and actor, actor and audience), the cubists' displaced body parts, the melodramatic, symbolic, and exaggerated mime-acting of silent films[26] were all fragments of this history of resistance.

Closer to our time, the phenomenon of that practice now known as deconstruction must also be seen as a determined effort to arrest speed and the instrumentalization of language. Deconstruction, as

we understand it from the writings of, say, Paul de Man, is first and
foremost obsessed with the *temporality* of language. For de Man,
the irony of language lies in the fact that it unfolds through time,
a process of negativity which undermines language's claim to rep-
resentational/symbolic fullness. De Man writes about time as the
materiality of the medium that cannot be short-circuited. If the
conventional uses of language *move* it toward a telos, then, deconstruction specializes in de-motioning—de-motivating—such a telos
by foregrounding its sequentiality—its temporal differentiation.
But the nihilism of deconstruction comes precisely from its disbelief in itself—from its demystification of its own undertaking. Language, we are told, "always already" contains the clues to its own
undoing; language takes itself apart before anyone else does. What
does this mean *in the light of speed*? We may say that, understood
in the deconstructionist sense, language is not simply an arresting
of speed as it is with the Russian Formalists and the New Critics;
rather, it is mediatized to the utmost—to the point where it de-
stroys its own existence as medium (fabricated sensation) *and* as
message. In other words, the practice of deconstruction, in spite of
its slowness, its patient negation of the presumed instantaneity of
consciousness and referentiality, is itself a form of speed—speed
not in the sense of the rapidity of motion but as the capacity to
anticipate, to foresee (to see before), and overtake oneself, so that
"arrival" is no longer possible because it is already (a thing of the)
past. In the simulacrum of a representational medium, language is
a constant departure from some place for nowhere, or from everywhere for the same kind of place: It is thus "allegorical" and
"empty." If Virilio is to have his fantasy of a museum of accidents,[27]
deconstructive readings with their *mise-en-abîmes*, failures, and
aporias should be among the foremost exhibits.

Backward Countries

If European and American cultures have been developing an
avant-garde "consciousness" in the form of deliberate slowness or
artful retardation against speed technology, how would we describe
the "other" cultures of the modern world?

The ascendency of transmission over storage has pronounced effects in the "third world." If China today still operates with an older notion of the political state as I indicated earlier, there are ways in which it had to give in to the mediatization of culture a long time ago. Here speed and transparency must be understood side by side with nationalism—as what facilitate an old civilization's entrance into the modern world. While the development of the media in countries like China and India might not have reached the level of technical sophistication they have in the West, upheavals experienced by these cultures in other quotidian areas in fact place them in the forefront of media revolution. I will briefly discuss one aspect of such a revolution—the modernization of language.

Although modern European intellectuals like Ezra Pound found in the Chinese language a fascinating inspiration for poetic revolution, the problem faced by Chinese intellectuals in the early twentieth century, notably around the May Fourth period, was how to rid their new nation of the retarding effects of the traditional language itself. For these intellectuals as for their counterparts in other "third world" countries, modernizing their language meant making it useful and usable in the new world. The first criterion for the construction of a "national" language was simplicity and expediency: Chinese was to be cleansed of all the traditional residues that stood in the way of the nation's progress. Because language is explicitly linked to a purpose—nation-building—it is thoroughly mediatized in its conception: Language is understood primarily in terms of a medium whose efficiency results from being stripped of its past and thus, we might say, of its memory. (Hence old "literary" qualities were the first to come under fire as obstacles that dragged the nation down.) Cleansing language meant speeding it up. Furthermore, as in linguistic and cultural revolutions elsewhere in history, the newly constructed Chinese language was said to be based on the vernacular—the people's *speech*.

A "third world" nation's need to reorient language toward speech is the other, forgotten side of the West's attempt, in the late stages of technologized culture, to deconstruct its own phonocentric logocentrism (as we find it in the early work of Derrida). While Western philosophers continue to be intrigued by the ideographic—the written—nature of Chinese, the development of Chinese in the twentieth century—in ways grossly ignored by our most sensitive deconstructionists—has been toward phoneticization (so that it can "catch up with" the rest of the world). We might describe China's modernization as a process in which the Chinese become increasingly "alphabetized" or "romanized" into a new literacy.[28] This new literacy involves the Japanization and Westernization of expressions and grammar, the reduction of complex characters to simplified ones, and the phonetic spelling of Chinese words. *Pinyin*, the romanization system used in the People's Republic, literally means "putting together by sound." As more and more words with similar sounds are indicated by the same character, what used to distinguish Chinese from many other languages—namely, differentiation of meanings through writing—gradually disappears. It will be interesting to see whether differentiation by tone, which is actually another effect of writing in Derrida's sense and which is still distinct, will survive in the coming decades.

In cultural production, speed leads to the ascendency of realism as the literary "mode" in which reality can be fixed. The point about realism is not simply that of finding a medium in which to reflect reality properly. Rather, it is the *pro-motion* of the linguistic medium to the point of transparency so that it will no longer be in the way. The result of this "promotion" is that those uses of language which depend upon language's materiality, such as philosophy and literature, are no longer possible if they do not conform to the realistic trend. Language is now appreciated with leisure (the opposite of speed) only if it is confined within the arena of the "classics," that is, when it is clearly no longer part of the present. There, in the glorious culture garden of bygone times, language is displayed for the visualism and taste of the connoisseur such as the sinologist. Meanwhile, the production of knowledge about China as a "modern" culture has long been divided among specialists in anthropology, sociology, political science, history, and so forth. These specialists do not need to have a good command of Chinese, but they must, in order to do their work, regard language as a transparent medium of communication.

Migrants

Perhaps nowhere are effects of speed more apparent than in the catastrophes of human bodies created by the continual confrontations between the "first" and "third" worlds.

On the side of world powers like the U.S., the mediatization of information and life has reached a point where incompatible realities are interchangeable. Murdering is as electronic as word processing. American teenagers who sat cross-legged on shag carpet playing video games on their TV screen eventually found themselves soaring above the Middle East during the Gulf War. The simulacra to which they had been accustomed appeared on their dashboards, requiring similar physical motions of pressing buttons. Miles above the land where people died, a clean and cohesive video game became the persuasive substitution for war. The dirtiness and bloodiness of what actually happened "down there" with the dropping of bombs were *not* part of the game, which preempted reality by the "virtual reality" it placed in front of the soldier-viewer.

The "aesthetics" of disappearance as such means not the disappearance of world politics but the disappearance of the damaged human body from the war screen. As Virilio and Lotringer put it: " . . . disappearance is not a complementary technique, but one which is becoming central. Bodies must disappear. People don't exist. There is a big future in this technology. . . . "[29] World politics will increasingly be played in the form of unequally competing discourse networks in which local intervention will be irrelevant. Speed overtakes local resistance not because it is faster but because it does not work by the same codes: A barricade on the ground, for instance, is useless when the enemy is speeding through the air; the misplacement of a book in some research archive would not hinder a user of hypertext; the cries of women and children in the villages of Iraq meant nothing to the American pilots bombing from the skies. As Alvin Toffler writes in his recent book, *Powershift*, the acute consequence of our electronic neural system is the "dangerous de-coupling of the fast economies from the slow,"[30] a de-coupling that has already reached irreparable proportions.

While some may still think that the way to resist speed as such is through body counts—for instance, by increasing the number of people in antiwar demonstrations—the bodies that really *matter* in the recent wars and confrontations between the "first" and "third" worlds are not those of the demonstrators but those who disappear *en masse*, in excess. Ironically, demonstrators for democracy (as in the China crisis) are themselves pro-speed—their requests are requests for governments to speed up their mediatization of life so that they would not be trapped in a backwater of military or authoritarian rule. But such speeding is precisely what the governments themselves want. In other words, in terms of interrupting "progress," the bodies that participate in demonstrations do not count simply because their intention does not contradict the general intention of their governments. Similarly, antiwar protests, whose goal is to "mobilize" people into the right consciousness/action, are unuseful because people are already mobilized by forces that work toward the same type of goal—and faster. How many antiwar demonstrations involving how many people would it take to crush the persuasive power of speed? My point here is not to criticize local interventions but rather to emphasize how, given the catastrophic pace of our machinery of speed, their effect can only be minimal.

The catastrophic pace of speed is the pace of vicious circles. Consider the Gulf War. This was a war about oil—the oil that is necessary for sustaining the European and American economies, industries, and standards of life. But the same oil was what kept the war going—what sustains Western military power, perpetuates the turmoil in countries like Iraq, and guarantees the permanence of the already lopsided division of world economies that lies at the source of warfare. Like "speed," oil is the "end" of war (its practical purpose) that has become the indispensable yet absolutely destructive "means."

Similarly in the China crisis, the "human rights" that were demanded as the ultimate end of confronting the Chinese government have become the means of diplomacy and trade negotiations. Like oil, "human rights" are what the West wants (to sustain its standard of life) and what the "third world" government refuses to release. In order to guarantee an unlimited supply of "human rights"—a demand that will perpetuate the present conflict between the West and China indefinitely—humans themselves are used to feed the speed machine that is "diplomatic exchange." While the Chinese government holds its own people hostage, releasing them only when it is necessary to show the West it is complying somewhat with respect for "human rights," the U.S. uses "human rights" to consider whether China should be granted the "most favored nation" treatment in trade relations. Such uses of humans (as bargaining chips, as hostages, as a means to an end) violate the explicit purpose of "human rights," which would have humans treated with equal respect everywhere and at all times. Instead, humans are now on a par with the oil and speed that sustain the machines of global relations. Chinese authorities like Deng Xiaoping were being *economically precise* when they said, around June 4, 1989, that China had too many people to care about the loss of a few thousand at Tiananmen. Humans for China have always been the main economic resource as oil is for Middle Eastern nations. So, if "human rights" are what the West wants, let the West pay for it. Turn the treasured goal into the lucrative means!

Despite their vast differences, both the China crisis and the Gulf War are logical consequences of a universal speed culture that, as part of its progress, continues to aggravate and enlarge the irreparable gaps it causes between those who are "quick" and those who have yet to "catch up." But "quick" and "catch up" in what sense? Who is closer to the end . . . of destruction? Who is slower . . . to die? The vicious circle of speed is like the paradox of the race between Achilles and the tortoise.

A direct result of this race for speed that dominates life across the globe is the emergence of the migrant—the involuntary passenger-in-transit between cultures, for whom homelessness is the only home "state." Be they Chinese student leaders in exile, refugees from the Gulf War, emigrants from the democratized Eastern Europe, or victims of other global conflicts, human bodies in the form of migrants are going to populate the earth in the decades to come. Precisely because the chief tendency of speed is to eliminate the presence of human persons, what we have to cope with now is the weight of the eliminated mass itself. Along the borders of countries in Asia, Africa, Europe, and America, as well as the internal boundaries of cities within those continents, migrants swell to make up a new ecology, the ecology of human waste, of humans-as-waste. While the American media are full of surreal dramas of triumphant soldiers returning home from a devastated Middle East, the refugees from the Gulf War and other wars, the unwanted and forgotten products of speed culture, will continue to deposit in the vacuum left by speed as unrecyclable matter, as destitute bodies.

The latest irony to mediatized culture is the electronification of migranthood itself. It is now possible to have surplus humans working for speed technology without physically crossing borders. A recent report indicates that computer companies in the U.S. have discovered a cheap means of data entry by employing "electronic immigrants" from countries like India and the Soviet Union where there exist a large number of well-trained but jobless technical professionals. These "immigrants" require neither resident permits nor health care insurance. Their labor is communicated through long-distance phone lines to the U.S. in a way that is free of import duties. Even though the use of humans rather than scanners means that more errors are likely to result, these "immigrants" cost so little (always much less than minimum wage in the U.S.) that the companies can pay them to enter the same data twice in order to eliminate the errors and still realize a higher profit than by using advanced scanning machinery.[31]

What this means is that what was still used by Marx in the nineteenth century as a metaphor—the alienation of human labor—is now literally true. Human labor is finally exchangeable in digitized form, without going through the stage of the concrete commodity whose mysteriousness Marx so memorably describes. In its bodiless form, electronic labor is the summation of what Virilio calls "the extermination of tangible culture in the West."[32] For a while perhaps, the body parts of the laborer linger—as waste matter stranded in the "homeland" after the useful labor has been extracted and fed into the global media machine. Such untransmitted matter will be the last brief, tangible record of our violence and our self-destruction.

GLOSSARY

Chapter 4

Names and Terms

A Cheng	阿城
douzheng	鬥爭
fan	反
Fang Lizhi	方勵之
gaige	改革
Haizi wang	孩子王
hunjun	昏君
junzi	君子
laoshi	老實
Liu Xiaobo	刘曉波
mingzhu	民主
pi	批
qingchu	清楚
qingguan	清官
renge	人格
renmin xinzhong de fating	人民心中的法庭
ren yan wei xin	人言為信
tanguan	貪官
Tansuo	探索
Wei Jingsheng	魏京生
xiaoren	小人
xin	信

xiushen   修身
zhuanzhi zhuyi   專制主義

Chapter 5

Names and Terms

jiaoxin   交心
Lunyü   論語
shanghen wenxue   傷痕文學
suku   訴苦
Xü Xiaodan   許曉丹
zhengming   正名
zuguo   祖國

Passages

(Confucius) 名不正，則言不順，
　　　　　　言不順，則事不成。

(Confucius) 故君子，名之必可言也，
　　　　　　言之必可行也，君子於其言，
　　　　　　無所苟而已矣。

(Xü Xiaodan) 我要以浪女的形象進入國會，
　　　　　　以聖女的靈魂愛護百姓。

1. Introduction

1. Stephen Owen, "The Anxiety of Global Influence: What Is World Poetry?" *The New Republic*, November 19, 1990: 28–32; hereafter page references are given in parentheses in the text. The piece is a review of Bei Dao, *The August Sleepwalker*, trans. Bonnie S. McDougall (London: Anvil Press, 1988; New Directions, 1990).

2. An indictment of contemporary Chinese poetry that is remarkably similar in its racist spirit to Owen's is another review of *The August Sleepwalker*, by W.J.F. Jenner. A few examples from Jenner: "great poetry can no longer be written in Chinese"; "Bei Dao's lines rarely have the inevitability, the weight, the structure, the authority of real poetry"; "[The modern Chinese poets] Wen Yidou and Xu Zhimo are not up there with Auden and Yeats"; "translations of modern Chinese poetry into English . . . do not lose all that much, because there is not much in the original language to be lost. . . . " *The Australian Journal of Chinese Affairs*, no. 23 (January 1990): 193–95. I am grateful to Gregory B. Lee for this reference.

3. Michelle Yeh, "The Anxiety of Difference—A Rejoinder," p. 8. This essay has been published in Chinese in *Jintian* (*Today*), no. 1 (1991), pp. 94–96. The page reference for the English version is taken from Yeh's manuscript.

4. Harry Harding, "From China, with Disdain: New Trends in the Study of China," *Asian Survey* 22.10 (October 1982): 934–58; hereafter page references are given in parentheses in the text.

5. Colin MacKerras, *Western Images of China* (Hong Kong: Oxford University Press, 1989), p. 3.

6. Rey Chow, "Violence in the Other Country: China as Crisis, Spectacle, and Woman," in *Third World Women and the Politics of Feminism*, ed. Chandra Talpade Mohanty, Lourdes Torres, and Ann Russo (Bloomington: Indiana University Press, 1991), pp. 81–100.

7. Sigmund Freud, "Mourning and Melancholia," *Collected Papers*, vol. iv, trans. Joan Riviere (New York: Basic Books, 1959), pp. 152–70.

8. The mutual implications between "translation" and "betrayal" as indicated in an expression like "*Traduttore, traditore*" and their etymological relations to "tradition" will have to be the subject of a separate study.

9. Naoki Sakai, "Modernity and Its Critique: The Problem of Universalism and Particularism," in *Postmodernism and Japan*, ed. Masao Miyoshi and H. D. Harootunian (Durham: Duke University Press, 1989) (formerly *South Atlantic Quarterly*, 87.3 [Summer 1988]), p. 105; my emphasis.

10. Naoki Sakai, "Modernity and Its Critique," pp. 113–14; emphases in the original.

11. Gayatri Chakravorty Spivak, "Who Claims Alterity?" in *Remaking History*, ed. Barbara Kruger and Phil Marian (Seattle: Bay Press, 1989), p. 281.

12. Tani Barlow, "Theorizing Woman: *Funu, Guojia, Jiating* [Chinese Women, Chinese State, Chinese Family]," *Genders* 10 (Spring 1991): 132–60.

13. G. Balandier, "The Colonial Situation: A Theoretical Approach (1951)," translated from the French by Robert A. Wagoner, in Immanuel Wallerstein, *Social Change: The Colonial Situation* (New York: John Wiley & Sons, Inc., 1966), pp. 34–61.

14. This paragraph and the next are taken, with modifications, from Rey Chow, "Digging an Old Well: The Labor of Social Fantasy," in *Feminismo y teoría fílmica*, ed. Giulia Colaizzi (Madrid: Ediciones Cátedra, forthcoming). This essay is part of a longer study of contemporary Chinese cinema. I am grateful to Teresa de Lauretis for telling me that I needed to clarify my point about "coloniality."

15. The official position in China today is that nothing of real significance happened in Tiananmen Square in May and June of 1989, and that it is best not to recall the demonstrations and the victims in public. In an interview with Chinese and non-Chinese reporters in early 1991, the Chinese Premier Li Peng responded to questions about the Tiananmen Massacre with the following kind of "rationality": "It has already been two years since the June Fourth incident; there is no need to discuss it any more. . . . Under the urgent circumstances of the time, had the Chinese government not acted decisively, we would not be able to have the stability and economic prosperity we see in China today." "Zhong wai jizhe zhaodaihui shang Li Peng huida wenti" (Li Peng's responses to questions at the press conference for Chinese and foreign reporters), *Ming Pao Daily News*, Vancouver Edition, April 11, 1991; my translation.

16. Arif Dirlik, "The Predicament of Marxist Revolutionary Consciousness: Mao Zedong, Antonio Gramsci, and the Reformation of Marxist Revolutionary Theory," *Modern China* 9.2 (April 1983): 186.

17. For a historical account of how Maoism inspired antiestablishment intellectuals' thinking in France in the 1960s and 1970s, see Lisa Lowe, *Critical Terrains: French and British Orientalisms* (Ithaca: Cornell University Press, 1991), pp. 136–89.

18. Nancy Armstrong and Leonard Tennenhouse, "Introduction: Representing Violence, or 'How the West Was Won,' " in *The Violence of Representation: Literature and the History of Violence*, ed. Nancy Armstrong and Leonard Tennenhouse (London: Routledge, 1989), p. 8.

19. Gayatri Chakravorty Spivak, "Three Women's Texts and a Critique of Imperialism," *"Race," Writing, and Difference* (formerly *Critical Inquiry* 12.1, and 13.1), ed. Henry Louis Gates, Jr. (Chicago: University of Chicago Press, 1986), p. 267; emphasis in the original.

20. Michel de Certeau, *The Practice of Everyday Life*, trans. Steven Rendall (Berkeley: University of California Press, 1984), p. 183; emphases in the original. Hereafter page references are given in parentheses in the text.

21. What Spivak criticizes as the "conflation of the indigenous elite women abroad with the subaltern" is but one prominent aspect of this current trend. "Who Claims Alterity?", p. 273.

22. Armstrong and Tennenhouse, "Introduction," p. 25.

23. Benjamin Disraeli, *Collected Edition of the Novels and Tales by the Right Honorable B. Disraeli, vol. IV—Tancred or The New Crusade* (London: Longmans, Green, 1871), p. 141. I am grateful to Prabhakara Jha for locating this reference for me.

24. Khachig Tölölyan, "The Nation-State and Its Others: In Lieu of a Preface," *Diaspora* 1.1 (Spring 1991): 6.

25. William Safran, "Diasporas in Modern Societies: Myths of Homeland and Return," *Diaspora* 1.1 (Spring 1991): 87.

26. Michel Foucault, "Intellectuals and Power: A Conversation between Michel Foucault and Gilles Deleuze," *Language, Counter-Memory, Practice: Selected Essays and Interviews*, edited and with an introduction by Donald F. Bouchard, translated from the French by Donald F. Bouchard and Sherry Simon (Ithaca: Cornell University Press, 1977), p. 208.

27. For a discussion of the limits imposed by "field" and "fieldwork," see James Clifford, "Traveling Cultures," *Cultural Studies*, ed. Lawrence Grossberg, Cary Nelson, Paula Treichler (New York: Routledge, 1991), pp. 96–116. In ethnography at least, Clifford advocates cross-cultural studies of travel and travelers as supplements to the more traditional notion of "fieldwork."

28. George J. Stigler, *The Intellectual and the Marketplace*, enlarged edition (Cambridge, Mass.: Harvard University Press, 1984), p. 145.

29. Even though Derrida points out in *Of Grammatology* that Chinese writing "functioned as a sort of European hallucination" (p. 80), his own project does not go beyond the ethnocentrism of a repeated reference to the other culture purely as a bearer—a sign—of the limits of the West. Gayatri Spivak puts it this way: "There is . . . the shadow of a geographical pattern that falls upon the first part of the book. The relationship between logocentrism and ethnocentrism is indirectly invoked in the very first sentence of the 'Exergue.' Yet, paradoxically, and almost by a reverse ethnocentrism, Derrida insists that logocentrism is a property of the *West*. He does this so frequently that a quotation would be superfluous. Although something of the Chinese prejudice of the West is discussed in Part I, the *East* is never seriously studied or deconstructed in the Derridean text. Why then must it remain, recalling Hegel and Nietzsche in their most cartological humors, as the name of the limits of the text's knowledge?" Translator's Preface, *Of Grammatology* (Baltimore: Johns Hopkins University Press, 1976), p. lxxxii; emphases in the original. By insisting that logocentrism is "Western," Derrida forecloses the possibility that similar problems of the

"proper" exist in as deep-rooted ways in the non-West and require a deconstruction that is at least as thorough and sophisticated as the one he performs for "his" tradition.

30. William Hinton, *Fanshen* (New York: Vintage Books, 1966). For an informative account of Western feminism's borrowings from the Chinese Communist Revolution, see Sally Taylor Lieberman, "Visions and Lessons: 'China' in Feminist Theory-Making, 1966–1977," *Michigan Feminist Studies*, no. 6 (Fall 1991), pp. 91–107.

31. For detailed critical discussions on this topic, see Arif Dirlik, *Revolution and History: Origins of Marxist Historiography in China, 1919–1937* (Berkeley: University of California Press, 1978), *The Origins of Chinese Communism* (New York: Oxford University Press, 1989), and *Anarchism in the Chinese Revolution* (Berkeley: University of California Press, 1991).

32. Terry Eagleton, "Defending the Free World," *Socialist Register 1990*, ed. Ralph Miliband, Leo Panitch, John Saville (London: The Merlin Press, 1990), p. 91; my emphasis.

33. Lynn Pan, *Sons of the Yellow Emperor: The Story of the Overseas Chinese* (London: Secker and Warburg, 1990), pp. 363, 373.

34. Dirlik, "Predicament," pp. 203, 184.

35. The danger of a book such as Nien Cheng's *Life and Death in Shanghai* (London: Penguin, 1988) lies precisely in its blindness to what is embraced as a heavenly alternative to Chinese communism—the United States of America.

36. "The non-analysis of fascism is one of the important political facts of the past thirty years. It enables fascism to be used as a floating signifier, whose function is essentially that of denunciation. The procedures of every form of power are suspected of being fascist, just as the masses are in their desires. There lies beneath the affirmation of the desire of the masses for fascism a historical problem which we have yet to secure the means of resolving." Michel Foucault, "Power and Strategies," in *Power/Knowledge: Selected Interviews and Other Writings 1972–1977 with Foucault*, ed. Colin Gordon, trans. Colin Gordon, Leo Marshall, John Mepham, Kate Soper (New York: Pantheon Books, 1980), p. 139.

37. Foucault, "Power and Strategies," p. 135.

38. Jay Branegan, "Fighter for a Paper Door," *Time*, May 27, 1991: 27.

39. Unofficially organized by a group of supporters for China's Democracy Movement in Hong Kong, the "Yellow Bird Operation" was aimed at assisting those persecuted by the mainland Chinese government to leave China. With over U.S. $2 million collected from traders and major networking aid from the triad societies in Asia, they have arranged secret escapes to the West for over 130 Chinese opposition intellectuals since June 1989, including the student leaders Wuer Kaixi and Li Lu, the government consultant Chen Yizi, and the scholars Yan Jiaqi and Su Xiaokang. Because of an error in one of the arranged trips, Yellow Bird Operation's actions are now known to the Chinese National Security Department (the equiva-

lent of a secret police). Some of its members revealed their identities and their work at an interview with the BBC's news program "Panorama" in mid-1991. My information is based on an account in *Xin Bao/Overseas Chinese Economic Journal* (the U.S. edition of the *Hong Kong Economic Journal*), June 7, 1991, p. 5. This account is a selected translation from a report on the "Yellow Bird Operation" in *The Washington Post*, June 2, 1991.

40. Donations from Taiwan were also enormous. A discussion of Taiwan's role in the China events will have to take into account the strong Taiwanese nativism that currently inspires political debates and artistic productions.

41. Safran, "Diasporas in Modern Societies," pp. 91–92.

42. David Yen-ho Wu, "The Construction of Chinese and Non-Chinese Identities," *Dædalus* 120.2 (Spring 1991): 176. This special issue of *Dædalus* is entitled "The Living Tree: The Changing Meaning of Being Chinese Today."

43. Vera Schwarcz, "No Solace from Lethe: History, Memory, and Cultural Identity in Twentieth-Century China," *Dædalus* 120.2 (Spring 1991): 105.

44. Participants at this conference can testify to this event.

45. Leo Ou-fan Lee recently criticizes what he calls the " 'centrist' frame of mind" by defining it as "the elitist belief" that intellectuals "can ultimately influence the reformist leaders in the party to their way of thinking." Lee associates this centrist frame of mind with some of the intellectuals and writers who left China partly because of the Tiananmen Massacre. See "On the Margins of the Chinese Discourse: Some Personal Thoughts on the Cultural Meaning of the Periphery," *Dædalus* 120.2 (Spring 1991): 219.

2. Where Have All the Natives Gone?

1. James Clifford, *The Predicament of Culture: Twentieth-Century Ethnography, Literature, and Art* (Cambridge, Mass.: Harvard University Press, 1988), p. 232; emphasis in the original.

2. Clifford, *The Predicament of Culture*, pp. 241, 245.

3. I discuss this in the first chapter of *Woman and Chinese Modernity: The Politics of Reading between West and East* (Minneapolis: University of Minnesota Press, 1991). One criticism that sinologists deeply invested in the culture of ancient China often make about contemporary Chinese people is that they are too "Westernized."

4. Fredric Jameson, *Signatures of the Visible* (New York: Routledge, 1990), p. 1; emphasis in the original. Jameson's notion of pornography owes its origins, in part at least, to fictional explorations of the relations between sexual images and technology such as J. G. Ballard's *Crash* (first published by Farrar, Strauss and Giroux in 1973), described by its author as "the first pornographic novel based on technology." See Ballard, "Introduction to the

French Edition" (first published in French in 1974 and in English in 1975), *Crash* (First Vintage Books Edition, 1985), p. 6. I am grateful to Chris Andre of Duke University for pointing this out to me.

5. Jean Baudrillard's theory of "seduction" offers a strong critique of modern theory's tendency to go toward depths, thus ignoring the subversive potential of the superficial. See his *Seduction*, trans. Brian Singer (New York: St. Martin's Press, 1990).

6. Slavoj Žižek, "Rossellini: Woman as Symptom of Man," *October* 54 (Fall 1990): 18–44 (the quote is on p. 21).

7. See Homi Bhabha, " 'What Does the Black Man Want?' " *New Formations*, no. 1 (Spring 1987), pp. 118–24. Bhabha's argument is that "the black man wants the objectifying confrontation with otherness" (p. 120). This essay is based on Bhabha's introduction to Fanon's *Black Skin, White Masks* (London: Pluto, 1986).

8. Julia Kristeva, *About Chinese Women*, trans. Anita Barrows (New York: Marion Boyars, 1977, 1986), p. 11.

9. Kristeva, *About Chinese Women*, p. 15.

10. Gayatri Chakravorty Spivak, "French Feminism in an International Frame," *In Other Worlds: Essays in Cultural Politics* (London: Methuen, 1987), p. 141; my emphasis.

11. Kristeva, *About Chinese Women*, p. 13.

12. Kristeva, *About Chinese Women*, p. 11.

13. Kristeva, *About Chinese Women*, p. 12; emphasis in the original.

14. As Jacques Derrida writes of Lévi-Strauss: "the critique of ethnocentrism, a theme so dear to the author of *Tristes Tropiques*, has most often the sole function of constituting the other as a model of original and natural goodness, of accusing and humiliating oneself, of exhibiting its being-unacceptable in an anti-ethnocentric mirror." *Of Grammatology*, trans. Gayatri Chakravorty Spivak (Baltimore: Johns Hopkins University Press, 1976), p. 114.

15. Alexandre Kojève, *Introduction to the Reading of Hegel: Lectures on the* Phenomenology of Spirit, assembled by Raymond Queneau, edited by Allan Bloom, translated by James H. Nichols, Jr. (Ithaca: Cornell University Press, 1980, 1989), p. 162; emphasis in the original. Barthes's reading of Japan is found in his *Empire of Signs*, trans. Richard Howard (New York: Hill and Wang, 1982). For a discussion of Kojève's conception of Japan's "post-historic" condition, see Masao Miyoshi and H. D. Harootunian, "Introduction: Postmodernism and Japan," *South Atlantic Quarterly* 87.3 (Summer 1988): 392–94. (This special issue is now the book *Postmodernism and Japan*, ed. Masao Miyoshi and H. D. Harootunian [Durham: Duke University Press, 1989].) In his *Suicidal Narrative in Modern Japan: The Case of Dazai Osamu* (Princeton: Princeton University Press, 1990), Alan Wolfe offers an astute reading of Kojève's problematic pronouncement and its Orientalist assumptions against the complex background of modern Japanese literature and culture. See especially pp. 216–17 and 220–22 of Wolfe's book.

16. Michel Serres, *Detachment*, trans. Genevieve James and Raymond Federman (Athens: Ohio University Press, 1989), p. 5.

17. Serres, *Detachment*, p. 6.

18. Serres, *Detachment*, p. 5.

19. "However impeccably the content of an 'other' culture may be known, however anti-ethnocentrically it is represented, it is its location as the 'closure' of grand theories, the demand that, in analytic terms, it be always the 'good' object of knowledge, the docile body of difference, that reproduces a relation of domination and is the most serious indictment of the institutional powers of critical theory." Homi K. Bhabha, "The Commitment to Theory," in *Questions of Third Cinema*, ed. Jim Pines and Paul Willemen (London: British Film Institute, 1989), p. 124; emphasis in the original.

20. Gayatri Spivak, "Can the Subaltern Speak?" in Cary Nelson and Lawrence Grossberg, eds., *Marxism and the Interpretation of Culture* (Urbana: University of Illinois Press, 1988), p. 308. The Spivak of this essay is very different from the one who speaks of "envy" on behalf of the silent Chinese women in "French Feminism in an International Frame," precisely because she does not read the subaltern in Oedipalized terms.

21. Benita Parry, "Problems in Current Theories of Colonial Discourse," *Oxford Literary Review* 9.1–2 (1987): 35.

22. Parry, "Problems," pp. 39–43. Bhabha's view is expressed in many of his essays. See, for instance, "The Other Question: The Stereotype and Colonial Discourse," *Screen* 24.6 (1983); "Of Mimicry and Man: The Ambivalence of Colonial Discourse," *October* 28 (Spring 1984); "Signs Taken for Wonders: Questions of Ambivalence and Authority under a Tree outside Delhi, May 1817," in *"Race," Writing, and Difference*, ed. Henry Louis Gates, Jr. (Chicago: University of Chicago Press, 1985, 1986), pp. 163–84. (The essays in the Gates volume were originally published in *Critical Inquiry* 12.1 [Autumn 1985] and 13.1 [Autumn 1986].) See also "DissemiNation: Time, Narrative, and the Margins of the Modern Nation," in *Nation and Narration*, ed. Homi K. Bhabha (London: Routledge, 1990), pp. 291–322.

23. Spivak, "Can the Subaltern Speak?" p. 308.

24. Spivak, "Can the Subaltern Speak?" p. 300. Jean-François Lyotard: "I would like to call a *differend* [*différend*] the case where the plaintiff is divested of the means to argue and becomes for that reason a victim. . . . A case of differend between two parties takes place when the 'regulation' of the conflict that opposes them is done in the idiom of one of the parties while the wrong suffered by the other is not signified in that idiom." See *The Differend: Phrases in Dispute*, trans. Georges Van Den Abbeele (Minneapolis: University of Minnesota Press, 1988), p. 9.

25. Spivak, "The New Historicism: Political Commitment and the Postmodern Critic," *Post-Colonial Critic: Interviews, Strategies, Dialogues*, ed. Sarah Harasym (London: Routledge, 1990), p. 158.

26. Spivak, "Can the Subaltern Speak?" pp. 307–308.

27. Slavoj Žižek, *The Sublime Object of Ideology* (London: Verso, 1989), p. 109.

28. Clifford, *The Predicament of Culture*, p. 5.

29. See, for instance, Sally Price, *Primitive Art in Civilized Places* (Chicago: University of Chicago Press, 1989); Marianna Torgovnick, *Gone Primitive: Savage Intellects, Modern Lives* (Chicago: University of Chicago Press, 1990); the many essays in *Writing Culture: The Poetics and Politics of Ethnography*, ed. James Clifford and George E. Marcus (Berkeley: University of California Press, 1986); and *Anthropology as Cultural Critique: An Experimental Moment in the Human Sciences*, ed. George E. Marcus and Michael M. J. Fischer (Chicago: University of Chicago Press, 1986).

30. Nancy Armstrong, "The Occidental Alice," *differences* 2.2 (Summer 1990): 33.

31. Clifford, *The Predicament of Culture*, p. 12.

32. This is T. S. Eliot's view of the poet's mind when it is "perfectly equipped for its work." See Eliot, "The Metaphysical Poets," *Selected Prose of T. S. Eliot*, edited and with an introduction by Frank Kermode (New York: Harcourt Brace Jovanovich; Farrar, Straus and Giroux, 1975), p. 64. This well-known discussion of the metaphysical poets' relevance to modernity was in part a criticism of Samuel Johnson's remark of them that "the most heterogeneous ideas are yoked by violence together" (Eliot, p. 60).

33. Cf. Lyotard's definition of the *différend*, cited in note 24.

34. Malek Alloula, *The Colonial Harem*, translated by Myrna Godzich and Wlad Godzich, with an introduction by Barbara Harlow (Minneapolis: University of Minnesota Press, 1986). Page references to this book are hereafter indicated in parentheses in the text.

35. Barbara Harlow, "Introduction," *The Colonial Harem*, p. xviii. Spivak's statement, "White men are saving brown women from brown men," is found in "Can the Subaltern Speak?" pp. 296–97. She is describing the British intervention in *sati* (widow sacrifice) in British India, whereby the colonizer attempted to co-opt native women under the pretext of freeing them from oppression by their own men.

36. See a similar criticism made by Winifred Woodhull in "Unveiling Algeria," *Genders* 10 (Spring 1991): 121–26. Because Alloula never really addresses the question of women's interests, Woodhull argues, he ultimately "repeats the gesture of the colonizer by making of the veiled woman the screen on which he projects *his* fantasy . . . of an Algerian nation untroubled by questions of women's oppression" (Woodhull, p. 126; emphasis in the original). See also Mieke Bal, "The Politics of Citation," *diacritics* 21.1 (Spring 1991): 25–45, for an argument about the complicity between the critic of colonial visual practice and colonial exploitation itself. Alloula's book is one of several Bal shows as lacking in a careful critique of the critic's own sexist and colonizing position.

37. Deconstructionist anticolonial critics such as Bhabha have, for instance, elaborated on the "ambivalence" of the image in the following terms: "the image—as point of identification—marks the site of an ambivalence. Its representation is always spatially split—it makes *present* something that is *absent*—and temporally deferred—it is the representation of

a time that is always elsewhere, a repetition. The image is only ever an *appurtenance* to authority and identity; it must never be read mimetically as the 'appearance' of a 'reality'. The access to the image of identity is only ever possible in the *negation* of any sense of originality or plenitude, through the principle of displacement and differentiation (absence/presence; representation/repetition) that always renders it a liminal reality." Bhabha, " 'What Does the Black Man Want?' " p. 120; emphases in the original.

38. For an example of a post-structuralist analysis of how pornography is in the eye of the beholder, see Judith Butler, "The Force of Fantasy: Feminism, Mapplethorpe, and Discursive Excess," *differences* 2.2 (Summer 1990): 105–25.

39. Paul de Man, *Blindness and Insight: Essays in the Rhetoric of Contemporary Criticism*, second edition, revised, with an introduction by Wlad Godzich (Minneapolis: University of Minnesota Press, 1983), p. 148.

40. Clifford, *The Predicament of Culture*, p. 244.

41. Francis Fukuyama, "The End of History?" *The National Interest* (Summer 1989): 18.

42. Arjun Appadurai, "Introduction: Commodities and the Politics of Value," in *The Social Life of Things: Commodities in Cultural Perspective*, ed. Arjun Appadurai (Cambridge: Cambridge University Press, 1986), p. 28.

43. Appadurai, "Introduction," p. 3.

44. *The Essential Frankfurt School Reader*, edited and with introductions by Andrew Arato and Eike Gebhardt (New York: Urizen, 1978), pp. 225–53.

45. *Illuminations*, edited and with an introduction by Hannah Arendt, translated by Harry Zohn (New York: Schocken, 1969), pp. 217–51, 253–64.

46. In the brief introduction to "Eduard Fuchs," the editors of *The Essential Frankfurt School Reader* write: "the presentation of Fuchs, the collector and often crude materialist, must also be read as one of Benjamin's self-presentations, and even as an *apologia pro vita sua* in the face of criticism" (p. 225).

47. Walter Benjamin, "Central Park," trans. Lloyd Spencer with the help of Mark Harrington, *New German Critique* 34 (Winter 1985): 41.

48. Price, *Primitive Art in Civilized Places*, p. 76.

49. Price, *Primitive Art in Civilized Places*, p. 74.

50. "History is the subject of a structure whose site is not homogeneous, empty time, but time filled by the presence of the now [*Jetztzeit*]. Thus, to Robespierre ancient Rome was a past charged with the time of the now which he blasted out of the continuum of history." "The awareness that they are about to make the continuum of history explode is characteristic of the revolutionary classes at the moment of their action." Benjamin, "Theses on the Philosophy of History," XIV and XV, *Illuminations*, p. 261.

51. See also Benjamin's similar argument in "The Author as Producer," *The Essential Frankfurt School Reader*, pp. 254–69.

52. J. Hillis Miller, "The Work of Cultural Criticism in the Age of Dig-

ital Reproduction." Page references to this essay are from the manuscript. Miller's reading of "aura" is post-structuralist. "The fact that the modern work of art is reproducible casts its shadow back not just to remove the aura from traditional works but to reveal that aura was always an ideological formation. That is what Benjamin means by saying film in itself, as a means of mechanical reproduction, is revolutionary criticism of traditional concepts of art. As the technological changes Benjamin describes have proceeded apace, the opposition between traditional man or woman and the masses disappears and with it the pertinence of the idea of a people with a specific culture. We are all to some degree members of what Benjamin invidiously calls the 'masses.' We are members of a transnational, multilinguistic, worldwide technological culture that makes the pieties of nationalism seem more and more outdated, nostalgic, perhaps even dangerously reactionary" (p. 10). Modified and extended versions of Miller's essay are forthcoming in *Genre* and in Miller's book *Illustration*.

53. "The problem with all Benjamin's symmetrical oppositions is that they tend to dissolve through the effort of thinking they facilitate." Miller, "The Work of Cultural Criticism," p. 10.

54. Miller, "The Work of Cultural Criticism," p. 18.

55. Miller, "The Work of Cultural Criticism," pp. 19–20.

56. The notion of a radical "antagonism" that structures sociality by making it incapable of self-identification or closure is argued by Ernesto Laclau and Chantal Mouffe, *Hegemony and Socialist Strategy: Towards a Radical Democratic Politics*, trans. Winston Moore and Paul Cammack (London: Verso, 1985). See especially chapter 3, "Beyond the Positivity of the Social: Antagonisms and Hegemony."

57. Jean-Jacques Rousseau, *A Discourse on Inequality*, translated and with an introduction by Maurice Cranston (London: Penguin, 1984), p. 136.

58. Gilles Deleuze and Félix Guattari make a comparable point when they, criticizing Freudian psychoanalysis as an anthropomorphic representation of sex, equate Lacan's "big Other" with what they call "nonhuman sex." See *Anti-Oedipus: Capitalism and Schizophrenia*, Preface by Michel Foucault, translated by Robert Hurley, Mark Seem, and Helen R. Lane (Minneapolis: University of Minnesota Press, 1983), pp. 295, 308–10. Deleuze and Guattari's notion of "part objects" or "partial objects" is, of course, very different. They are not "part" of any "whole," but molecular machinic flows and breaks.

59. I take this phrase from Abdul R. JanMohamed, *Manichean Aesthetics: The Politics of Literature in Colonial Africa* (Amherst: University of Massachusetts Press, 1983).

60. Bhabha, " 'What Does the Black Man Want?' " p. 121.

61. In Saussure, the linguistic sign (made up of a relationship between signifier and signified) is arbitrary because it is conventional—in the sense that it works only within a system of differences.

62. This chapter was completed in mid-1991. The subsequent verdict on the King beating (that the policemen were "not guilty") demonstrated once again the dominant culture's ability to manipulate images to its own advan-

tage by sabotaging the witnessing function crucial to any "evidence" of abuse. Once it succeeds in divorcing the act of witnessing from the image, the dominant culture can appoint itself as the "true" witness whose observation and interpretation of the image is held as the most accurate and just one. The Rodney King video and the racial riots that followed the verdict thus became "evidence" not for the historical white discrimination against blacks but for how necessary that discrimination is!

63. Brian Spooner, "Weavers and Dealers: The Authenticity of an Oriental Carpet," in *The Social Life of Things*, ed. Arjun Appadurai, p. 226.

64. Jonathan Elmer, review of Slavoj Žižek, *The Sublime Object of Ideology, Qui Parle* 4.1 (Fall 1990): 122.

65. Žižek, "How the Non-Duped Err," *Qui Parle* 4.1 (Fall 1990): 3. Žižek quotes the Freudian joke about Polish Jews often mentioned by Lacan: "one of them asks the other in an offended tone: 'Why are you telling me that you are going to Lemberg, when you are really going to Lemberg?' " (p. 3). See also Žižek, *The Sublime Object of Ideology*, p. 197.

66. Žižek, "How the Non-Duped Err," p. 12.

3. Postmodern Automatons

1. I am grateful to Amitava Kumar and Peter Canning for their comments on an early version of this chapter.

2. Jameson, "Postmodernism and Consumer Society," in *The Anti-Aesthetic: Essays on Postmodern Culture*, edited and with an introduction by Hal Foster (Port Townsend: Bay Press, 1983), p. 112.

3. Ross, ed., *Universal Abandon? The Politics of Postmodernism* (Minneapolis: University of Minnesota Press, 1988).

4. Introduction to *South Atlantic Quarterly* 87.3 (Summer 1988) (special issue on postmodernism and Japan): 388.

5. I argue this in the context of modern Chinese literature in "Mandarin Ducks and Butterflies: A Response to the 'Postmodern' Condition," *Cultural Critique*, no. 5 (Winter 1986–87): 69–93.

6. See, for instance, Daryl McGowan Tress's response (*Signs* 14.1 [1988]: 200) to Jane Flax's "Postmodernism and Gender Relations in Feminist Theory" (*Signs* 12.4 [Summer 1987]: 621–43): "Postmodernism, with its 'deep skepticism' and 'radical doubts' is not the medicine required to cure intellectual and social life of the afflictions of various orthodoxies (e.g., Marxist, Enlightenment, Freudian). What is sorely needed instead of theory that denies the self and integrity or reason is theory that permits us to achieve appropriate and intelligent trust in the self and in its various abilities to come to know what is real."

7. See Kenneth Frampton, "Towards a Critical Regionalism: Six Points for an Architecture of Resistance," in Foster, pp. 16–30.

8. Frazer and Nicholson, "Social Criticism without Philosophy: An Encounter between Feminism and Postmodernism," in Ross, pp. 88, 90.

9. Hayden White's argument about history in *Tropics of Discourse:*

Essays in Cultural Criticism (Baltimore: Johns Hopkins University Press, 1978) remains exemplary in this regard.

10. Craig Owens, "The Discourse of Others: Feminists and Postmodernism," in Foster, p. 58.

11. George Yúdice, "Marginality and the Ethics of Survival," in Ross, p. 215.

12. See Naomi Schor's argument in "Dreaming Dissymmetry: Barthes, Foucault, and Sexual Difference," in Alice Jardine and Paul Smith, eds., *Men in Feminism* (New York: Methuen, 1987), pp. 98–110.

13. In Ross, pp. 91, 102. The phrase "endless variety and monotonous similarity" is from Gayle Rubin, "The Traffic in Women," in *Toward an Anthropology of Women*, ed. Rayna R. Reiter (New York: Monthly Review Press, 1975), p. 160.

14. This notion is Walter Benjamin's.

15. A similar point can be made about pornography. Attacks on pornography that focus only on its abuse of women cannot deal with the question why pornography always exists.

16. James Smith, *Melodrama* (London: Methuen, 1973), p. 18.

17. Freud, *Jokes and Their Relation to the Unconscious*, trans. and ed. James Strachey (New York: Norton, 1963), p. 193.

18. Freud, *Jokes*, p. 195.

19. Freud, "The 'Uncanny,' " *Collected Papers*, vol. IV (London: Hogarth Press, 1946), pp. 368–407.

20. Freud, "The 'Uncanny,' " p. 385 (note 1).

21. De Lauretis, "The Violence of Rhetoric: Considerations on Representation and Gender," *Semiotica* 54.1–2 (1985), special issue on "The Rhetoric of Violence," ed. Nancy Armstrong; rpt. in *Technologies of Gender: Essays on Theory, Film, and Fiction* (Bloomington: Indiana University Press, 1987), pp. 31–50, and in *The Violence of Representation: Literature and the History of Violence*, ed. Nancy Armstrong and Leonard Tennenhouse (London: Routledge, 1989).

22. Huyssen, *After the Great Divide: Modernism, Mass Culture, Postmodernism* (Bloomington: Indiana University Press, 1986), p. 53.

23. Huyssen, *After the Great Divide*, p. 46.

24. See especially Baudrillard, *In the Shadow of the Silent Majorities or the End of the Social and Other Essays*, trans. Paul Foss, Paul Patton, and John Johnston (New York: Semiotext(e), 1983), and *Simulations*, trans. Paul Foss, Paul Patton, and Philip Beitchman (New York: Semiotext(e), 1983).

25. Huyssen, *After the Great Divide*, p. 62.

26. Cixous, "Fiction and Its Phantoms: A Reading of Freud's *Das Unheimliche* (The 'Uncanny')," *New Literary History* 7.3: 538; emphasis in the original.

27. Donna Haraway, "A Manifesto for Cyborgs: Science, Technology, and Socialist Feminism in the 1980s," *Socialist Review*, no. 80 (March–April 1985); rpt. in Elizabeth Weed, ed., *Coming to Terms: Feminism, Theory, Politics* (London: Routledge, 1989), pp. 173–204.

28. De Lauretis deals with this problem by reintroducing narrative. See

especially her chapter on "Imaging" in *Alice Doesn't: Feminism, Semiotics, Cinema* (Bloomington: Indiana University Press, 1984). Neil Hertz makes a similar argument about Freud's reading of Hoffmann by showing the necessity of "literature" for "psychoanalysis": "we know that the relation between figurative language and what it figures cannot be adequately grasped in metaphors of vision. . . . " See "Freud and the Sandman," in *Textual Strategies: Perspectives in Post-Structuralist Criticism*, edited and with an introduction by Josué V. Harari (Ithaca: Cornell University Press, 1979), p. 320.

29. Freud, *Jokes*, p. 194.

30. Spivak, "The Political Economy of Women as Seen by a Literary Critic," in Weed, p. 220.

31. Spivak, "The Political Economy of Women," p. 221; emphases in the original.

32. Schor, *Reading in Detail: Aesthetics and the Feminine* (London: Methuen, 1987), p. 97.

33. Weed, "Introduction: Terms of Reference," in Weed, pp. xvii–xviii.

34. Lyotard, "Presentations," in *Philosophy in France Today*, ed. Alan Montefiore (Cambridge: Cambridge University Press, 1983), p. 133; quoted by Warren Montag, "What Is at Stake in the Debate on Postmodernism?" in E. Ann Kaplan, ed., *Postmodernism and Its Discontents: Theories, Practices* (London: Verso, 1988), p. 91.

35. See Haraway, "Cyborgs"; Ebert, "The Romance of Patriarchy: Ideology, Subjectivity, and Postmodern Feminist Cultural Theory," *Cultural Critique*, no. 10 (Fall 1988): 19–57.

36. " . . . women's insistence on difference and incommensurability may not only be compatible with, but also an instance of postmodern thought." In Foster, pp. 61–62.

37. See Flax, "Postmodernism and Gender Relations," p. 638.

38. Weed, "Introduction: Terms of Reference," in Weed, p. xxiv.

4. Pedagogy, Trust, Chinese Intellectuals in the 1990s

1. A Cheng, "Haizi wang," in *A Cheng xiaoshuo* (Taipei: Haifeng chubanshe youxian gongsi, 1988), p. 194. All translations from this story are mine.

2. A Cheng, "Haizi wang," p. 203.

3. A Cheng, "Haizi wang," pp. 211–12.

4. Roland Barthes, *Mythologies*, selected and translated from the French by Annette Lavers (London: Paladin, 1972), p. 109; emphasis in the original.

5. Barthes, *Mythologies*, pp. 145–46; emphases in the original.

6. A Cheng, "Haizi wang," p. 192.

7. The issues of gender raised by the interactions of Lao Gan, Laidi, and Wang Fu require a much more detailed discussion than can be provided here. They are the focus of my essay, "Male Narcissism and National Culture: Subjectivity in Chen Kaige's *King of the Children*," *camera obscura* 25/26 (1991): 9–41.

8. Contrast this with the much more extreme and deconstructive view of Chen Kaige, who made the film *King of the Children* (1987) from A Cheng's story and who sees copying as the summation of the emptiness of culture: "Culture is precisely this: it's a matter of copying." See Chen Wanying, "Interview with Chen Kaige, Director of *King of the Children* and *Yellow Earth*," in the Chinese edition of *Playboy* 22 (May 1988): 42–51. Chen's notion of copying is part of a complex understanding of the meaning of repetition in post-technological mass production in a "backward" "third world" nation. I argue this in the essay "Silent Is the Ancient Plain: Music, Film-Making, and the Conception of Reform in China's New Cinema," *Discourse* 12.2 (Spring 1990): 82–109.

9. For a succinct discussion of the problem of reflection in Marxist literary criticism, see Pierre Macherey and Etienne Balibar, "Literature as an Ideological Form: Some Marxist Propositions," *Praxis: A Journal of Cultural Criticism*, no. 5 (1981): 43–58.

10. Liu Xiaobo, "Zhongguo dangdai zhishifenzi yu zhengzhi," *Cheng Ming*, no. 137 (March 1989): 68–71. This is the first part of a longer essay. All translations are mine.

11. The Chinese term is consistently *zhuanzhi zhuyi*, which is sometimes translated as "authoritarianism" rather than "despotism."

12. Liu, "Zhongguo dangdai zhishifenzi," p. 69.

13. Liu, "Zhongguo dangdai zhishifenzi," p. 69.

14. Sandra Burton, "One Year Later," *Time*, June 4, 1990: 60.

15. Liu, "Zhongguo dangdai zhishifenzi," pp. 70–71.

16. Tsao Hsing-yuan: "I know a Party hack who at the beginning of the protest cursed the students as troublemakers. When the hunger strike started, he said: 'The Communist Party is not afraid of these kinds of threats. We couldn't care less if someone dies.' Then, I saw him again on the morning of June 4 in front of the Union Medical Hospital. His eyes were red with tears; he was very emotional and kept saying: 'They really opened fire! They did it! I can't believe the Party would do such a thing.' He felt totally betrayed. This tragedy awakened many people as well." See the interview with Chinese intellectuals called "The Hopes of China," *Mother Jones* (December 1989): 26.

17. This imperative to cultivate one's self appears in *Daxue (The Great Learning)*, one of the *Four Books*. As in the case of many Chinese idioms, the concept of *xiushen* is "traditional" not so much because it originated in a specific ancient text as because it is a familiar part of popular usage.

18. I take this phrase from Carol Lee Hamrin and Timothy Cheek, eds., *China's Establishment Intellectuals* (Armonk, New York: M. E. Sharpe, Inc., 1986).

19. See Richard Kraus, "Bai Hua: The Political Authority of a Writer," and Vera Schwarcz, "Afterword," in *China's Establishment Intellectuals*, pp. 185–211, 249–50. In Fall 1989 I attended a speech by Liu Binyan at the "Voices of China" Conference at the University of Minnesota. Like many Chinese people after the Tiananmen Massacre, Liu has clearly abandoned his loyalty to the current regime.

20. Nadine Gordimer, "A Writer's Freedom," *Index on Censorship*, 1976; reprinted in George Theiner, ed., *They Shoot Writers, Don't They?* (London: Faber and Faber, 1984), p. 135.

21. Wei Jingsheng, "Yao minzhu haishi yao xin de ducai," reprinted in *Cheng Ming*, no. 137 (March 1989), pp. 29–31. All translations are mine. An extract from Wei's unpublished autobiography, written in prison, appeared in *Index on Censorship* in 1981 and was reprinted under the title "Searching for the Truth," trans. Peter Harris, in Theiner, ed., pp. 74–83.

22. Wei, "Yao minzhu," p. 31.

23. Wei, "Yao minzhu," p. 30; my emphasis.

24. Wei, "Yao minzhu," p. 31.

25. Orville Schell, "China's Andrei Sakharov," *The Atlantic Monthly* (May 1988): 42.

26. See *Cheng Ming*, no. 137 (March 1989); *Jiushi niandai (The Nineties)* (March 1989). For an account in English, see Schell, "An Act of Defiance," *New York Times Magazine* (April 16, 1989): 27, 30, 43.

27. Schell, "China's Andrei Sakharov," p. 42.

28. John Israel, "Foreword," *China's Establishment Intellectuals*, p. x.

29. Israel, "Foreword," *China's Establishment Intellectuals*, p. xv.

30. Ralph Miliband, "Reflections on the Crisis of Communist Regimes," *New Left Review*, no. 177 (September/October 1989): 35.

31. Lu Yuan, "Beijing Diary," *New Left Review*, no. 177 (September/October 1989): 7.

32. Since this chapter was first completed in December 1989, some changes have occurred. In June 1990, Fang and his wife, Li Shuxian, were allowed to leave China after signing an affidavit to the effect that they would not criticize the Chinese government. As a visiting scholar, Fang went first to Cambridge University, England, and then to the Institute for Advanced Study in Princeton, New Jersey. In October 1991, Fang received the Sidney Hook Memorial Award from the National Association of Scholars [*sic*] in Minneapolis for championing intellectual freedom. Wei was reported to have been transferred from Qinghai to a labor camp in Hebei Province and is supposedly "in good health." *Ming Pao Daily News*, Vancouver Edition, July 10, 1991, p. 8.

33. Ernesto Laclau and Chantal Mouffe, *Hegemony and Socialist Strategy: Towards a Radical Democratic Politics*, trans. Winston Moore and Paul Cammack (London: Verso, 1985), p. 190; my emphasis.

34. I discuss this in greater detail in "Violence in the Other Country: China as Crisis, Spectacle, and Woman," in Chandra Talpade Mohanty et al., eds., *Third World Women and the Politics of Feminism* (Bloomington: Indiana University Press, 1991), pp. 81–100.

35. See, for instance, Mikhail Bakhtin, *Problems of Dostoyevsky's Poetics*, edited and translated by Caryl Emerson, introduction by Wayne C. Booth (Minneapolis: University of Minnesota Press, 1984).

36. Laclau and Mouffe, *Hegemony and Socialist Strategy*, p. 96; emphasis in the original.

37. Laclau and Mouffe, *Hegemony and Socialist Strategy*, p. 109.

38. Laclau and Mouffe, *Hegemony and Socialist Strategy*, p. 113; emphasis in the original.

39. Private conversation with C. H. Chow, my father.

40. Hu Kan, " 'Zhiyou zhongguo cai neng jiu shehui zhuyi,' " *Ming Pao Daily News*, Vancouver Edition, December 13, 1989, p. 1.

41. Laclau and Mouffe, *Hegemony and Socialist Strategy*, p. 182.

42. The subject matter of this chapter is such that what is argued here is by necessity incomplete. I am grateful to Kwan-man Kwok, Yao-chung Li, Kwai-cheung Lo, Austin Meredith, and Ming-bao Yue for their comments and criticisms.

5. Against the Lures of Diaspora

1. "Genitalism," per Gayatri Spivak, is the attitude that "depending on what kind of genitals you have, you can or cannot speak in certain situations." "Questions of Multi-culturalism," *The Post-Colonial Critic: Interviews, Strategies, Dialogues*, ed. Sarah Harasym (London: Routledge, 1990), p. 62.

2. Abdul R. JanMohamed and David Lloyd, "Introduction: Minority Discourse—What Is to Be Done?" *Cultural Critique*, no. 7 (Fall 1987): 7.

3. Nativism is not necessarily an attitude held by "natives." Scholars who study a particular culture can espouse nativism as a way to fence off disciplinary territories, and this often happens in non-Western fields such as Asian studies. For an extended argument on this point, see the next chapter.

4. I have in mind Allan Bloom, *The Closing of the American Mind* (New York: Simon & Schuster, 1987), and E. D. Hirsch, Jr., *Cultural Literacy* (Boston: Houghton Mifflin, 1987).

5. In his study of the history of Chinese communism, Arif Dirlik shows that, beginning in the earliest period of their acquaintance with the ideas of Marx, the Chinese Communists have tended to be most fascinated with what is arguably Marx's most problematic area—his economism. See Dirlik, *The Origins of Chinese Communism* (Oxford: Oxford University Press, 1989), especially chapters 2 through 6.

6. Arif Dirlik, "Culturalism as Hegemonic Ideology and Liberating Practice," *Cultural Critique*, no. 6 (Spring 1987): 37.

7. Gayatri Spivak, "Can the Subaltern Speak?" in Cary Nelson and Lawrence Grossberg, eds., *Marxism and the Interpretation of Culture* (Urbana: University of Illinois Press, 1988), pp. 271–313.

8. For an argument of this predicament characterizing minority discourse, see Abdul R. JanMohamed, *Manichean Aesthetics: The Politics of Literature in Colonial Africa* (Amherst: University of Massachusetts Press, 1983).

9. Gayatri Spivak, "The New Historicism: Political Commitment and the Postmodern Critic," *The Post-Colonial Critic*, p. 158.

10. *Confucian Analects*, Chapter III, 5, 7; *The Four Books: The Great Learning, The Doctrine of the Mean, Confucian Analects, and The Works*

of Mencius, with English translation and notes by James Legge (Taipei: Culture Book Co., 1973), p. 298; emphases in the translation.

11. Slavoj Žižek, *The Sublime Object of Ideology* (London: Verso, 1989), p. 95.

12. Žižek, *Sublime Object*, p. 98.

13. As I am writing this in April 1991, a controversy over the ethics of naming rape victims has just broken out across the U.S. media. The immediate cause is the naming by several news institutions (*The Globe*, NBC, and *The New York Times*) of the female victim in an alleged case of rape by a member of the Kennedy family. The pros and cons of whether the victim should be named touch on individual rights to privacy, media consumer needs, the dissemination of news for financial profit, abuses suffered by rape victims at legal proceedings, and more, all of which have to do with social relationships rather than with the pure act of naming itself.

14. Kwai-cheung Lo, "The Real in Lacan: Some Reflections on 'Chinese Symptoms,' " *Polygraph*, no. 4 (1990–91): 86–87.

15. "With great trepidation I would say that Marxism in fact is a critical philosophy. Its transformation into a substantive philosophy, a utopian philosophy that can be adequately represented by revolution and social reform has been in fact a centrist mistake." Spivak, "The *Intervention* Interview," *The Post-Colonial Critic*, p. 131.

16. Fredric Jameson, "Third-World Literature in the Era of Multinational Capital," *Social Text*, no. 15 (Fall 1986): 69.

17. See Spivak's discussion of this point in "The New Historicism," pp. 161–62.

18. Nancy Armstrong, *Desire and Domestic Fiction: A Political History of the Novel* (Oxford: Oxford University Press, 1987), p. 8.

19. Quoted in Juliet Mitchell, *Psychoanalysis and Feminism* (New York: Vintage Books, 1975), p. 416.

20. Kwai-cheung Lo, "The Real in Lacan," p. 89.

21. Spivak, "The New Historicism," p. 158.

22. Spivak, "The New Historicism," p. 156.

23. *Xin Bao/Overseas Chinese Economic Journal* (the U.S. edition of *The Hong Kong Economic Journal*), January 1991.

24. Writing about colonial India, Ranajit Guha uses the term "elite" to describe the dominant social groups, made up of "mainly British officials of the colonial state and foreign industrialists, merchants, financiers, planters, landlords and missionaries," on the one hand, and of powerful indigenous elements at the "all-India" and the "regional and local" levels, on the other. See "On Some Aspects of the Historiography of Colonial India," *Subaltern Studies I: Writings on South Asian History and Society*, ed. Ranajit Guha (Delhi: Oxford University Press, 1986), p. 8. Spivak, while defining the "subaltern" as "all that is not elite" ("The New Historicism," p. 158), points also to the "gendered subaltern" as being paradigmatic of the subaltern subject ("Practical Politics of the Open End," *The Post-Colonial Critic*, p. 103). Because education traditionally plays such an important role in determining class difference in Chinese society, I think the relation

between the "elite" and the "subaltern" in China needs to be formulated *primarily* in terms of the way education and gender work together.

25. The conference "Sexuality and Gender in Twentieth-Century Chinese Literature and Society" at the University of Iowa, March 1991, and the panel "Gender, Class, and Twentieth-Century Chinese Fiction" at the Annual Meeting of the Association for Asian Studies, New Orleans, April 1991.

26. *Hegel's* Phenomenology of Spirit, trans. A. V. Miller, with analysis of the text and foreword by J. N. Findlay (New York: Oxford University Press, 1977), pp. 54–55; emphases in the original.

27. The extensiveness of the philosophical, political, and feminist arguments about "essentialism" is such that I can merely point to it here. Two recent publications readers can consult are Diana Fuss, *Essentially Speaking* (New York: Routledge, 1989), and *differences* 1.2 (Summer 1989), a special issue on essentialism.

28. "In 'woman' I see something that cannot be represented, something that is not said, something above and beyond nomenclatures and ideologies." Kristeva, "Woman Can Never Be Defined," trans. Marilyn A. August, in Elaine Marks and Isabelle de Courtivron, eds., *New French Feminisms* (New York: Schocken Books, 1981), p. 137.

29. I want to acknowledge those who have contributed to the final version of this chapter. I have benefited from comments made by Wendy Larson and Lydia Liu at the conferences at Iowa and in New Orleans. Continual discussions with Kwai-cheung Lo, Tonglin Lu, and Ming-bao Yue about this chapter and other related issues give me the support of a strong critical community. Most of all, I am indebted to Yu-shih Chen for a forceful and enabling critique, which made me restate my concerns with a clarity that had been previously missing.

6. The Politics and Pedagogy of Asian Literatures in American Universities

1. This was the theme of *differences* 2.3 (Fall 1990), in which this chapter was first published.

2. Pauline Yu, "Alienation Effects: Comparative Literature and the Chinese Tradition," in *The Comparative Perspective on Literature: Approaches to Theory and Practice*, edited and with an introduction by Clayton Koelb and Susan Noakes (Ithaca: Cornell University Press, 1988), p. 162. Yu defines "mutual parochialism" in terms of the difficulties facing someone attempting to study Chinese literature from a comparative perspective. These include the impatience of scholars of Western literatures who often consider the linguistic and cultural differences too profound to make any serious comparative study meaningful, and the hostility of sinologists who distrust anyone who claims to "know about China *and* something else as well" (emphasis in the original).

3. Wlad Godzich, "Emergent Literature and the Field of Comparative Literature," in *The Comparative Perspective on Literature*, p. 22.

4. The dismissal of Edward Said's account of Orientalism by some si-

nologists is typical of the ideology of "nativist elitism" described here. See, for instance, Simon Leys, "Orientalism and Sinology," in *The Burning Forest: Essays on Chinese Culture and Politics* (New York: Holt, Rinehart and Winston, 1986), pp. 95–99. Leys, a French sinologist, speaks as someone steeped in knowledge about the Chinese culture. While he shows some humility toward the "natives" (since he regards the Chinese as his teachers), Leys's attack on Said's work clearly indicates that he is not merely "protecting" the Chinese. What comes across strongly in his brief essay is an arrogant sense of disdain, often encountered in European intellectuals, toward the U.S. and the American university, of which Said, the critic of European Orientalism, is viewed as a representative.

5. Edward Said, "Raymond Schwab and the Romance of Ideas," in *The World, the Text, and the Critic* (Cambridge, Mass.: Harvard University Press, 1983), p. 264.

6. Hal Foster, "Postmodernism: A Preface," *The Anti-Aesthetic: Essays on Postmodern Culture*, edited and with an introduction by Hal Foster (Port Townsend: Bay Press, 1983), p. xii.

7. Godzich, "The Culture of Illiteracy," *enclitic* 8.1-2 (Spring/Fall 1984): 29.

8. Said, "Opponents, Audiences, Constituencies and Community," in Foster, p. 137; emphasis in the original.

9. This is the basic argument made by Benjamin I. Schwartz, "Presidential Address: Area Studies as a Critical Discipline," *Journal of Asian Studies* XL.1 (November 1980): 15–25. In what is a defense of area studies against Said's attack on area studies as a mode of intellectual imperialism, Schwartz cites the "desire to communicate" (p. 15) as the reason for the multidisciplinary makeup of area studies programs. Area specialists "do aspire to achieve a complex and deep understanding of other societies, cultures, and historic experiences" (p. 25). I have two major difficulties with Schwartz's argument. First, I cannot agree with his view that area specialists are, like historians, "humble gatherers of facts" (page 17 and *passim*). Second, given the fact that area specialists should be comparative and interdisciplinary by inclination, why would "theory" present such a problem for them? Though it is an issue specially raised by Schwartz, the conflict between theoreticians and "humble gatherers of facts" is not, to my mind, sufficiently politicized. As I indicate throughout this chapter, that conflict has much to do with what, in spite of claims of interdisciplinarity, remains the untheorized stable point of reference for area specialists—the notion of a fixed geographical "area" itself.

10. Gayatri Chakravorty Spivak, "Reading the World: Literary Studies in the Eighties," in *In Other Worlds: Essays in Cultural Politics* (London: Methuen, 1987), p. 95.

11. Said, "Opponents," p. 153; emphasis in the original.

12. Hsia, "Chinese Novels and American Critics: Reflections on Structure, Tradition, and Satire," in Peter H. Lee, ed., *Critical Issues in East Asian Literature* (Seoul: International Cultural Society of Korea, 1983), p. 179.

13. Spivak, "The Political Economy of Women as Seen by a Literary

Critic," in Elizabeth Weed, ed., *Coming to Terms: Feminism, Theory, Politics* (New York: Routledge, 1989), p. 228.

14. Spivak, "Reading the World," p. 100.

15. Barbara Harlow, *Resistance Literature* (London: Methuen, 1987), p. 14.

16. Nathan Glazer, "The Emergence of an American Ethnic Pattern," in Ronald Takaki, ed., *From Different Shores: Perspectives on Race and Ethnicity in America* (New York: Oxford University Press, 1987), p. 23.

17. Vine Deloria, Jr., "Identity and Culture," in Ronald Takaki, ed., *From Different Shores*, p. 101.

18. Stuart Hall, "Minimal Selves," in ICA Document 6: *Identity* (1987): 44.

19. Spivak, "Reading the World," p. 97.

20. See, for instance, Trinh T. Minh-ha, "Difference: 'A Special Third World Women Issue,' " *Discourse* 8 (Fall–Winter 1986–87): 11–37.

21. See Harlow, *Resistance Literature*.

22. I am indebted for an insightful discussion of "translation" to Kwai-cheung Lo, "Crossing Boundaries: A Study of Modern Hong Kong Fiction from the Fifties to the Eighties" (M. Phil. Dissertation, University of Hong Kong, 1990).

23. Hall, "Minimal Selves," p. 44.

24. Said, "Opponents," p. 157.

25. See Deleuze and Guattari, *Kafka: Toward a Minor Literature*, trans. Dana Polan, foreword by Réda Bensmaïa (Minneapolis: University of Minnesota Press, 1986).

26. Hall, "Minimal Selves," p. 46.

7. Listening Otherwise, Music Miniaturized

1. "Comrade Lover" ("Airen tongzhi"), theme song of a film of the same name, music and lyrics by Luo Dayou, published by Praiseplan Ltd., Hong Kong, 1989. The translation is mine.

2. *Inscriptions* 5 (1989). "Traveling Theory" is the title of a chapter in Edward Said's *The World, the Text, and the Critic* (Cambridge, Mass.: Harvard University Press, 1983), pp. 226–47. Said means by "traveling theory" the borrowing of ideas between persons, situations, and time periods.

3. Theodor Adorno, *Philosophy of Modern Music*, trans. Anne G. Mitchell and Wesley V. Blomster (New York: The Seabury Press, 1973), p. 200.

4. Raymond Williams uses the term "practical consciousness" to refer to areas of experience which fall outside the attention and hence, by implication, the absolute control of the dominant culture. See *Marxism and Literature* (Oxford: Oxford University Press, 1971), p. 125.

5. Adorno's position on mass culture is one that requires a more lengthy discussion than I can provide here. A recent article on this topic I find very interesting is Thomas Y. Levin's "For the Record: Adorno on Music in the Age of Its Technological Reproducibility," *October* 55 (Winter 1990): 23–47. (See also the articles by Adorno in the same issue.) Levin shows that

in his writings on the gramophone and the phonograph record, Adorno was formulating a position on mechanical reproduction that was much closer to Walter Benjamin's than most critics are hitherto led to believe. Levin argues that Adorno was advocating "gramophonic montage" and that his ideological critique of the culture industry and its commodification of popular culture is in fact inseparable from his fascination with and call for a dialectical interpretation of mechanical reproducibility (an interpretation Adorno first associated with the techniques of mass produced music but subsequently also with the techniques of film). However, the careful details of Levin's essay give us an Adorno who was, as always, cultured and refined in the highbrow sense: He was captivated by the new technological forms such as the phonograph record because they were, for him, a materialization of phenomenal events that amounted to a determined but encrypted *trace* or *writing*. Despite its reified and commodified aspects, in other words, the mass musical technology ironically presented Adorno with a supreme example of a *mediated* inscription/performance that he consistently privileged in his notion of progressive art. To this extent at least (i.e., that mass culture is interesting only because its mediatedness requires *contemplation* in such a way as to lead to a discerning and rigorous *cognition* on the part of the critic/consumer), I would contend that the popularized reading of Adorno as "elitist" remains—even if unwittingly—on the mark.

6. Fredric Jameson, "Postmodernism: Or the Cultural Logic of Late Capitalism," *New Left Review*, no. 146 (July/August 1984): 55.

7. Katrina Irving, "Rock Music and the State: Dissonance or Counterpoint?" *Cultural Critique*, no. 10 (Fall 1988): 158.

8. Roland Barthes, "Of What Use Is an Intellectual?" *The Grain of the Voice: Interviews 1962–1980*, trans. Linda Coverdale (New York: Hill and Wang, 1985), p. 268.

9. Mao Dun, "From Guling to Tokyo," trans. Yu-shih Chen, *Bulletin for Concerned Asian Scholars* (Jan.–Mar., 1976): 40.

10. Susan Stewart, *On Longing: Narratives of the Miniature, the Gigantic, the Souvenir, the Collection* (Baltimore: Johns Hopkins University Press, 1984), p. 71.

11. Friedrich Kittler, "The Mechanized Philosopher," *Looking after Nietzsche*, ed. Laurence A. Rickels (Albany: State University of New York Press, 1990), p. 201.

12. Stephen Schiff, "Havel's Choice," *Vanity Fair* (August 1991): 158.

13. Cui Jian did not make any public appearances during the period immediately after the Tiananmen Massacre in 1989. In January 1990, however, he gave a series of concerts in China to raise funds for the Asian Games. The concerts, during which he sang many of his controversial songs, drew extremely large crowds. On the eve of the second anniversary of the Tiananmen Massacre in June 1991, the Chinese authorities again canceled a rock concert in Beijing where Cui Jian was planning to appear. Around the same period he appeared in Hong Kong as part of the concerted effort by musicians and performers to raise funds for China's flood relief.

14. Sun Shen, Vice-President of the Chinese Musicians Association, criticized "Rock and Roll on the Road of the New Long March" in public as "slandering and distorting" the Long March. *Yazhou zhoukan* (Asia Weekly), April 21, 1991, p. 28. This issue of the journal features the recent developments of rock music in Hong Kong, Taiwan, the PRC, and S.E. Asia.

15. Julia Kristeva, *Language—The Unknown: An Initiation into Linguistics*, trans. Anne M. Menke (New York: Columbia University Press, 1989), p. 309; emphases in the original.

16. Lawrence Grossberg, " 'I'd Rather Feel Bad Than Not Feel Anything at All': Rock and Roll, Pleasure and Power," *enclitic* 8.1-2 (Spring/Fall 1984): 101.

17. Grossberg, " 'I'd Rather Feel Bad,' " p. 102.

18. Grossberg, " 'I'd Rather Feel Bad,' " p. 103.

19. In his substantial rereading of Hegel, Slavoj Žižek describes the analysis of religious alienation as developed by Feuerbach in these terms, which are appropriate to an analysis of the Communist state if we substitute the word "collective" for "God": Alienation "means that man presupposes, perceives *himself*, his own creative power, in the form of an external substantial Entity; it means that he 'projects', transposes his innermost essence into an alien Being ('God'). 'God' is thus man himself, the essence of man, the creative movement of mediation, the transforming power of negativity, but perceived in the form of externality, as belonging to some strange Entity existing in itself, independently of man." *The Sublime Object of Ideology* (London: Verso, 1989), p. 225; emphasis in the original. Žižek's analyses of the theoretical pitfalls of Communist ideology are found throughout his book.

20. Zhang Xianliang, *Half of Man Is Woman*, trans. Martha Avery (New York: Norton, 1988), p. 61.

21. Jacques Attali, *Noise: The Political Economy of Music*, trans. Brian Massumi, foreword by Fredric Jameson, afterword by Susan McClary (Minneapolis: University of Minnesota Press, 1985), pp. 134–35.

22. Jean Baudrillard's *For a Critique of the Political Economy of the Sign*, translated and with an introduction by Charles Levin (St. Louis: Telos Press, 1981), remains a helpful critique of the idealism attached to "use" in the classical Marxist understanding of labor.

23. *Yazhou zhoukan*, April 21, 1991, p. 28.

24. Attali, *Noise*, p. 137.

25. Attali, *Noise*, p. 135.

26. Lyrics and music by Luo Dayou; my translation.

27. Luo Dayou, *Queen's Road East* (*Huanghou da dao dong*) production notes, Music Factory, Hong Kong, 1991; my translation.

28. The notion that music is a language with a syntax but no semiotics is Benveniste's, as Barthes mentions at the conclusion to "Rasch," *The Responsibility of Forms: Critical Essays on Music, Art, and Representation*, trans. Richard Howard (New York: Hill and Wang, 1985), p. 311.

29. Hence the regular media accounts of how "decadent" and "Westernized" Chinese youths have become by liking disco dancing, for instance.

30. A recent news report on China indicates the Chinese bureaucracy's wish for "different voices but one 'common' language." Editorial to *Ming Pao Daily News*, Vancouver Edition, March 27, 1990.

31. Muzak, the most obvious example of a "listening otherwise," is always criticized for its effects of blurring distinctions. Its unstoppable flow makes it impossible, precisely, to listen clearly and attentively. However, if we are to look for a contemporary "expression" of the idealist infinity traditionally associated with music, Muzak is exactly that—an infinity, but an infinity vulgarized. What is still lacking in most theories, on the other hand, is not the discussion of how Muzak numbs people, but how the listener operates it.

32. This is the last statement in an ad for the Sony "Discman" in *Esquire*, January 1990.

33. For a nuanced argument about how we cannot understand the contemporary structure of listening (together with the changes in the meaning of "memory" it demands) without understanding the social significance of our reproductive technologies, see John Mowitt, "The Sound of Music in the Era of Its Electronic Reproducibility," in *Music and Society: The Politics of Composition, Performance and Reception*, ed. Richard Leppert and Susan McClary (New York: Cambridge University Press, 1987), pp. 173–97.

34. Iain Chambers, "A Miniature History of the Walkman," *New Formations* 11 (Summer 1990): 1.

35. Chambers, "A Miniature History of the Walkman," p. 3.

36. Adolf Hitler wrote in 1938 in the *Manual of German Radio*: "Without the loudspeaker, we could never have conquered Germany," quoted in Attali, *Noise*, p. 87.

37. Stewart, *On Longing*, p. 55.

38. Stewart, *On Longing*, p. 54; emphasis in the original.

39. Barthes, "Of What Use Is an Intellectual?" p. 268.

40. Adorno, *Introduction to the Sociology of Music*, trans. E. B. Ashton (New York: Continuum, 1989), p. 30.

41. Barthes: "the scandal of individualist positions . . . it's a scandal for every thought and theory since Hegel! Any philosophy that tries to free itself from these collective imperatives is extremely unusual and, I would say, carries a bad trademark." See "On the Subject of Violence," *The Grain of the Voice*, p. 311.

42. "The fascination of the image of the Walkman, apart from the inner secret it brazenly displays in public (what is s/he listening to?), is the ambiguous position that it occupies between autism and autonomy. . . . " Chambers, "A Miniature History of the Walkman," p. 2.

8. Media, Matter, Migrants

1. Paul Virilio and Sylvère Lotringer, *Pure War*, trans. Mark Polizzotti (New York: Semiotext(e), 1983), p. 43. See also Virilio, *Speed and Politics: An Essay on Dromology*, trans. Mark Polizzotti (New York: Semiotext(e), 1977).

2. Paul Virilio, *Popular Defense & Ecological Struggles*, trans. Mark Polizzotti (New York: Semiotext(e), 1990), p. 104.

3. Virilio and Lotringer, *Pure War*, p. 45.

4. Virilio, *Popular Defense*, p. 100.

5. Virilio and Lotringer, *Pure War*, p. 83.

6. For a sustained argument about how modern culture in the West needs to be understood through its visualism, see Johannes Fabian, *Time and the Other: How Anthropology Makes Its Object* (New York: Columbia University Press, 1983).

7. I owe the foregoing analysis to a conversation with Nancy Armstrong.

8. Friedrich A. Kittler, *Discourse Networks 1800/1900*, trans. Michael Metteer, with Chris Cullens, foreword by David E. Wellbery (Stanford: Stanford University Press, 1990); *Gramophone, Film, Typewriter* (English translation forthcoming from the University of Minnesota Press). The references in this essay are drawn exclusively from Kittler, "Gramophone, Film, Typewriter," translated by Dorothea von Mücke with the assistance of Philippe L. Similon, *October* 41 (1987–88): 101–18.

9. See Peter H. Lewis, "A Circus Is on Its Way to the Stores," Science Section, *The New York Times*, May 14, 1991.

10. See Seiichi Kanise, "Grand Illusions," Technology Section, *Time*, June 3, 1991.

11. See Karen de Witt, "How Best to Teach the Blind: A Growing Battle over Braille," *The Sunday New York Times*, May 12, 1991.

12. Kittler, "Gramophone," p. 104.

13. Theodor W. Adorno, "The Form of the Phonograph Record," trans. Thomas Y. Levin, *October* 55 (Winter 1990): 58.

14. Theodor W. Adorno, "The Form of the Phonograph Record," pp. 58 (emphasis in the original), 59.

15. See Henry and Elizabeth Urrows, "Kodak's Photo CD Promised for 1992," *Document Image Automation* 11.2 (March–April 1991): 89–97.

16. See Virilio and Lotringer, *Pure War*, p. 32.

17. See Walter Benjamin, "The Work of Art in the Age of Mechanical Reproduction" and "On Some Motifs in Baudelaire," in *Illuminations*, edited and with an introduction by Hannah Arendt, translated by Harry Zohn (New York: Schocken, 1969), pp. 217–51 and 155–200; "The Author as Producer," in *Reflections: Essays, Aphorisms, Autobiographical Writings*, trans. Edmund Jephcott, edited and with an introduction by Peter Demetz (New York: Schocken, 1986), pp. 220–38.

18. The distinction between the "writerly" and "readerly" texts made by Roland Barthes in the early 1970s (in *S/Z*, for instance) seems in retrospect to be still reliant on an avant-garde, humanistic notion of creativity: The "writerly" text is what an imaginative and nonconforming reader produces in defiance to the familiar notion of a finished "work," while a "readerly" text reproduces the existing social order in conformity with "common sense."

19. For a sampling of Jean Baudrillard, see *The Mirror of Production*, translated and with an introduction by Mark Poster (St. Louis: Telos Press,

1975); *For a Critique of the Political Economy of the Sign*, translated and with an Introduction by Charles Levin (St. Louis: Telos Press, 1981); *In the Shadow of the Silent Majorities, or, the End of the Social and Other Essays*, trans. Paul Foss, John Johnston, and Paul Patton (New York: Semiotext(e), 1983); *Simulations*, trans. Paul Foss, Paul Patton, and Philip Beitchman (New York: Semiotext(e), 1983); *The Ecstasy of Communication*, trans. Bernard and Caroline Schutze (New York: Semiotext(e), 1988); *Seduction*, trans. Brian Singer (New York: St. Martin's Press, 1990).

20. Virilio and Lotringer, *Pure War*, p. 88; Virilio is referring to his argument in *L'Esthétique de la disparition* (Paris: Ballard, 1981).

21. Virilio and Lotringer, *Pure War*, p. 28; emphasis in the original.

22. Victor Shklovsky, "Art as Technique," in *Russian Formalist Criticism: Four Essays*, ed. L. Lemon and M. J. Reis (Lincoln: University of Nebraska Press, 1965), p. 12.

23. Shklovsky, "Art as Technique," p. 23.

24. See Cleanth Brooks, *The Well Wrought Urn* (London: Dobson, 1968).

25. See I. A. Richards, *Practical Criticism* (New York: Harcourt, Brace, 1929); *Principles of Literary Criticism* (New York: Harcourt, Brace, 1925). In what remains a remarkable study of speed culture, *Mythologies*, Roland Barthes writes that modern poetry, precisely because it tries to resist the mediatization of language (what Barthes calls myth), tends to fall prey to it completely: "as in the case of mathematical language, the very resistance offered by poetry makes it an ideal prey for myth: the apparent lack of order of signs, which is the poetic facet of an essential order, is captured by myth, and transformed into an empty signifier, which will serve to *signify* poetry. This explains the improbable character of modern poetry: by fiercely refusing myth, poetry surrenders to it bound hand and foot." See *Mythologies*, selected and translated from the French by Annette Lavers (London: Paladin, 1973), p. 134; emphasis in the original.

26. As is well known, the coming of sound was looked upon with dismay by admirers of silent film. We may explain this as the apprehension that sound, being faster than images, would increasingly naturalize and neutralize the film medium by speed.

27. "Every technology, every science should choose its specific accident, and reveal it as a product . . . to be 'epistemo-technically' questioned. At the end of the nineteenth century, museums exhibited machines; at the end of the twentieth century, I think we must grant the formative dimension of the accident its rightful place in a new museum. They ought to exhibit—I don't know how yet—train derailments, pollution, collapsing buildings, etc. I believe that the accident is to the social sciences what sin is to human nature. It's a certain relation to death, that is, the revelation of the identity of the object." Virilio and Lotringer, *Pure War*, p. 33.

28. Kittler uses the notion of the "alphabetized individual" to refer to a literate person. See "Gramophone," p. 108. This notion applies well to twentieth-century Chinese intellectuals' *modernized* education.

29. Virilio and Lotringer, *Pure War*, p. 89.

30. Alvin Toffler, *Powershift: Knowledge, Wealth, and Violence at the Edge of the 21st Century* (New York: Bantam Books, 1990), p. 406.

31. See Fred Davis, "Electronic Immigrants: Cheap Labor without Green Cards," *PC Week*, June 3, 1991: 142.

32. Virilio, *Popular Defense*, p. 86.

WORKS CITED

A Cheng. "Haizi wang." *A Cheng xiaoshuo*. Taipei: Haifeng chubanshe youxian gongsi, 1988.

Adorno, Theodor W. "The Form of the Phonograph Record." Translated by Thomas Y. Levin. *October* 55 (Winter 1990): 56–61.

———. *Introduction to the Sociology of Music*. Translated by E. B. Ashton. New York: Continuum, 1989.

———. *Philosophy of Modern Music*. Translated by Anne G. Mitchell and Wesley V. Blomster. New York: The Seabury Press, 1973.

Alloula, Malek. *The Colonial Harem*. Translated by Myrna Godzich and Wlad Godzich. Introduction by Barbara Harlow. Minneapolis: University of Minnesota Press, 1986.

Appadurai Arjun. "Introduction: Commodities and the Politics of Value." Appadurai, ed., pp. 3–63.

———, ed. *The Social Life of Things: Commodities in Cultural Perspective*. Cambridge: Cambridge University Press, 1986.

Arato, Andrew, and Eike Gebhardt, eds. *The Essential Frankfurt School Reader*. New York: Urizen, 1978.

Arendt, Hannah, ed. *Illuminations*. Translated by Harry Zohn. New York: Schocken, 1969.

Armstrong, Nancy. *Desire and Domestic Fiction: A Political History of the Novel*. Oxford: Oxford University Press, 1987.

———. "Introduction: Representing Violence, or 'How the West Was Won.' " Armstrong and Tennenhouse, pp. 1–26.

———. "The Occidental Alice." *differences* 2.2 (Summer 1990): 3–40.

———, ed. Special Issue on "The Rhetoric of Violence." *Semiotica* 54.1–2 (1985).

Armstrong, Nancy, and Leonard Tennenhouse, eds. *The Violence of Representation: Literature and the History of Violence*. London: Routledge, 1989.

Attali, Jacques. *Noise: The Political Economy of Music*. Translated by Brian Massumi. Foreword by Fredric Jameson. Afterword by Susan McClary. Minneapolis: University of Minnesota Press, 1985.

Bakhtin, Mikhail. *Problems of Dostoyevsky's Poetics*. Edited and translated by Caryl Emerson. Introduction by Wayne C. Booth. Minneapolis: University of Minnesota Press, 1984.

Bal, Mieke. "The Politics of Citation." *diacritics* 21.1 (Spring 1991): 25–45.

Balandier, G. "The Colonial Situation: A Theoretical Approach (1951)." Translated from the French by Robert A. Wagoner. Wallerstein, pp. 34–61.

Barlow, Tani. "Theorizing Woman: *Funu, Guojia, Jiating* [Chinese

Women, Chinese State, Chinese Family]." *Genders* 10 (Spring 1991): 132–60.

Barthes, Roland. *Empire of Signs*. Translated by Richard Howard. New York: Hill and Wang, 1982.

———. *Mythologies*. Selected and translated from the French by Annette Lavers. London: Paladin, 1972.

———. "On the Subject of Violence" and "Of What Use Is an Intellectual?" *The Grain of the Voice: Interviews 1962–1980*. Translated by Linda Coverdale. New York: Hill and Wang, 1985, pp. 306–11; 258–80.

———. "Rasch." *The Responsibility of Forms: Critical Essays on Music, Art, and Representation*. Translated by Richard Howard. New York: Hill and Wang, 1985, pp. 299–312.

Baudrillard, Jean. *The Ecstasy of Communication*. Translated by Bernard and Caroline Schutze. New York: Semiotext(e), 1988.

———. *For a Critique of the Political Economy of the Sign*. Translated and with an introduction by Charles Levin. St. Louis: Telos Press, 1981.

———. *In the Shadow of the Silent Majorities, or, the End of the Social and Other Essays*. Translated by Paul Foss, Paul Patton, and John Johnston. New York: Semiotext(e), 1983.

———. *The Mirror of Production*. Translated and with an introduction by Mark Poster. St. Louis: Telos Press, 1975.

———. *Seduction*. Translated by Brian Singer. New York: St. Martin's Press, 1990.

———. *Simulations*. Translated by Paul Foss, Paul Patton, and Philip Beitchman. New York: Semiotext(e), 1983.

Benjamin, Walter. "The Author as Producer." *The Essential Frankfurt School Reader*. Edited by Andrew Arato and Eike Gebhardt. Introduction by Paul Piccone. New York: Urizen Books, 1978, pp. 254–69.

———. "The Author as Producer." *Reflections: Essays, Aphorisms, Autobiographical Writings*. Translated by Edmund Jephcott. Edited and with an introduction by Peter Demetz. New York: Schocken, 1986, pp. 220–38.

———. "Central Park." Translated by Lloyd Spencer with the help of Mark Harrington. *New German Critique* 34 (Winter 1985): 32–58.

———. "The Work of Art in the Age of Mechanical Reproduction," "On Some Motifs in Baudelaire," and "Theses on the Philosophy of History." *Illuminations*. Edited and with an introduction by Hannah Arendt. Translated by Harry Zohn. New York: Schocken, 1969, pp. 217–51; 155–200; 253–64.

Bhabha, Homi K. "The Commitment to Theory." Pines and Willemen, pp. 111–32.

———. "DissemiNation: Time, Narrative, and the Margins of the Modern Nation." Bhabha, ed., *Nation and Narration*, pp. 291–322.

———. "Of Mimicry and Man: The Ambivalence of Colonial Discourse." *October* 28 (Spring 1984): 125–33.

———. "The Other Question: The Stereotype and Colonial Discourse." *Screen* 24.6 (November/December 1983): 18–36.

————. "Signs Taken for Wonders: Questions of Ambivalence and Authority under a Tree Outside Delhi, May 1817." Gates, pp. 163–84.

————. " 'What Does the Black Man Want?' " *New Formations* 1 (Spring 1987): 118–24.

————, ed. *Nation and Narration*. London: Routledge, 1990.

Bloom, Allan. *The Closing of the American Mind*. New York: Simon & Schuster, 1987.

Branegan, Jay. "Fighter for a Paper Door." *Time*, May 27, 1991: 26–27.

Brooks, Cleanth. *The Well Wrought Urn*. Revised Edition, London: Dobson, 1968.

Burton, Sandra. "One Year Later." *Time*, June 4, 1990: 58–60.

Butler, Judith. "The Force of Fantasy: Feminism, Mapplethorpe, and Discursive Excess." *differences* 2.2 (Summer 1990): 105–25.

Certeau, Michel de. *The Practice of Everyday Life*. Translated by Steven Rendall. Berkeley: University of California Press, 1984.

Chambers, Iain. "A Miniature History of the Walkman." *New Formations* 11 (Summer 1990): 1–4.

Chen Wanying. Interview with Chen Kaige, director of *King of the Children* and *Yellow Earth*. Chinese edition of *Playboy* 22 (May 1988): 42–51.

Cheng Ming, no. 137 (March 1989). Hong Kong.

Nien Cheng. *Life and Death in Shanghai*. London: Penguin, 1988.

Chow, Rey. "Digging an Old Well: The Labor of Social Fantasy." Colaizzi, ed., *Feminismo y Teoría Filmica*.

————. "Male Narcissism and National Culture: Subjectivity in Chen Kaige's *King of the Children*." *camera obscura* 25/26 (1991): 9–41.

————. "Mandarin Ducks and Butterflies: A Response to the 'Postmodern' Condition." *Cultural Critique* 5 (Winter 1986–87): 69–93.

————. "Silent Is the Ancient Plain: Music, Film-Making, and the Conception of Reform in China's New Cinema." *Discourse* 12.2 (Spring 1990): 82–109.

————. "Violence in the Other Country: China as Crisis, Spectacle, and Woman." Mohanty et al., eds., pp. 81–100.

————. *Woman and Chinese Modernity: The Politics of Reading between West and East*. Minneapolis: University of Minnesota Press, 1991.

Cixous, Hélène. "Fiction and Its Phantoms: A Reading of Freud's *Das Unheimliche* (The 'Uncanny')." *New Literary History* 7.3: 525–48.

Clifford, James. *The Predicament of Culture: Twentieth-Century Ethnography, Literature, and Art*. Cambridge, Mass.: Harvard University Press, 1988.

————. "Traveling Cultures." *Cultural Studies*. Ed. Lawrence Grossberg, Cary Nelson, and Paula Treichler. New York: Routledge, 1991, pp. 96–116.

Clifford, James, and George E. Marcus, eds. *Writing Culture: The Poetics and Politics of Ethnography*. Berkeley: University of California Press, 1986.

Colaizzi, Giulia, ed. *Feminismo y Teoría del discurso*. Madrid: Ediciones Cátedra, Colección Teorema, 1990.

————, ed. *Feminismo y Teoría Fílmica*. Madrid: Ediciones Cátedra, Colección Teorema (forthcoming).

Cui Jian. "Rock and Roll on the Road of the New Long March." Music and lyrics by Cui Jian. EMI Music Publishing Ltd., S.E. Asia, 1989.

Davis, Fred. "Electronic Immigrants: Cheap Labor without Green Cards." *PC Week*, June 3, 1991.

de Lauretis, Teresa. In *Alice Doesn't: Feminism, Semiotics, Cinema*. Bloomington: Indiana University Press, 1984.

————. "The Violence of Rhetoric: Considerations on Representation and Gender." *Technologies of Gender: Essays on Theory, Film, and Fiction*. Bloomington: Indiana University Press, 1987.

Deleuze, Gilles, and Félix Guattari. *Kafka: Toward a Minor Literature*. Translated by Dana Polan. Foreword by Réda Bensmaïa. Minneapolis: University of Minnesota Press, 1986.

Deloria, Vine, Jr. "Identity and Culture." Takaki, pp. 94–103.

de Man, Paul. *Blindness and Insight: Essays in the Rhetoric of Contemporary Criticism*. Second Edition. Revised. Introduction by Wlad Godzich. Minneapolis: University of Minnesota Press, 1983.

Derrida, Jacques. *Of Grammatology*. Translated by Gayatri Chakravorty Spivak. Baltimore: Johns Hopkins University Press, 1976.

differences 1:2 (Summer 1989). "Another Look at *Essentialism*."

Dirlik, Arif. *Anarchism in the Chinese Revolution*. Berkeley: University of California Press, 1991.

————. "Culturalism as Hegemonic Ideology and Liberating Practice." *Cultural Critique* 6 (Spring 1987): 13–50.

————. *The Origins of Chinese Communism*. New York: Oxford University Press, 1989.

————. "The Predicament of Marxist Revolutionary Consciousness: Mao Zedong, Antonio Gramsci, and the Reformation of Marxist Revolutionary Theory." *Modern China* 9.2 (April 1983): 182–211.

————. *Revolution and History: Origins of Marxist Historiography in China, 1919–1937*. Berkeley: University of California Press, 1978.

Disraeli, Benjamin. *Collected Edition of the Novels and Tales by the Right Honorable B. Disraeli. Volume IV: Tancred or The New Crusade*. London: Longmans, Green, 1871.

Eagleton, Terry. "Defending the Free World." Miliband, ed., pp. 85–94.

Ebert, Teresa. "The Romance of Patriarchy: Ideology, Subjectivity, and Postmodern Feminist Cultural Theory." *Cultural Critique* 10 (Fall 1988): 19–57.

Eliot, T. S. "The Metaphysical Poets." Kermode, pp. 59–67.

Elmer, Jonathan. Review of Slavoj Žižek's *The Sublime Object of Ideology*. *Qui Parle* 4.1 (Fall 1990): 117–23.

Fabian, Johannes. *Time and the Other: How Anthropology Makes Its Object*. New York: Columbia University Press, 1983.

Fanon, Frantz. *Black Skin, White Masks*. Trans. Charles Lam Markmann. New York: Grove Press, 1967.

Flax, Jane. "Postmodernism and Gender Relations in Feminist Theory." *Signs* 12.4 (Summer 1987): 621–43.

Foster, Hal, ed. *The Anti-Aesthetic: Essays on Postmodern Culture.* Port Townsend: Bay Press, 1983.

Foucault, Michel. "Intellectuals and Power: A Conversation between Michel Foucault and Gilles Deleuze." In *Language, Counter-Memory, Practice: Selected Essays and Interviews with Foucault.* Edited and with an introduction by Donald F. Bouchard. Translated by Donald F. Bouchard and Sherry Simon. Ithaca: Cornell University Press, 1977, pp. 205–17.

———. "Power and Strategies." *Power/Knowledge: Selected Interviews and Other Writings 1972–1977 with Foucault.* Translated by Colin Gordon, Leo Marshall, John Mepham, and Kate Soper. New York: Pantheon Books, 1980, pp. 134–45.

Frampton, Kenneth. "Towards a Critical Regionalism: Six Points for an Architecture of Resistance." Foster, pp. 16–30.

Frazer, Nancy, and Linda Nicholson. "Social Criticism without Philosophy: An Encounter between Feminism and Postmodernism." Ross, pp. 83–104.

Freud, Sigmund. *Jokes and Their Relation to the Unconscious.* Translated and edited by James Strachey. New York: Norton, 1963.

———. "Mourning and Melancholia." *Collected Papers.* Edited by Joan Riviere. London: Hogarth Press, 1946; New York: Basic Books, 1959. Volume IV, pp. 152–70.

———. "The 'Uncanny.' " *Collected Papers.* Edited by Joan Riviere. London: The Hogarth Press, 1946; New York: Basic Books, 1959. Volume IV, pp. 368–407.

Fukuyama, Francis. "The End of History?" *The National Interest* (Summer 1989): 3–18.

Fuss, Diana. *Essentially Speaking.* New York: Routledge, 1989.

Gates, Henry Louis, Jr., ed. *"Race," Writing, and Difference.* Chicago: University of Chicago Press, 1986. Originally published in *Critical Inquiry* 12.1 (Autumn 1985) and 13.1 (Autumn 1986).

Glazer, Nathan. "The Emergence of an American Ethnic Pattern." Takaki, pp. 13–25.

Godzich, Wlad. "The Culture of Illiteracy." *enclitic* 8.1–2 (Spring/Fall 1984): 27–35.

———. "Emergent Literature and the Field of Comparative Literature." Koelb and Noakes, pp. 18–36.

Gordimer, Nadine. "A Writer's Freedom." *Index on Censorship*, 1976. Reprinted in Theiner, pp. 134–40.

Grossberg, Lawrence. " 'I'd Rather Feel Bad Than Not Feel Anything at All': Rock and Roll, Pleasure and Power." *enclitic* 8.1–2 (Spring/Fall 1984): 94–111.

Guha, Ranajit. "On Some Aspects of the Historiography of Colonial India." Guha, ed., *Subaltern Studies I*, pp. 116–35.

———, ed. *Subaltern Studies I: Writings on South Asian History and Society.* Delhi: Oxford University Press, 1986.

Hall, Stuart. "Minimal Selves." ICA Document 6: *Identity* (1987): 44–47.

Hamrin, Carol Lee, and Timothy Cheek, eds. *China's Establishment Intellectuals*. Armonk, New York: M. E. Sharpe, 1986.

Harari, Josué V., ed. *Textual Strategies: Perspectives in Post-Structuralist Criticism*. Ithaca: Cornell University Press, 1979.

Haraway, Donna. "A Manifesto for Cyborgs: Science, Technology, and Socialist Feminism in the 1980s." *Socialist Review* 80 (March/April 1985). Reprinted in Weed, pp. 173–204.

Harding, Harry. "From China, with Disdain: New Trends in the Study of China." *Asian Survey* 22.10 (October 1982): 934–58.

Harlow, Barbara. *Resistance Literature*. London: Methuen, 1987.

Hegel, Georg Wilhelm Friedrich. *Hegel's* Phenomenology of Spirit. Translated by A. V. Miller, with analysis of the text and foreword by J. N. Findlay. New York: Oxford University Press, 1977.

Hertz, Neil. "Freud and the Sandman." Harari, pp. 296–321.

Hinton, William. *Fanshen*. New York: Vintage Books, 1966.

Hirsch, E. D., Jr. *Cultural Literacy*. Boston: Houghton Mifflin, 1987.

Hsia, C. T. "Chinese Novels and American Critics: Reflections on Structure, Tradition, and Satire." Peter H. Lee, 133–52.

Hu Kan. " 'Zhiyou zhongguo cai neng jiu shehui zhuyi.' " *Ming Pao Daily News*, Vancouver Edition, December 13, 1989: 1.

Huyssen, Andreas. *After the Great Divide: Modernism, Mass Culture, Postmodernism*. Bloomington: Indiana University Press, 1986.

Inscriptions 5 (1989).

Irving, Katrina. "Rock Music and the State: Dissonance or Counterpoint?" *Cultural Critique* 10 (Fall 1988): 151–70.

Israel, John. "Foreword." Hamrin and Cheek, pp. ix–xix.

Jameson, Fredric. "Postmodernism and Consumer Society." Foster, pp. 111–25.

———. "Postmodernism: Or the Cultural Logic of Late Capitalism." *New Left Review*, no. 146 (July/August 1984): 53–92.

———. *Signatures of the Visible*. New York: Routledge, 1990.

———. "Third-World Literature in the Era of Multinational Capital." *Social Text* 15 (Fall 1986): 65–88.

JanMohamed, Abdul R. *Manichean Aesthetics: The Politics of Literature in Colonial Africa*. Amherst: University of Massachusetts Press, 1983.

———, and David Lloyd. "Introduction: Minority Discourse—What Is to Be Done?" *Cultural Critique* 7 (Fall 1987), pp. 5–17.

Jardine, Alice, and Paul Smith, eds. *Men in Feminism*. New York: Methuen, 1987.

Jiushi niandai (The Nineties) (March 1989). Hong Kong.

Kanise, Seiichi. "Grand Illusions." Technology Section, *Time*, June 3, 1991.

Kaplan, E. Ann, ed. *Postmodernism and Its Discontents: Theories, Practices*. London: Verso, 1988.

Kermode, Frank, ed. *Selected Prose of T. S. Eliot*. New York: Harcourt Brace Jovanovich; Farrar, Straus and Giroux, 1975.

Kittler, Friedrich A. *Discourse Networks 1800/1900*. Translated by Michael

Metteer, with Chris Cullens. Foreword by David E. Wellbery. Stanford: Stanford University Press, 1990.

———. "Gramophone, Film, Typewriter." Translated by Dorothea von Mücke with the assistance of Philippe L. Similon. *October* 41 (1987–88): 101–18.

———. "The Mechanized Philosopher." *Looking after Nietzsche.* Edited by Laurence A. Rickels. Albany: State University of New York Press, 1990.

Koelb, Clayton, and Susan Noakes, eds. *The Comparative Perspective on Literature: Approaches to Theory and Practice.* Ithaca: Cornell University Press, 1988.

Kojève, Alexandre. *Introduction to the Reading of Hegel: Lectures on the Phenomenology of Spirit.* Assembled by Raymond Queneau. Edited by Allan Bloom. Translated by James H. Nichols, Jr. Ithaca: Cornell University Press, 1980, 1989.

Kraus, Richard. "Bai Hua: The Political Authority of a Writer." Hamrin and Cheek, pp. 185–211.

Kristeva, Julia. *About Chinese Women.* Translated by Anita Barrows. New York: Marion Boyars, 1977, 1986.

———. *Language—The Unknown: An Initiation into Linguistics.* Translated by Anne M. Menke. New York: Columbia University Press, 1989.

———. "Woman Can Never Be Defined." Translated by Marilyn A. August. Marks and de Courtivron, pp. 137–41.

Kruger, Barbara, and Phil Marian, eds. *Remaking History.* Seattle: Bay Press, 1989.

Laclau, Ernesto, and Chantal Mouffe. *Hegemony and Socialist Strategy: Towards a Radical Democratic Politics.* Translated by Winston Moore and Paul Cammack. London: Verso, 1985.

Lee, Leo Ou-fan. "On the Margins of the Chinese Discourse: Some Personal Thoughts on the Cultural Meaning of the Periphery." *Dædalus* 120.2 (Spring 1991): 207–26.

Lee, Peter H., ed. *Critical Issues in East Asian Literature.* Seoul: International Cultural Society of Korea, 1983.

Legge, James, ed. and trans. *The Four Books: The Great Learning, The Doctrine of the Mean, Confucian Analects, and The Works of Mencius.* Taipei: Culture Book Co., 1973.

Leppert, Richard, and Susan McClary, eds. *Music and Society: The Politics of Composition, Performance and Reception.* New York: Cambridge University Press, 1987.

Levin, Thomas Y. "For the Record: Adorno on Music in the Age of Its Technological Reproducibility." *October* 55 (Winter 1990): 23–47.

Lewis, Peter H. "A Circus Is on Its Way to the Stores." Science Section, *The New York Times,* May 14, 1991.

Leys, Simon. *The Burning Forest: Essays on Chinese Culture and Politics.* New York: Holt, Rinehart and Winston, 1986.

Li Peng. "Zhong wai jizhe zhaodaihui shang Li Peng huida wenti" (Re-

sponses to questions at the press conference for Chinese and foreign
reporters). *Ming Pao Daily News*, Vancouver Edition, April 11, 1991.

Lieberman, Sally Taylor. "Visions and Lessons: 'China' in Feminist Theory-
Making, 1966–1977." *Michigan Feminist Studies*, no. 6 (Fall 1991):
91–107.

Liu Xiaobo. "Zhongguo dangdai zhishifenzi yu zhengzhi." *Cheng Ming*, no.
137 (March 1989): 68–71.

Lo Kwai-cheung. "The Real in Lacan: Some Reflections on 'Chinese Symptoms.'" *Polygraph* 4 (1990–91): 77–91.

———. "Crossing Boundaries: A Study of Modern Hong Kong Fiction
from the Fifties to the Eighties." M. Phil. Dissertation, University
of Hong Kong, 1990.

Lowe, Lisa. *Critical Terrains: French and British Orientalisms*. Ithaca:
Cornell University Press, 1991.

Lu Yuan. "Beijing Diary." *New Left Review*, no. 177 (September/October
1989): 3–26.

Luo Dayou. "Comrade Lover." Theme song of film "Airen tongzhi," music
and lyrics by Luo Dayou. Hong Kong: Praiseplan Ltd., 1989.

———. "Song of the Dwarf" ("Zhuru zhi ge"). Music and lyrics by Luo
Dayou. Hong Kong: Praiseplan Ltd., 1989.

———. *Queen's Road East* (*Huanghou da dao dong*) production notes.
Hong Kong: Music Factory, 1991.

Lyotard, Jean-François. *The Differend: Phrases in Dispute*. Translated by
Georges Van Den Abbeele. Minneapolis: University of Minnesota
Press, 1988.

———. "Presentations." Montefiore, pp. 116–35.

Macherey, Pierre, and Etienne Balibar. "Literature as an Ideological Form:
Some Marxist Propositions." *Praxis: A Journal of Cultural Criticism*
5 (1981): 43–58.

MacKerras, Colin. *Western Images of China*. Hong Kong: Oxford University Press, 1989.

Mao Dun. "From Guling to Tokyo." Translated by Yu-shih Chen. *Bulletin
for Concerned Asian Scholars* (January/March 1976): 38–44.

Marcus, George E., and Michael M. J. Fischer, eds. *Anthropology as Cultural Critique: An Experimental Moment in the Human Sciences*.
Chicago: University of Chicago Press, 1986.

Marks, Elaine, and Isabelle de Courtivron, eds. *New French Feminism*.
New York: Schocken Books, 1981.

Miliband, Ralph. "Reflections on the Crisis of Communist Regimes." *New
Left Review*, no. 177 (September/October 1989): 27–39.

Miliband, Ralph, Leo Panitch, and John Saville, eds. *Socialist Register
1990*. London: Merlin Press, 1990.

Miller, J. Hillis. "The Work of Cultural Criticism in the Age of Digital
Reproduction." Typed manuscript.

Ming Pao Daily News, Vancouver Edition.

Mitchell, Juliet. *Psychoanalysis and Feminism*. New York: Vintage Books,
1975.

Miyoshi, Masao, and H. D. Harootunian, eds. *Postmodernism and Japan*.

Durham: Duke University Press, 1989 (*South Atlantic Quarterly* 87.3 [Summer 1988]).

Mohanty, Chandra Talpade, Lourdes Torres, and Ann Russo, eds. *Third World Women and the Politics of Feminism*. Bloomington: Indiana University Press, 1991.

Montag, Warren. "What Is at Stake in the Debate on Postmodernism?" Kaplan, pp. xx–yy.

Montefiore, Alan, ed. *Philosophy in France Today*. Cambridge: Cambridge University Press, 1983.

Mother Jones (December 1989). "The Hopes of China." Interview with Chinese intellectuals, pp. 21–57.

Mowitt, John. "The Sound of Music in the Era of Its Electronic Reproducibility." Leppert and McClary, pp. 173–97.

Nelson, Cary, and Lawrence Grossberg, eds. *Marxism and the Interpretation of Culture*. Urbana: University of Illinois Press, 1988.

Owen, Stephen. "The Anxiety of Global Influence: What Is World Poetry?" *The New Republic*, November 19, 1990: 28–32.

Owens, Craig. "The Discourse of Others: Feminists and Postmodernism." Foster, pp. 57–82.

Pan, Lynn. *Sons of the Yellow Emperor: The Story of the Overseas Chinese*. London: Secker and Warburg, 1990.

Parry, Benita. "Problems in Current Theories of Colonial Discourse." *Oxford Literary Review* 9.1–2 (1987): 27–58.

Pines, Jim, and Paul Willemen, eds. *Questions of Third Cinema*. London: British Film Institute, 1989.

Price, Sally. *Primitive Art in Civilized Places*. Chicago: University of Chicago Press, 1989.

Reiter, Rayna R., ed. *Toward an Anthropology of Women*. New York: Monthly Review Press, 1975.

Richards, I. A. *Practical Criticism*. New York: Harcourt, Brace, 1929.

———. *Principles of Literary Criticism*. New York: Harcourt, Brace, 1925.

Ross, Andrew, ed. *Universal Abandon? The Politics of Postmodernism*. Minneapolis: University of Minnesota Press, 1988.

Rousseau, Jean-Jacques. *A Discourse on Inequality*. Translated and with an introduction by Maurice Cranston. London: Penguin, 1984.

Rubin, Gayle. "The Traffic in Women." Reiter, pp. 157–210.

Safran, William. "Diasporas in Modern Societies: Myths of Homeland and Return." *Diaspora* 1.1 (Spring 1991): 83–99.

Said, Edward. *The World, the Text, and the Critic*. Cambridge, Mass.: Harvard University Press, 1983.

———. "Opponents, Audiences, Constituencies and Community." Foster, pp. 135–59.

Sakai, Naoki. "Modernity and Its Critique: The Problem of Universalism and Particularism." Miyoshi and Harootunian, pp. 93–122; *South Atlantic Quarterly* 87.3: 475–504.

Schell, Orville. "An Act of Defiance." *New York Times Magazine*, April 16, 1989: 27–43.

———. "China's Andrei Sakharov." *The Atlantic Monthly* (May 1988): 35–52.

Schiff, Stephen. "Havel's Choice." *Vanity Fair* (August 1991): 124–28 and 156–63.

Schor, Naomi. "Dreaming Dissymmetry: Barthes, Foucault, and Sexual Difference." Jardine and Smith, pp. 98–110.

———. *Reading in Detail: Aesthetics and the Feminine.* London: Methuen, 1987.

Schwarcz, Vera. "Afterword." Hamrin and Cheek, pp. 247–56.

———. "No Solace from Lethe: History, Memory, and Cultural Identity in Twentieth-Century China." *Dædalus* 120.2 (Spring 1991): 85–112.

Schwartz, Benjamin I. "Presidential Address: Area Studies as a Critical Discipline." *Journal of Asian Studies* XL.1 (November 1980): 15–25.

Shklovsky, Victor. "Art as Technique." *Russian Formalist Criticism: Four Essays.* Edited by L. Lemon and M. J. Reis. Lincoln: University of Nebraska Press, 1965.

Serres, Michel. *Detachment.* Translated by Genevieve James and Raymond Federman. Athens: Ohio University Press, 1989.

Smith, James. *Melodrama.* London: Methuen, 1973.

South Atlantic Quarterly 87.3 (Summer 1988). Special issue on postmodernism and Japan.

Spivak, Gayatri Chakravorty. "Can the Subaltern Speak?" Nelson and Grossberg, pp. 271–313.

———. *In Other Worlds: Essays in Cultural Politics.* London: Methuen, 1987.

———. "The Political Economy of Women As Seen by a Literary Critic." Weed, pp. 218–29.

———. *The Post-Colonial Critic: Interviews, Strategies, Dialogues.* Edited by Sarah Harasym. London: Routledge, 1990.

———. "Three Women's Texts and a Critique of Imperialism." Gates, pp. 262–80.

———. "Who Claims Alterity?" Kruger and Marian, pp. 269–92.

Spooner, Brian. "Weavers and Dealers: The Authenticity of an Oriental Carpet." Appadurai, ed., pp. 195–235.

Stewart, Susan. *On Longing: Narratives of the Miniature, the Gigantic, the Souvenir, the Collection.* Baltimore: Johns Hopkins University Press, 1984.

Stigler, George J. *The Intellectual and the Marketplace.* Cambridge, Mass.: Harvard University Press, 1984 enlarged edition.

Takaki, Ronald, ed. *From Different Shores: Perspectives on Race and Ethnicity in America.* New York: Oxford University Press, 1987.

Theiner, George, ed. *They Shoot Writers, Don't They?* London: Faber and Faber, 1984.

Toffler, Alvin. *Powershift: Knowledge, Wealth, and Violence at the Edge of the 21st Century.* New York: Bantam Books, 1990.

Tölölyan, Khachig. "The Nation-State and Its Others: In Lieu of a Preface." *Diaspora* 1.1 (Spring 1991): 3–7.

Torgovnick, Marianna. *Gone Primitive: Savage Intellects, Modern Lives.* Chicago: University of Chicago Press, 1990.

Tress, Daryl McGowan. "Comment on Flax's 'Postmodernism and Gender Relations in Feminist Theory.' " *Signs* 14.1 (1988): 196–200.

Trinh T. Minh-ha. "Difference: 'A Special Third World Women Issue.' " *Discourse* 8 (Fall/Winter 1986–87): 11–37.

Urrows, Henry, and Elizabeth Urrows. "Kodak's Photo CD Promised for 1992." *Document Image Automation* 11:2 (March/April 1991): 89–97.

Virilio, Paul. *Popular Defense and Ecological Struggles.* Translated by Mark Polizzotti. New York: Semiotext(e), 1990.

———. *L'Esthétique de la disparition.* Paris: Ballard, 1981.

———. *Speed and Politics: An Essay on Dromology.* Translated by Mark Polizzotti. New York: Semiotext(e), 1977.

———, and Sylvère Lotringer. *Pure War.* Translated by Mark Polizzotti. New York: Semiotext(e), 1983.

Wallerstein, Immanuel. *Social Change: The Colonial Situation.* New York: John Wiley & Sons, 1966.

Weed, Elizabeth, ed. *Coming to Terms: Feminism, Theory, Politics.* London: Routledge, 1989.

Wei Jingsheng. "Yao minzhu haishi yao xin de ducai." Reprinted in *Cheng Ming,* no. 137 (March 1989): 29–31.

———. "Searching for the Truth." Translated by Peter Harris. Theiner, pp. 74–83.

White, Hayden. *Tropics of Discourse: Essays in Cultural Criticism.* Baltimore: Johns Hopkins University Press, 1978.

Williams, Raymond. *Marxism and Literature.* Oxford: Oxford University Press, 1971.

Witt, Karen de. "How Best to Teach the Blind: A Growing Battle over Braille." *The Sunday New York Times,* May 12, 1991.

Wolfe, Alan. *Suicidal Narrative in Modern Japan: The Case of Dazai Osamu.* Princeton: Princeton University Press, 1990.

Woodhull, Winifred. "Unveiling Algeria." *Genders* 10 (Spring 1991): 112–131.

Wu, David Yen-ho. "The Construction of Chinese and Non-Chinese Identities." *Dædalus* 120.2 (Spring 1991): 159–79.

Xin Bao/Overseas Chinese Economic Journal (the U.S. edition of the *Hong Kong Economic Journal*).

Yazhou zhoukan, (Asia Weekly) April 21, 1991.

Yeh, Michelle. "The Anxiety of Difference—A Rejoinder." *Jintian (Today)* 1 (1991): 94–96.

Yu, Pauline. "Alienation Effects: Comparative Literature and the Chinese Tradition." Koelb and Noakes, pp. 162–75.

Yúdice, George. "Marginality and the Ethics of Survival." Ross, pp. 214–36.

Zhang Xianliang. *Half of Man Is Woman.* Translated by Martha Avery. New York: Norton, 1988.

Žižek, Slavoj. "How the Non-Duped Err." *Qui Parle* 4.1 (Fall 1990): 1–20.

———. "Rossellini: Woman as Symptom of Man." *October* 54 (Fall 1990): 18–44.

———. *The Sublime Object of Ideology.* London: Verso, 1989.

INDEX

REY CHOW was educated in the British Crown Colony of Hong Kong and in the United States. She is Associate Professor of English and Comparative Literature at the University of California at Irvine and the author of *Woman and Chinese Modernity: The Politics of Reading between West and East* (1991). Her writings in English have been translated into Chinese, Spanish, French, and Japanese.